MIMI
—— and her ——
DAUGHTERS

REMARKABLE LIVES REVEALED
THROUGH LETTERS & JOURNALS

BRIDGET DOLE

Mimi and Her Daughters:
Remarkable Lives Revealed Through Letters & Journals
Copyright © 2025 Bridget Dole

www.AcornPublishingLLC.com
Acorn Publishing, LLC
3943 Irvine Blvd. Ste. 218, Irvine, CA 92602

Cover design by Damonza
Interior formatting by Debra Cranfield Kennedy
Map by Eowyn Cwper
Author photo by Alex Kemp
Peter Gowland's photo used with the permission of Lauren Kahler.
All other photographs are from the author's collection.
Cover Photos: Jane in the WACs, Mimi writing aboard ship, Gwen in the 1940s.

All rights reserved. No part of this book may be used or reproduced in any manner whatsoever, including Internet usage, without written permission from the author. Printed in the United States of America

Publisher's Cataloging-in-Publication provided by
Cassidy Cataloguing Services, Inc.

Names: Dole, Bridget, author.
Title: Mimi and her daughters : remarkable lives revealed through letters & journals / Bridget Dole.
Description: First edition. | Irvine, CA : Acorn Publishing, LLC, [2025] | Includes bibliographical references.
Identifiers: ISBN: 979-8-88528-041-9 (hardcover) |
  979-8-88528-040-2 (paperback) |
  979-8-88528-096-9 (ebook) | LCCN: 2022919166
Subjects: LCSH: Friedman, Mona Tate (Mimi). | Dole, Gwendolyn Kramer (Scottie). | Anderson, Jane Kramer (Jay). | Mothers and daughters--Biography. | Tate family--Genealogy. | Brittany (France)--Social life and customs--19th century.
Classification: LCC: CT275.F75 D65 2025 | DDC: 920.72--dc23

Additional bibliographic information available from OCLC's WorldCat and from SkyRiver.

To Kent & Caitlin

With gratitude to

those who preceded us

And faith in

those who follow

Author's Note: This is a family history and every effort has been made to ensure its accuracy. Mimi's words and those of her daughters are as they spoke or wrote them. I edited them, and the words of others, only to the extent necessary for clarity and brevity.

CONTENTS

Preface .... *xi*
Family Trees and Map *1, 34, 62, 119*

BOOK I *Victorian England*

1 A Chance Meeting.. *3*
2 The First George & First Henrietta *7*
3 The Canadian Railroad *11*
4 A Poor Choice *16*
5 An Unexpected Inheritance *21*
6 A Bleak Beginning *25*

BOOK II *Brittany, France*

7 A Brittany Childhood *35*
8 Unhallowed Ground *44*
9 Making Mischief *51*
10 A Different Sensibility *57*
11 Queeny *61*
12 Being Helpful *68*
13 Zizi, Coco, and Caramel *74*
14 Bravo, Mona! *80*
15 Crossings *83*
16 First Beau *89*
17 The Mexican Railroad *92*
18 The Lusitania *101*

BOOK III *New England*

19	A Redcoat in New England	*111*
20	Herbert Hayford	*116*
21	A Hard, Hard Life	*124*
22	Farewell to Villa St. George	*131*
23	Dresses in the Closet	*137*
24	Chestnut Ridge	*144*
25	A Wife's Curse	*149*
26	Starting Over	*153*
27	When Is That Child Going Home?	*161*

BOOK IV *Upstate New York*

28	The Kramers of Albany	*171*
29	Left on the Farm	*181*
30	A Lovely Strand of Golden Hair	*187*
31	Route 66	*192*

BOOK V *Southern California*

32	West Coast	*199*
33	End of an Era	*206*
34	Ye Gods and Little Fishes	*214*
35	Reconciliation	*221*
36	Out on Their Own	*226*
37	A Close Call in the Pacific	*235*
38	The War in France	*242*
39	We Are Free!	*248*
40	A Fruitless Marriage	*254*
41	A Delightful Chap	*258*

42	Mrs. Dole	*263*
43	The Matriarch	*269*
44	Return to Brittany	*276*
45	Sebec Lake, Maine	*281*
46	The Grand Tour	*289*
47	Fate, Who Picked Me	*297*
48	Facing the Ocean	*300*
49	That Name Means You to Me	*308*
50	The Third Act	*315*
51	God Show Me the Way!	*319*
52	Power of the Mind	*325*
53	At Long Last	*335*
54	Like Mother, Like Daughter	*341*
55	Goodbye, Mon Amour Chéri	*349*
56	Mimi's Will	*354*
57	Legacy	*362*

Epilogue	*371*
Notes and Sources	*375*
Acknowledgments	*389*

Preface

Mimi made herself comfortable in Papá's easy chair and patted the narrow space beside her flowered skirt. Her charm bracelet, with an engraved coin for each of us grandkids, jingled invitingly as I climbed in beside her. She put her arm around me and I reached for the dangling coins, turning each until I found the small one showing Queen Victoria on the front and my name, Biddy, on the back. Then Mimi picked up her book and started to read.

Photo of Mimi by Peter Gowland.

Soon I forgot about the silver bangles. With her resonant voice, distinct British accent, and past experience playing bit parts in Hollywood, my grandmother had a flair for the dramatic. Before long, the view out her French doors of a well-tended yard faded as that naughty Peter Rabbit ate his way through Mr. McGregor's garden.

After Mrs. Rabbit had given Peter his medicinal spoonful of chamomile tea, and Mimi was satisfied I no longer had the slightest concern about where my parents had gone, she suggested a bath.

Her bathroom, with its spotless walls and tile floor, was full of fancy ladies' things—except for the odd-shaped sea sponge, so out of place in a room that smelled more of perfume than the ocean. I was as unseemly as the sponge.

Mimi switched on the wall heater to break the chill and ran the water. When I took off my clothes, she brought out her cold cream and applied a generous layer to the ground-in patches of dirt on my neck and arms. After letting the cream sit a moment, she wiped it off vigorously with tissues, leaving my skin red but cleaner, all the while tsking over ears that could grow potatoes and piggies that had clearly wallowed in mud.

Once I was good enough for the tub, she knelt on the bath rug and washed me with the efficiency of a nurse, soaping and rinsing, from top to bottom. She scrubbed my skin—which hadn't seen a washcloth since my last stay—as hard as she could without my yowling. Next, she took the manicure brush and had a go at my fingernails. Standing me up, she worriedly assessed my knobby knees—a sure sign of rickets, she said—and lifted me out of the tub. I looked back and noticed the wide ring of scum.

"Don't worry, dear," she said. "I'll tidy up later. The important thing is that you're clean now and ready for a proper holiday."

"What holiday?"

"Our holiday, our little vacation together," she said, wrapping me in a plush towel monogrammed with her initials, MTK, for Mona Tate Kramer. "Shall we finish up and have a cup of tea?"

Although I didn't particularly enjoy the zealous washing that marked the start of the "holiday," I looked forward to the fancy cup of tea with milk and a cube of sugar.

That's my earliest memory of Mimi. My big brother Mike and I stayed with our grandparents for a couple of weeks at a time while Mother and Father were on their annual summer trip. Our little brother Tim wasn't born yet so I was probably four that year. After the first day of settling into their home in Los Angeles' affluent Cheviot Hills, Mike and I would fall into an easy routine that included afternoons of classic books with yellowing pages and sparse pictures. Mimi piqued my imagination with dark forest worlds inhabited by disobedient children, evil witches, and fearless woodsmen. My favorite story, though, was Rudyard Kipling's

"Rikki-Tikki-Tavi." I admired the brave mongoose and liked the way Mimi said his name.

Sometimes, instead of pulling a volume from the shelf, she told us about her own experiences as an English girl growing up in Brittany on the northern coast of France. Pets bounded through these stories... her monkey, her parrot, and lots of dogs. Mimi loved dogs and frequently regaled us with tales of loyal canines who gave up their lives to protect their masters.

I didn't connect the heroic creatures in her stories with the two Scottish Terriers that shared the flea-ridden backyard with my brother and me at home. Perhaps Mimi suspected as much.

"Now, Biddy dear, you have little dogs," she said. "Are you being nice to them? Hmm?"

I wrinkled my nose at the mention of Mother's smelly old Silas and Gollywog.

"You know, they have emotions just like people. You can tell by looking. They wag their tails if they're happy or cower if they're afraid. Do your little dogs wag their tails for you?"

It hadn't occurred to me that animals had feelings, but when Mimi told me they did, I was ashamed of the time I'd kicked Silas out of my way.

But my grandmother, a decades-long Christian Scientist, also taught me how to pray, so that evening we made it right with God before our nightly recital of Mary Baker Eddy's prayer:

> *Father-Mother God, Loving me,*
> *Guard me when I sleep;*
> *Guide my little feet*
> *Up to Thee.*

Even when I was older and Mimi had sufficiently civilized me, she continued to share her stories. The new tales, however, had less to do with dogs or childhood exploits and more to do with her family, the Tates. I was often confused since her grandmother, aunt, and sister were all named Henrietta; and her grandfather, father, and brother were all named George. I couldn't keep them straight or remember which old George was looking down at me from the gilt-framed portrait in her living room. But I never had to ponder long before Mimi moved on to her favorite subject, romance.

She loved to tell the story of her grandparents' impetuous one-day courtship, as well as her father's patient seven-year wait for her mother's hand in marriage. Eventually, Mimi revealed her own search for love, and shared the longing, betrayal, and potent curse that accompanied it.

My last memory of Mimi is of her lying, barely conscious, in a careworn nursing home. It was winter and I had come to say goodbye. I stood by the bed with my children, Kent and Caitlin, then thirteen and ten, and wished I knew what to do. I took Mimi's withered hand in mine and promised to write about her so her great-grandchildren would know her stories as I had. I felt her squeeze my hand . . . or I think I did. A few days after our visit, she passed away.

I wished later that I'd thought to read to her, or comfort her with our prayer . . . *guide my little feet up to Thee.*

BOOK I

Victorian England

George Tate b. 1808 — Henrietta Gliddon b. 1819

Edward B. Gudgeon b. 1820 — Jane Bennett b. 1819

George James Frederick Tate b. 1857

Agnes Mary (Queeny) Gudgeon b. 1855

Henrietta Agnes (Rita) b. 1890

Mary Kathleen b. 1892

Maud Isabelle Mona (Mimi) b. 1893

George Edward Cecil b. 1894

1

A Chance Meeting

They met on a train and married the next day.

That was the beginning of Mimi's favorite story, the courtship of her grandparents. Their accidental meeting and spur-of-the-moment wedding set a standard for great love, and Mimi expected no less for herself.

She wasn't unreasonable. It didn't have to be on a train. Perhaps it would start with a chance meeting on a ship, or the sudden locking of eyes with a dashing stranger at the annual dance on the village green. But it would happen. After all, it had happened to George and Henrietta.

The year was 1847, and the train was a railway carriage on the new Le Havre-Paris line. The track had been laid to link London and Paris via a channel crossing from Southampton. If a vessel was available upon arrival at the English port, and if the boat passengers were lucky enough to reach Le Havre in time to catch the train, the entire journey could be completed in as little as eleven hours.

Even at that unprecedented pace, though, the trip was never easy. The ocean crossing was notoriously rough, and seasick travelers faced new discomforts as they waited to board the train in Le Havre. They could barely see for the steam spewing from the engines, and many cringed in anticipation of the upcoming assault on their backsides; the carriages, lacking suspension, often bounced and jerked mercilessly. The train was also known to be hard on the ears—the infernal screeching of wheels on tracks frequently made polite conversation all but impossible.

Many of the riders making their way aboard this unpleasant mode of transportation also feared for their safety. The line had opened only six months earlier, after a lengthy delay caused by the collapse of France's hundred-foot-high Barentin Viaduct. But the brick arches, twenty-seven in all, had recently been replaced using better mortar, and the overpass was now deemed reliable.

Thirty-nine-year-old George Tate, hurrying to catch the train, was not one to worry about the span crumbling beneath him. He trusted the repairs of the contractor, with whom he had dined just the week before.

George worked as a civil engineer specializing in the construction of tracks, bridges, and tunnels. After finishing his university education, he had compiled an enviable record of successful projects that secured him a home on Parliament Street in Westminster. Most recently he'd accepted a job as one of the chief engineers on England's Great Northern Railway. He was a confident, handsome man, with a full head of dark, wavy hair.

Henrietta Gliddon, seated with her lady companion, may have fretted about the advisability of enclosing herself in the entrails of an iron horse hurtling across deep gorges, but it isn't likely. An independent-minded twenty-eight-year-old, she enjoyed travel and was probably excited about leaving her home in dreary London to visit Paris. Adventure aside, as an artist, musician, and poet, she may have looked forward to the rhythm of the swaying coaches and the pastoral view of the French landscape.

What undoubtedly concerned her, however, were the limited conveniences of train travel. Those on board for the seven-hour stretch from Le Havre to Paris couldn't stroll down the corridor to a dining car, or even to a lavatory, because the only doors in each compartment opened directly to the outside. If riders had personal needs, they had to wait; and if they were uncomfortable with those who shared their confined space, they had to suffer their presence . . . at least until the next station.

Henrietta, who came from a respectable family, had her attendant for company and protection. But as a stylish brunette, she surely endured her fair share of eager men seeking to engage her in conversation.

Mimi, who was especially fond of romantic tales with strong, proud heroines who utterly succumb to love, told how the two railway passengers met.

> At the last minute, George Tate boarded the train and took a seat in Henrietta's compartment. He was struck by her beauty and charm and, although she was aloof and reserved, he kept addressing her through her companion. But while he made conversation about points of interest and the countryside, Henrietta refused to look at him and pretended he wasn't even there.

Undeterred by the jostling carriage and occasional scream of the wheels, George, a bachelor, must have found a way to get her to look at him because later he would remark on her lively eyes. *Gypsy eyes,* he called them. They captivated him.

> While at one station, where the train stopped for water and coal, he bought her a beautiful bouquet of red roses, which he presented to her through her chaperone.
>
> Shocked by such fast proceedings, unknown at that time to ladies of her class, she threw the flowers on the floor and stamped on them—which was very rude indeed—although she was quite a lady.

Henrietta's reaction might seem extreme by today's standards, but in the Victorian era, a gift of red roses was recognized as an offering of love. Given too soon, however, the romantic gesture could be mistaken for ungentlemanly presumption.

Mimi never said how George responded to Henrietta's rejection. He was known, however, to be as determined as he was personable, and he had the benefit of several hours in close quarters to make a favorable impression.

Another unseen force may also have been at play.

> Eros must have been traveling in their compartment, for when they reached Paris, their hearts had already been welded for life. They made a date to meet the next day, chaperoned by her companion. But what really happened the following day is another matter. They went to the British Embassy and were married ... then and there.

This headlong rush to marriage—which Mimi characterized as ordained from the beginning of time—took place on Tuesday, September 14, 1847.

Mimi's father told her the story many times. After all, George and Henrietta were his parents and he was a sentimental man who loved telling of their courtship as much as Mimi loved hearing about it.

2

The First George & First Henrietta

Upon their return from Paris, the engineer and his bride traveled to Yorkshire, where he was overseeing work on the Doncaster section of the railway. After a search for suitable housing, they found Bawtry Hall, a two-story brick mansion set in acres of parkland just south of the town of Bawtry.

Until a decade earlier, the manor house, consisting of about forty thousand square feet, had been the home of the Dowager Galway. But after she died, Lord Galway's heirs put the sprawling estate up for lease.

George and Henrietta moved in and assembled the staff necessary to care for them and the property. It was certainly a bigger residence than the couple would need, but finding a place befitting George's professional standing may have been difficult in the countryside. Besides, it's doubtful they moved in alone. Each came from a large family.

The groom was the tenth and last child of a medical practitioner who died when George was twenty-one. As the only surviving son, he had assumed head-of-household duties, providing for his aging mother and four spinster sisters.

Henrietta was also one of ten children. She was the next-to-last child of James John Gliddon, a Londoner from the merchant class. He had expected to become a lawyer, and as a youth was studying at his uncle's law office when a regulation was passed requiring a new £200 apprenticeship fee. Not having the money, his family instead apprenticed him to a watchmaker. Although he dabbled in various interests—he was known as an ingenious mechanic—he went on to make his livelihood as a goldsmith, crafting fine watchcases. He lived and worked in the rooms he inherited from his parents at 16 Red Lion Passage, a block-long street of narrow shops topped by three floors of living space.

When James John was twenty-one, he married eighteen-year-old Esther Knocker, who presented him with a new son or daughter every couple of years until she died at forty-four. At the time, Henrietta was only seven.

Henrietta eventually gained a stepmother, but even though the new woman of the house was past her child-bearing years—escaping one of the greatest threats to a woman's life in Victorian England—she, too, died long before Henrietta married.

However, Henrietta's father and several siblings still lived in London, along with many artistic, avant-garde cousins. These relatives, as well as George's family, had the means to travel, and if they wanted a respite from the city, Bawtry Hall was the perfect place to accommodate both short-term and long-term guests.

The home itself was stately, but it was the surroundings that were particularly enchanting. Aside from having its own woods and lake, the property included a formal, tiered garden complete with an aviary that once housed Chinese pheasants and other rare birds. Inclement weather was probably the only thing that discouraged the newlyweds from strolling the grounds or taking their afternoon tea outside . . . that is, when George had time.

He was not a man to sit by idly while there was work to be done, and his job brought with it a demanding schedule. Supervising seven hundred men engaged in laying track, he spent long hours away from home. But his heart was always there, particularly after the birth of their daughter.

Baby Henrietta arrived a few days before the couple's second Christmas at Bawtry Hall. It's not clear how this little girl was distinguished in name from her mother, but much later Mimi knew her as Aunty Harrie, so presumably she was called Harrie as a child, too.

George was a man popular with both those above and those below him. Success, however, begets success, and two years after joining the Great Northern Railway, he was called to London to work on another prestigious engineering project.

His men gave him a rousing farewell. In an age when poetry was recognized as a manly skill, they presented him with two poems, one rigorously exhorting him on to ever greater heights—*Waving the sword of the Spirit with might, resolved not to lose in the world's noblest fight*—and another, by W.H. Scott, wishing him good fortune:

> Wherever thou goest,
> By land or by sea,
> Apart from thy home—still
> May peace be with thee!
>
> And when thou art sleeping,
> May bright forms divine
> Ever hover in fondness
> Around thee and thine;
>
> The friend of thy bosom—
> So feeling and mild,
> And her tender floweret,
> Thy sweet, artless child;
>
> And thus, when your short dreams
> Of earth have gone by,
> Ye all shall awake—safe,
> And dreamless—on high.

The grandeur and pastoral beauty of Bawtry Hall remained in their hearts, but the family's elegant new home in London was not apt to have been a disappointment. George, Henrietta, and Harrie moved into No. 10 Hanover Terrace in Kensington. Although built on the order of a townhouse—there were nine apartments on each side of the one occupied by the Tates—it was a regal, three-story building fronted by Greek columns and topped with goddess statuary. From their upstairs windows, the residents—which then included George's older sister, a niece, and a nine-year-old page boy—enjoyed a grand view of Regent's Park directly across the street.

George was led to London, at least in part, by a competition to design a building to house the 1851 *Great Exhibition of the Works of Industry of All Nations.* Of the 245 plans submitted, however, none could compete with Joseph Paxton's Crystal Palace, a magnificent glass conservatory that soon covered nineteen acres of Hyde Park.

Even without winning the contract, it was an exciting time to live in the capital. The international exhibition lasted only five months, but over six million people viewed thousands of displays from all over the world. Queen Victoria herself was said to have visited more than thirty times.

Prince Albert presented George with a bronze medal marked *for services,* perhaps in recognition of his participation in the competition, and a second medal of which even less is known.

George, however, wasn't the only one in the family to receive an award. While his focus had been on great engineering feats, his wife, like her gold-working father before her, had been crafting smaller items. She created decorated chests—each about the size of a small jewelry box—for the keeping of valuables. Entering at least one of them in the event's competitions, Henrietta won a bronze medal of her own.

3

The Canadian Railroad

Throughout his time in London, George stayed active in a number of railroad ventures, including talks with Portuguese officials for a Lisbon line. He lived in an era of boundless industrial expansion. A year after the Great Exhibition, the contracting firm of Peto, Brassey, Betts & Jackson was negotiating to lay track for the Grand Trunk Railway of Canada. They asked George to survey the proposed route and he boarded a steamer for the twelve-day crossing.

In 1852, most of the British colony was a pioneer land of rivers that froze over in the winter, dirt roads that dissolved to mud in the spring, and dense forests that were impenetrable year-round. The vast wilderness limited the movement of people and goods, so the proposed line between Montreal and Toronto was deemed vital to Canada's development.

After George surveyed the terrain, he returned home, where an elite cadre of civil engineers, mostly from England and Scotland, were selected to oversee the work. George was tapped to serve as resident engineer supervising the construction of seventy-five miles of track between Toronto and Belleville.

While he was wrapping up projects in London, his wife had business endeavors of her own. She was seeking to obtain Queen Victoria's patronage for her jeweled boxes. Thirty-four-year-old Henrietta, who was the same age as the queen and favored the monarch's sleek parted-down-the-middle hairstyle, twice came close to securing an audience at Buckingham Palace. But both attempts failed, the last due to the birth of the queen's eighth child, Prince Leopold.

"Her Majesty having been confined this morning," said the royal letter of April 7, 1853, "Mrs. Tate will see it is not possible as yet to name a day and hour for sending her work to the Palace."

Mimi wasn't sure if Henrietta ever had the honor of being presented to Queen Victoria in court, but only three weeks after Leopold's birth, Henrietta, George, and five-year-old Harrie were boarding a ship to Canada. It's unlikely the Queen's confinement would have ended before their departure.

In the beginning, the family lived in Port Hope at the midpoint of George's assigned section. But by October 1856, when the colony celebrated the opening of the Grand Trunk Railway, they resided in the heart of Toronto. They appear to have lived in an apartment above George's office in the brick railway building on the busy corner of Bay and Wellington.

It was there, on February 4, 1857, that they welcomed their second child, George James Frederick Tate. Like his sister, who was named after her mother, the boy was named after his father. His second name honored his grandfathers, who had both been christened James. Although the newborn grew up to proudly use all four of his names—or at least their initials—for simplicity's sake, he'll be referred to here by the shortened George James.

The Tate family stayed in Canada another five years. George leased part of the rail line and ran it for two years, and also worked on the design and construction of the Great Victoria Bridge, the first to span the St. Lawrence River. At the time of its completion in 1859, it was the longest bridge in the world.

The official opening came eight months later when the Prince of Wales, the future King Edward VII, made his first formal visit to British North America. The ceremony was held at the center of the bridge, where the eighteen-year-old prince took up the last rivet—which had dutifully been set aside for him—and drove it in. A banquet followed, along with a festive week of boat races, concerts, and balls.

George and Henrietta had a personal occasion to celebrate as well. Just three months before the royal opening ceremonies, she had given birth to another baby, a girl they named Maud. By then, the family was living in a residential neighborhood in a two-story, wood-framed home kept in running order by two servants. The following year, at forty-two, Henrietta delivered their fourth and last child, Ethel.

After a decade in Canada, George took his family of six—now with an infant and toddler in tow—on the long crossing back to England. Traveling with them was another man, George's twenty-six-year-old secretary, William Whitehead. British by blood but Canadian by birth, he was devoted to his employer.

Upon their homecoming, George embarked on a position constructing new harbor facilities on the Isle of Man, where he and his family took up residence. After the project was completed, the Tates finally moved back to London and settled into an urbane life in the upper-class neighborhood of Kilburn.

It's not known if George and Henrietta had sought out a return to the big city with its theaters, museums, and proper gardens, but they certainly made the most of what London had to offer. They collected religious works of art, including one of Raphael's many depictions of the *Holy Family*. Theirs was a cultured home of scholarship and fine arts. Henrietta herself was an accomplished composer and performer, playing the piano, harp, and guitar. She also sang.

Young George James became proficient at composing and was an excellent pianist, often serving as accompanist to his mother. Gifted with a rich singing voice, too, he sang in the choir at the renowned St. Paul's Cathedral, occasionally performing solos.

In the Victorian era, however, success was thought best acquired through rigid discipline, and Henrietta was strict with her children. Aside from teaching them music and art, she oversaw their academics too, never sparing the rod for a wrong answer. When it came to the world at large, Henrietta was said to have held compassionate and humanitarian views, but at home with her children she was dictatorial. She demanded perfection and absolute obedience.

George James was whipped if he didn't do exactly as he was instructed. Two generations later, his granddaughter, Jane, related a story she had once heard.

"One winter, George had a cold. Pneumonia was always a fear because in the 1800s it was often fatal. So George's mother told him, 'You are not to go outside or so much as put your feet on the porch.' He knew enough to obey, but a package arrived and since the maid was out, he answered the door. As he stepped out to get the package, he couldn't help but place his feet on the threshold. When his mother returned, she asked her son, 'Did you touch the porch with your feet?' When he admitted he had, he received a thrashing."

Even if Henrietta's response was tough, her fear of illness was common before the age of modern medicine. Aside from the untimely death of Henrietta's mother, her grandmother—who had become a Baptist late in life—was reported to have died of a cold caused by her baptismal immersion. And when Henrietta was ten, she'd lost her six-year-old brother. Life was precarious, even for those strong in body and spirit.

One day in February 1866, George was invited to Germany to give advice on an important railway project he was to take part in. It was a promising business opportunity, but it led him to stop at a hotel where he passed a night in damp bedding.

The account is short on details. Why was he in a damp bed? Had his ceramic hot-water bottle, then popular with travelers, leaked during the evening? Had he experienced a bout of night sweats? Whatever happened, Mimi grew up hearing that he suffered a drenching chill from sleeping in wet sheets and returned to London sick with pneumonia.

Perhaps chill-induced pneumonia was an easier tale to tell a child, but what ailed George didn't have to do with his lungs. He had a urinary blockage. With the medical limits of the 1860s, it was difficult to treat. And carried a frightful prognosis.

Despite the doctor's efforts, Henrietta's fervent prayers, and the bedside vigil of his faithful secretary, George's condition worsened. Neither his great passion for life, nor the unfailing determination that had made him so successful, was able to save him. On the third day, at the unfinished age of fifty-seven, he died.

The doctor recorded his cause of death as "Extravasation of urine—48 hours," and below that, "Exhaustion—12 hours."

After his body had been bathed and dressed for his final journey, an artist, Otto Brauer, was called to render his likeness. George's eyes were closed, but his thick unruly curls framed a serious face that, even in death, gave the appearance of a vital man resting.

The following week, his body was taken by horse-drawn hearse to East Finchley Cemetery. Five miles away, it was not the closest burial ground, but it was where Henrietta's father had been interred a few years earlier. The old goldsmith's coffin had been placed twelve feet down, leaving space for four more above him.

On Henrietta's forty-seventh birthday, the grown-over grave was reopened and her husband's casket was slowly lowered to rest on top of her father's.

George Tate—the man who had won Henrietta's heart on a Paris-bound train, warmed that same heart through long Canadian winters, and then shattered it with his final departure—was gone. Their marriage had ended as unexpectedly as it had started.

4

A Poor Choice

George Tate died many years before Mimi was born, so she knew him only through family portraits and her father's stories. But tales of her grandfather's ability to achieve whatever he set out to do—whether to win the hand of a woman or build a bridge—exerted a strong influence on her. She inherited his considerable vitality, passion, and willpower, and what she didn't inherit, she absorbed from her father's anecdotes. Hearing George's story, and knowing his blood coursed through her veins, empowered her with the belief that anything was possible.

His legacy, however, served not just as a lesson in the opportunities of life, but in the pitfalls as well. George's early death had a devastating effect on his loved ones and their future. Although he reportedly left the family rich in furnishings, paintings, and heirlooms, probate papers note his effects at under £50, worth less than $8,000 in today's value.

According to family lore, Henrietta was independently wealthy, but the records are a bit contradictory. Her father, James John Gliddon, was the watchcase maker who couldn't afford the fee to apprentice to a lawyer. He was, in fact, the son of tripe sellers. They'd had an offal business in the very same shop he later used for crafting his fine gold watches. At his death, James John's effects were valued at under £20. The Gliddons were successful tradesmen, but not exactly affluent.

However, Henrietta's mother came from the Knocker family, headed by a Customs and Excise man. They may have had money since one of Henrietta's aunts owned prime rental property in an era when women weren't commonly landlords.

So, between her father's business income and holdings on her mother's side, Henrietta no doubt had an adequate dowry to fall back on. Even if she had her own resources, though, without her husband's income, she would need to be prudent.

The widow—now solely responsible for seventeen-year-old Harrie, nine-year-old George James, five-year-old Maud, and four-year-old Ethel—turned to her older brother Joshua.

A parliamentary official and shorthand writer for the courts, Joshua lived in Abbey Gardens, a block-long row of fashionable three-story townhouses. Serving as man of the family since their father's death, he took in his bereaved sister and her children.

As grief-stricken as Henrietta was that year, when the period of mourning ended, she was urged to think about remarrying. Aside from financial considerations and the societal expectations of nineteenth-century England, her temperament may have required it. For, along with the skills of an artist, she was said to have shared those personality traits often seen as common to their kind; she was imaginative, intuitive, and emotional. She needed a practical, down-to-earth man on whom to lean.

With four children to rear, Henrietta may not have had many suitors, but she was soon courted by the man who had been with her during her darkest hours. Her late husband's secretary, William, a widower with a three-year-old boy, asked her to marry him.

Even if trusted by Henrietta, William was not the steadfast influence others wanted for her. That may have been due, in part, to his youth. He was only thirty-two, sixteen years younger than Henrietta. But the greater cause for concern had less to do with his age and more to do with a flaw in his character.

Family historian Alain Tate noted that Henrietta's lawyer and her closest relatives advised against the marriage. "Although he came from a good social background," wrote Tate, "she failed to perceive that he was of a weak and frivolous disposition."

But in the same way that Henrietta did as she pleased when she rushed into her first marriage, she heeded no one's counsel in her second. Fourteen months after George died, with her brother standing as witness, she married William.

It began well enough. In 1871, five years into their marriage, they resided a short walk from her brother's place. Henrietta's children lived at home while her eight-year-old stepson, Henry, attended a distant boarding school. William worked as an auctioneer and estate agent. As before, a couple of live-in servants took care of the house. The only thing that appeared unusual about their lives was Henrietta's age, which seemed to have decreased rather than increased. When the census taker came to their door that year, Henrietta shaved off nine years, reporting herself to be forty-three.

A decade later, they lived in a narrow, two-story row house in Lambeth, a less-desirable neighborhood on the other side of London. Thirty-two-year-old Harrie was by now a true spinster, confirmed not just by age, but by misfortune. In her youth, a piece of ceiling plaster had broken off and fallen on her. Perhaps she'd been sleeping, or maybe she'd heard the cracking and looked up at the last moment. In any case, she suffered a frightful injury. She was left disfigured and blind in one eye. With no hope of marriage, she had settled into the unpromising life of companion to her mother.

Twenty-four-year-old George James, a slightly built man with a serious demeanor, had received his degree in accounting and administration. He worked as a clerk. Maud, under Henrietta's tutelage, sketched and painted, and the youngest, Ethel, had recently married a salesman in the hardware business. The newlyweds lived in a flat around the corner.

But in an era when household help was almost as much a necessity as status symbol, the Whiteheads no longer had live-in servants. Perhaps William told Henrietta cutbacks were necessary because of the "Long Depression" which began in 1873 and still held a grip on England. Perhaps there truly were fiscal forces beyond his control. Perhaps.

According to Mimi, though, William had been secretly spending Henrietta's money from the beginning and it was dwindling.

It all came to a head a couple of years later. George James, a sensitive man who occasionally exhibited powers of perception that others lacked, had an eerie vision that his stepfather killed himself. It was 1883 and things hadn't felt right for some time. That summer, his premonition turned into a reality.

On July 26, the *Sheffield Daily Telegram* reported William's demise. The authorities, however, didn't rule it a suicide, possibly to avoid adding disgrace to the grief of a stunned widow.

> "An inquest was held yesterday morning at St. John's Vestry Hall, Horselydown, concerning the death of William Henry Whitehead, aged 48, civil engineer, late of Overton road, Brixton, who was found dead in bed at the Terminus Hotel, London Bridge, last Sunday. It was stated that the deceased had been for some time harassed by pecuniary difficulties, and the medical evidence was to the effect that death was due to syncope, brought about by anxiety and excitement. A verdict was returned accordingly."

Syncope, defined as a temporary loss of consciousness, was often given as a cause of unexplained or sudden death, in this case leaving mourners to believe William had checked himself into the Terminus Hotel, gone to bed, and simply "fainted dead away."

Henrietta's brother, Joshua, responsible for two family plots at the East Finchley Cemetery, arranged to have William buried in the same grave as Henrietta's first husband.

After George Tate's interment seventeen years earlier, the plot had become the final resting place for two more family members. Now with William's coffin added and the grave full, it would have been customary to erect the headstone for the five resting below: Henrietta's father, her two husbands, a cousin, and a nephew. It may have been the shameful circumstances of William's death, or perhaps Henrietta's lack of funds, but the grave was left unmarked.

She was a widow again, but this time no longer young... and no longer solvent. Only after William's death did she become aware of the extent of his financial mismanagement.

There was nothing left.

To pay William's outstanding debts, sixty-four-year-old Henrietta was told she'd have to sell her treasures—heirlooms passed down from the Tate and Gliddon families, as well as the beloved objects of art she had acquired with her first husband.

Stepping into the role of man of the house, twenty-six-year-old George James took charge of the monetary affairs and made sure his mother was occupied elsewhere when the estate sale was held. Her friends attended, however, and bought many of her things, which they then quietly returned to her home. George James was deeply impressed by their loyalty and kindness.

Even as he shielded his mother from the worst of the financial problems, he'd also suffered a substantial loss. A year earlier he'd wanted to propose to the girl who had captured his heart, Agnes Mary Gudgeon, a strawberry blonde with impossibly curly hair. But at the time, he didn't have enough money to provide for a wife. Now, after his family's terrible reversal of fortune, there was even less.

Like his father before him, George James was responsible for supporting a widowed mother and unmarried sisters. Unlike his father, he had to do it while climbing out of debt.

5

An Unexpected Inheritance

George James was a fairly successful accountant, but he didn't develop the strong driving force that had defined his father. He was more like his mother.

"He was a musician and a poet," according to Alain Tate, "a dreamer more than a man of action, an emotive personality with occasional fits of anger, but on the whole, a very affectionate and lovable person."

His affections had for years focused on Agnes Mary, known to all by her nickname, Queeny. She was slender and petite—almost a head shorter than George James—but a practical and self-assured woman.

Her family wasn't rich but quite comfortable. Queeny's father, balding and sporting the mutton-chop sideburns fashionable at the time, was Edward Barnaby Gudgeon. He came from a family of upholsterers and cabinet makers in Winchester, but as a young man he had moved to London and secured a job at the Bank of England. There he worked his way up to a trusted position in the gold-weighing room.

After retiring, he had been elected to the school board, was active in several charitable organizations, and served as a parish vestryman and guardian, where he was tasked with overseeing relief to the poor. Having proven himself at the local level, he was appointed London's Consul General of Liberia.

Edward was an important man with certain monetary standards to uphold, and, unfortunately, George James did not meet them. If Queeny's mother had still been alive, she might have served as a balance to her banker husband, but she had died when the girl was only two, leaving Queeny to be raised by nannies and nuns.

Although George James was a man who had endured fiscal misfortune, he finally enjoyed a fair share of luck, even if he was past thirty by the time it came his way.

A long-time friend of his family, Mary Ann Fleschelle, loved George James like a son and was distressed by his circumstances. When she died, she left him her home and all her money. He suddenly had close to £6,000, equivalent in today's dollars to almost $100,000.

By then, however, Queeny no longer lived in London, nor even in England for that matter. She hadn't for some time. Seven years earlier, when George James hadn't been able to offer a proposal of marriage, she'd moved to France.

It was not a foreign land to her. When she was a teenager, her father, a staunch Catholic, had sent her across the channel to attend the Sacred Heart Convent in Amiens, eighty miles north of Paris. It was an exclusive Catholic girls' boarding school where the Gudgeon sisters were enrolled to better their French and further their religious education. While there, Queeny met the daughters of a few French noble families, including one who was to become the Countess de Bélizal. The two became close friends.

When Queeny was twenty-six, she returned to France to visit her friend, who had in the meantime married the count and moved into his eighteenth-century castle in Brittany. The countess asked Queeny to stay with her as a companion.

In the 1880s, there were hardly any occupations suitable for unmarried women of privileged backgrounds. But a "lady's companion" was a well-respected position, not unlike the role of a lady-in-waiting in the royal family.

A lady's companion provided a much-needed service for a woman of rank or wealth. In a society that held many restrictions for upper-class women—and a degree of isolation even in one's own castle—loneliness and boredom were common. A noblewoman required someone of genteel birth with whom to converse and confide while sewing, having tea, or taking a leisurely walk in the gardens. Because a lady's companion was deemed acceptable company in the best of circles, she helped her mistress entertain guests, joined her in charity work, and accompanied her to social events or on her travels.

This, then, was the life Queeny was living, in a chateau in the medieval town of Moncontour, when George James came into his fortune. He sent her a cable to announce he'd be calling on her, and while taking a walk together in the picturesque countryside of Brittany, he asked her to marry him. She said yes.

In spite of now having the finances to wed—and her acceptance of his proposal—yet another obstacle remained. George James, like most of the British population, was a member of the Church of England rather than the Roman Catholic Church that was so important to Queeny's father.

Edward Gudgeon had not only sent his children to Catholic schools, he was active in the Church and one of the founders of a local convent. His religion permeated even his role as Consul General of Liberia, as revealed in a sixteen-page address he presented in 1888 to the Manchester Geographical Society.

In it, he praised Liberia's weather and natural resources, decried the liquor traffic carried on by British and foreign traders and, most pointedly, promoted the spread of the Roman Catholic Church. He noted it was "of the deepest importance to counteract the spread of Mohammedanism, the direst and most powerful enemy of Christianity in Africa."

Although partisan-thinking Edward didn't deem the Church of England as powerful an enemy as Islam, it still wasn't acceptable for the Gudgeons. Queeny would have to marry a Catholic. So she urged George James to consult a Catholic Church canon, a family friend, about converting. In short order, he was confirmed in the Catholic faith.

The nuptials were set for June 11, 1889, at the gothic-spired Church of the Sacred Heart in Camberwell. Notwithstanding the seven-year delay, Queeny—who had a reputation for being late—nearly missed her own wedding. In the rush to dress, she misplaced a silk stocking. A frantic search proved fruitless, but Queeny was a levelheaded woman not to be stopped by a missing piece of hosiery. She slipped on the one stocking, donned a regal air, and took her place at the altar.

With the bride's father, Edward Gudgeon, and the groom's stepbrother, Henry Whitehead, acting as witnesses, they married. George James was thirty-two and Queeny was thirty-three.

These were Mimi's parents.

6

A Bleak Beginning

George James brought Queeny to the London residence he had inherited from Mrs. Fleschelle. The generous-sized three-story terrace house at 219 Brixton Road easily accommodated the newlyweds, as well as a couple of servants in the fourth-floor attic.

Queeny, however, missed the bucolic life in Brittany, so she and George James sailed across the English Channel to find a vacation home where they could spend their summer months.

With its pleasant beaches and favorable rate of exchange for the pound, the French province was popular with British tourists. Many visiting Englishmen bought holiday villas in the lively towns of Saint-Malo and Dinard, but Queeny wasn't interested in resort living. She and George James called on the Countess de Bélizal, who suggested a place ten miles north of her castle.

Surrounded by farmland, the old fieldstone house they went to inspect had no modern amenities. Paved roads, electric lights, and running water—conveniences the Tates enjoyed in London—hadn't yet made their way to rural Brittany. But the property boasted a freshwater spring and was well situated. Although only a short walk from the large Bay of Saint-Brieuc, the house stood on a slight rise that guaranteed it wouldn't flood.

The structure itself—three stories with matching chimneys at each end and dormer windows in the roof—had a drawing room, dining room, six bedrooms, kitchen, and a stable with rooms above it for servants.

Making the house livable required some work, but soon it stood in the French countryside like a proper manor. Hedges and roses lined the courtyard in front, and even more flowers adorned the back. Beyond the rear garden, they also planted an orchard of fruit trees.

George James, who was an Englishman to the core and proud of carrying the name of the patron saint of England, dubbed his domain Villa St. George.

On the other side of the bay lay the nearest city, Saint-Brieuc. It was five miles away, far enough to ensure the Tates a quiet rural life, but close enough, by horse-drawn buggy, to provide them with urban necessities and diversions.

Nearer still were the small villages of Hillion to the north, and Yffiniac to the south, each a brisk thirty-minute walk along a dirt road. Yffiniac had more conveniences, namely a post office and an outlying train station. However, the Tates' home was in Hillion's jurisdiction, so they regularly followed the tree-lined *rue d'Hillion* to get their mail from a little pub, buy the provisions they couldn't get from nearby farmers, and attend church.

Most of the year, however, the Tates spent in England and it was there that Queeny gave birth to their first child, Henrietta Agnes. They distinguished her from the other Henriettas—her artist grandmother and blind-in-one-eye Aunt Harrie—by calling her Rita. The baby was baptized in the Catholic Church with her grandfather, Edward Gudgeon, serving as godfather.

The seventy-year-old diplomat and promoter of good works, however, didn't live to see his granddaughter past her infancy. He suffered from bronchitis, not an unusual ailment in the dirty air of London with its coal-burning factories and fireplaces. But in the end, it was a cerebral hemorrhage that caused his death. Just three months after Rita's christening, Edward Gudgeon was laid to rest in Camberwell Old Cemetery, next to his second wife, who had died the year before.

Following her father's death, there was less to keep Queeny in crowded London with its noise and pollution. So the Tate family found a home in Acton, a suburb farther out and west of London proper. Their second daughter, Mary Kathleen, was born there eighteen months after Rita.

The next year brought the last of three closely spaced girls. That was Mimi.

She arrived on August 9, 1893, well before her due date and critically premature. She weighed less than three pounds. To keep her warm in the damp English air, her nurse put her in a cotton-lined box next to the oven. Mimi was not expected to live, but even in her earliest hours she exhibited a tenacious grip on life.

Back then, no one called her Mimi. She was christened Maud Isabelle Tate. Her parents also gave her a nickname and just as her mother, Agnes Mary, was most commonly known as Queeny, Maud Isabelle was known as Mona. It wasn't until many years later that she chose the moniker Mimi.

By the time she was born, the family had made plans to move permanently to their summer home. After four years in the greater London area, Queeny wanted to live year-round in France. George James's inheritance, however, was not great enough to allow him a life of leisure, and since professional positions in Brittany were scarce—especially for someone with limited French—he decided to keep his job in England. He planned to spend half of each year working at the accounting firm, and the other half with his family at Villa St. George.

It's likely their move to Brittany was based in part on health concerns. Aside from air pollution, the greater London area suffered a high concentration of infectious diseases in an era before the development of medications to treat them. Child mortality was high. George James had a keen interest in medicine and was probably as anxious as his wife to get their children out of England's unwholesome capital.

Queeny may have intended to be settled in Villa St. George before Mimi's birth, allowing the family to enjoy the summer holidays there. The baby's early arrival, however, surely forced them to wait a few months until the tiny girl was strong enough to travel. By then, the season was over and George James was back at work. Queeny and her girls, accompanied by their servants and nannies, embarked on the rough crossing to Brittany. November now, the beaches were cold and the flowers no longer in bloom, but autumn crops were being harvested and the air was clean.

Despite the healthier environment, shortly after their move, Queeny's middle daughter, twenty-two-month-old Mary Kathleen, was stricken with spinal meningitis. It's not known whether she had brought the infection—spread through coughing and sneezing—with her from England, or if she caught it on the boat or even in France. Regardless, the toddler was dreadfully sick. Mimi related the story she'd been told.

> **"** My sister was ill for about three days. At that time, my father was in London and it was difficult to reach him because in this village we had no telephone. Finally my mother sent a telegram to my father acquainting him with the fact that my sister was seriously ill and requesting him to please come home.
>
> Now, to come home to Hillion meant crossing the English Channel, which took twelve hours. After landing in a small place called Saint-Malo, he had to take either the morning train or, if he arrived later in the day, board a night train and ride until the next morning. Hillion had no station, so he had to get off at Yffiniac and ask some farmer for a ride to the house.
>
> When my father finally arrived, the courtyard was filled with Brittany peasants and friends. Just then this

little coffin was carried out through the front door, followed by my mother.

There was a law that anyone dying of spinal meningitis was to be buried immediately, within a day, so my mother had had to start the funeral without him.

A man said to my father, 'Would you like to look at your child?' He replied, 'No, the last time I saw this dear little thing she was waving and saying *bye-bye* to me.' **"**

It was a late November day when the somber entourage walked behind the small casket to Hillion. The ancient graveyard beside the church had already been filled to capacity, so Mary Kathleen was buried in the new cemetery. A bit removed from the village center, it was a stark piece of land overlooking the frigid waters of the bay.

That night, Queeny, mourning her little girl left alone in that bleak burial ground, was unable to sleep.

" It was well after midnight and my mother was feeling so bad, she walked down to the cemetery and stood at Mary Kathleen's grave. It was dark, and she was smoking a cigarette. Suddenly, out of nowhere, came a shot, and the cigarette was knocked out of her mouth! Terrified, she immediately hurried home.

The next day a story spread around, as it does in a little village. A man was in the pub drinking and said that when he was going out to hunt ducks, very early in the morning, that he passed by the cemetery and saw a ghost!

'So,' he said, 'believe me, I shot that ghost!'

The people there were very superstitious. I'm quite sure my mother didn't try to visit my sister's grave at night again. It was simply too dangerous. **"**

Mary Kathleen's fifty-eight-year-old nanny, Adele, was heartbroken. Queeny, who regarded the older French woman as part of the family, put her in charge of caring for Mimi.

Two weeks later, the family's sorrow deepened further with the death of George James's sister, Ethel. Only thirty-two, she died a week after giving birth to her fifth child, a boy they named Herbert. In an era when infant mortality was already high, it was even higher for the motherless. Five months later, Ethel's baby followed her in death.

Before the first anniversary of Mary Kathleen's passing, at a time when Mimi was taking her first steps, the family finally had cause to look ahead. Queeny was expecting another baby.

An active woman who enjoyed vigorous walks far into her pregnancies, she was out on an autumn day when she suddenly found herself in close quarters with a neighbor's bull. He chased her through a field, but Queeny, heavy with child, managed to outrun him.

This slightly-more-than-vigorous outing brought on labor. Although anxious about having another early delivery, she and George James were happy when, after three daughters, she gave birth to a small but healthy son.

Queeny had trouble nursing her born-too-soon baby, so she hired Bobonne, a wet nurse from a neighboring village. Three weeks later, they took the infant to the church in Hillion and baptized him George Edward Cecil. The Countess de Bélizal was named godmother.

In less than fifteen months, Queeny had given birth to a premature baby, moved to France, buried a toddler, narrowly escaped being shot, and delivered a second preterm infant. What's more, she'd spent most of that time without the company of her husband, who likewise, was forced to bear much of his own worry and sorrow alone. Even with servants to lighten the load and nannies to take care of the children, Mimi's first year was spent in a home most likely darkened by stress and grief.

Before the age when her earliest memories were formed, however, easier times had arrived. Mimi always spoke glowingly of her childhood in Brittany and especially of life with her little brother, George Edward, who soon became her playmate and best friend.

BOOK II

Brittany, France
1893–1909

QUEENY—Mimi's mother, Agnes Mary Gudgeon.

GEORGE JAMES—Mimi's father, George James Frederick Tate.

HENRIETTA—Mimi's grandmother, Henrietta Gliddon.

HARRIE—Mimi's aunt, Henrietta Alexandriana Ross Tate.

RITA—Mimi's oldest sibling, Henrietta Agnes.

MARY KATHLEEN—Mimi's older sister, who died at 22 months.

GEORGE EDWARD—Mimi's brother, George Edward Cecil.

ADELE LESAGE—Mimi's aging nursemaid.

MIMI—Christened Maud Isabelle and commonly called Mona.

COUNTESS DE BÉLIZAL—Queeny's dearest friend.

VILLA ST. GEORGE—The Tates' home in Hillion, Brittany.

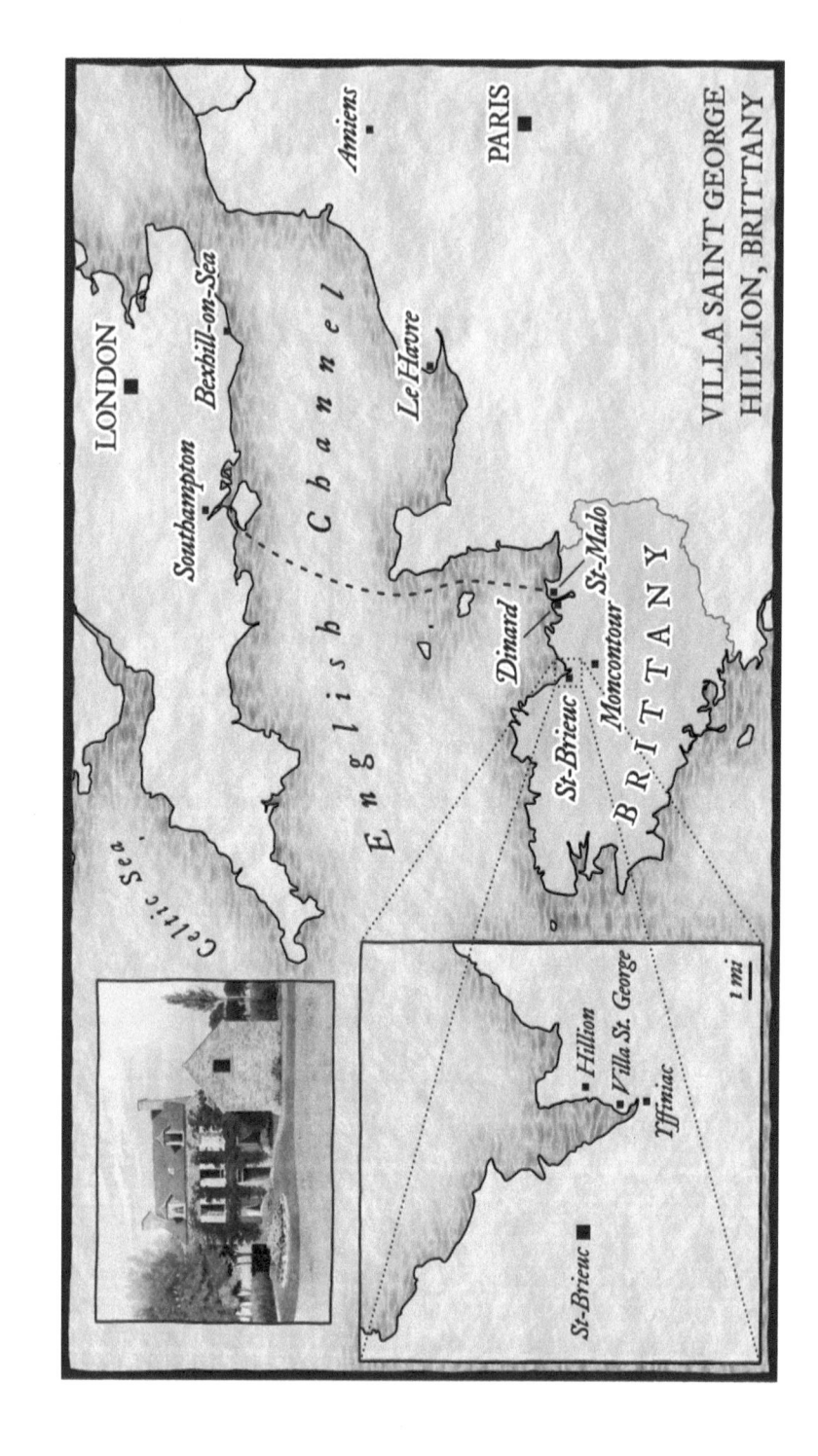

7

A Brittany Childhood

Life at Villa St. George reflected a mix of British and French influences. The small manor was a proper English home, at least when George James was in residence. Still, the household staff and nannies were French and, not surprisingly, Mimi and her siblings grew up speaking the language of the land. Queeny was comfortable in either tongue, but George James, who demanded flawless English of his children, wasn't in favor of them speaking *en français*. Luckily, frequent guests from London kept the Tate children's English fluent.

George James's recently married sister, Maud, visited with her husband, William Rogers. Both artists, they enjoyed capturing the Brittany countryside and produced watercolors of the farmers' thatched-roof homes. The rural yards lacked the colorful flowers of England's picturesque cottages, but the everyday mishmash of barrels and brooms, chickens and pigs, held a quaint charm of their own.

Although George James didn't seem to have inherited his mother's artistic talent, he had great respect for art, especially in its ability to preserve history. Once, he commissioned an artist to create a large oil painting of the inside of a typical Breton home. It depicted a traditionally attired country family—men sporting black hats with black ribbons and the women in white lace caps and wooden sabot shoes—gathered around the hearth as they entertained city relatives in modern garb.

George James's mother, Henrietta, visited on occasion, but she lived in London with Harrie, in three rooms paid for by her son. He stayed there during his working months.

Henrietta was the only grandparent Mimi knew, the others having died before she was born. Even if Mimi had very few first-hand recollections of her straight-backed Grandmamma, one of her favorite stories was of the time Henrietta carved a likeness of Queeny from stone.

A man, perhaps a neighbor or acquaintance, had scoffed at the art of sculpting, asserting that anyone with the proper tools could do it. According to Mimi, Henrietta was not pleased.

"You don't need the tools," she'd said, "you need the skills. If you give me a piece of marble, a hammer, and an old nail, I can carve out a respectable figure."

Her challenger brought her a ten-pound slab of marble and a bent nail. Queeny, wearing what looked like a medieval headscarf, posed as the Virgin Mary. Then Henrietta proceeded to silence the scoffer by carefully hammering out, without the benefit of a chisel, a neoclassical bas-relief profile.

Mimi, who grew up admiring the white marble carving, loved this display of determination. Not many girls had a grandmother who was self-assured enough to accept such a challenge... talented enough to win a medal from Prince Albert... or bold enough to request an audience with Queen Victoria. Henrietta's life inspired Mimi in much the same way that George Tate's had, fueling in her a spirit of independence and confidence.

The last story about her Grandmamma had an equally enduring effect. In her old age, Henrietta—in a bid to confer lasting protection on her son—told George James, "Whoever does you good will flourish, but whoever wounds you will have my curse until the day they die."

It's doubtful anyone greatly benefited or suffered from her solemn invocation, since George James would have shared that part of the story with Mimi as well. But it was perhaps the beginning of Mimi's belief in the power of the mind. At the very least, she grew up believing in the ability, and occasional necessity, of placing curses.

But that was to come later. Mimi wasn't yet five when Henrietta lived out her final days. She was seventy-nine and residing on England's southern coast at a Catholic home for the "aged poor, orphans and destitute children." Despite the humble status of the residents, Nazareth House was a new three-story building with gables and corner turrets.

It's not clear why the family matriarch—raised in the Church of England and supported by her son—was in a Catholic facility for the indigent, much less one seventy miles from her last address in London. Why wasn't she living at Villa St. George? Was she perhaps as demanding in old age as she'd been as a mother? Or was she a softened Grandmama who simply couldn't climb the stairs to the bedrooms?

As to the location—Bexhill-on-Sea in Sussex—the home was only four miles from a seaside convent where Queeny had lived as an adolescent, so maybe Henrietta's practical daughter-in-law had connections with the nuns.

In any case, it was at Nazareth House, with a matron by her side, that seventy-nine-year-old Henrietta died of asthenia—loss of strength—and old age. She was buried at St. Peter's in Bexhill.

Fifty-year-old Harrie, who had spent her life at her mother's side, was then living at Villa St. George. Aside from her, the residents included George James, Queeny, their three children, two nannies, a cook, and an assortment of household help. For months at a time, it also housed one or another of Mimi's cousins, who visited from England to better their French.

These were the children of Queeny's oldest sister, Emily, who had married a handsome bank clerk named John Westley and over the following two decades gave birth to seventeen children. Three died early, but she raised the others—with the help of a number of nannies—to adulthood. Although most of Emily's children were much older, her last was born just a year before Queeny's first, and the age gaps were not so great as to preclude friendships and fun when the youngest Westleys came to visit.

As Mimi later recounted, summer days typically found them all walking to the beach five minutes beyond the village church.

> "The road from Villa St. George to Hillion was delightful. It was about three kilometers, on an avenue with chestnut trees on either side. It was the most beautiful avenue that I think I've ever seen.
>
> We used to walk to Hillion often, and then take the road to the beach, where I would play for hours. It had beautiful silver sand and I could sit there all day and still be perfectly clean.
>
> Mummy had long, blond hair, well past her waist. And she was an excellent swimmer. Many times I would see my mother swimming with her hair floating on the water, as she took these great, strong strokes."

The sun turned Mimi's own hair lighter and her fair skin darker. It also brought out, to her dismay, the freckles that gilded her face. But Mimi loved the sunshine and the family spent as much time as they could outside, especially in the warmer months.

> "In the front garden there was an enormous old weeping willow. We had a table and chairs under the branches, where we sat when we didn't go to the beach. We ate all our meals under this tree.
>
> In the tree itself was a big nest that had been there for many years. It belonged to a couple of old jackdaws or magpies. They were black-blue birds with beautiful white

wings. They raised their babies, and when they were of flying age, the parents just threw them out of the nest and continued living there.

They were very tricky birds and used to steal everything. They would fly down on the table and pick up anything they could find. If Mummy or Aunty Harrie had been sewing and had run into the house for something and left a thimble, they would not be able to find it when they came back. Once, one of these cheeky birds came down and nipped my mother's earring right off her ear and took it up to the nest!

When the summer was over, someone would go up into the willow tree to retrieve all these items—the thimbles and spoons and things. **"**

In the autumn, a time of fewer visitors, the children enjoyed the simple pleasures of gathering fresh food. They picked apples from their trees, and what they didn't eat they carefully placed in a straw-lined room over the stable to save for cider. They were responsible for checking on the harvest and throwing out any bad apples before they could spoil the rest.

Aside from the easy pickings in their own orchard, Queeny took the children to hunt for wild mushrooms. Often as big as saucers, each one could serve three or four people. Brittany was known for its wheat, onions, and vegetables, too. And sometimes the family—passing fields tended by farmers stooped over their sickles—received a special treat.

" They had a great many fields with potatoes, which ripen in the fall when their foliage is dead and brown. The peasants would dig up the potatoes, then take all the dead weeds and make a huge pile of them. They would put the potatoes inside, next to the ground, and set fire to the weeds. We'd be walking in the country and stop and talk to a farmer, and he'd say to my mother, 'Oh, Madame, would you have a potato? They are just about ready to eat.' I tell you, no potato ever tasted better, with neither salt nor butter, than those potatoes. They were absolutely delicious. **"**

Although not a gregarious woman, Queeny was friendly with her neighbors, whether they were the dirt-poor sharecroppers or the local aristocracy who lived in the two nearby chateaux. She was a frequent guest of the latter, having met them years earlier through the Countess de Bélizal. They often played cards together. One couple, the Count and Countess de la Noue, had daughters about the ages of Rita and Mimi, so the girls were regular visitors to each other's homes.

Queeny, however, was not the high-society type. She never lacked the credentials or propriety that made her welcome in upper class circles, but she was a down-to-earth woman most content riding her bike along the dirt roads or taking her children on afternoon outings in the countryside.

One would think that a woman who had been shot at in the cemetery and chased by a bull on the eve of her son's birth might have grown fearful, but it was not in her nature to shy away from the occasional hazards of life in Brittany. She enjoyed all that the rural setting had to offer.

One sunny day—perhaps in the spring when the sweet scent of flowering gorse filled the air—she took Rita, Mimi, George Edward, and their small dog for a picnic in a nearby meadow. They had just set out their things under a tree when a group of bellicose bovines appeared and rushed at them. She hurried the youngsters up the tree and passed them the dog. Gathering up her long skirt, she bolted up behind them. The cows butted the tree for a while, but even when they'd finally calmed down, they couldn't be persuaded to go away. Queeny, who was cautious when her children's safety was at stake, kept them entertained in the tree until the farmer came out to get his herd for milking.

She also led her brood on nocturnal adventures a few times a year. On those full-moon nights when the tides were so high the seawater overflowed the banks, the family, as well as most of the villagers, walked to the Hillion levee to take in the sight.

But evenings were normally spent in the drawing room, lit by oil lamps and candles, with the household entertaining themselves. Queeny or Aunty Harrie would play the piano while the children sang, at least until the little ones started lessons and were able to supply the musical accompaniment on their own.

At some point, they acquired a Gramophone, which the children took turns cranking, although probably only those with the steadiest of hands were allowed to place the needle in the record groove. The phonograph was likely a gift from their father on one of his semi-annual trips home.

George James continued to spend at least half of the year in England. Earlier, his company had sent him to Texas to conduct an audit at a British-owned mining company, where he proudly solved a case of embezzlement, but for the most part, his work was in London. He no longer, however, kept a permanent flat in the city. After his mother was moved to Nazareth House, he stayed with other relatives or lodged with an old friend. He was always eager, though, to return to his family.

"Leaving Villa St. George in mid-September," wrote Alain Tate, "he used to come back home for the Christmas and New Year season and leave again in early January for the next three months. His children remembered that he was always loaded with toys and sweets for them, whenever coming back home to Brittany."

With Mimi's father home for the holidays, Christmas was a festive time, especially after the children were old enough to be included in an invitation to Midnight Mass at one of the nearby castles. Mimi recalled celebrating at the Chateau des Aubiers.

> Two families, friends of ours, lived on the hill, each in their own castle. They were nobility, of course, and one couple, the Count and Countess de la Noue, always had a Midnight Mass on Christmas Eve.
>
> Each of these castles had a chapel on the grounds. A priest lived in the castle with them so that every morning they could have communion in their own private church. On Christmas Eve, my father and mother and we children, when we were old enough, were always invited to the big celebration, the Midnight Mass, after which we enjoyed a sumptuous banquet.
>
> I'll never forget this beautiful castle. The chandeliers along the great mahogany hall were enormous. Of course at that time they did not have electricity; they lit candles. It was simply magnificent, like a fairyland. And there was a huge table where we all sat, sometimes twenty-five or thirty of us.

The head of the family missed some annual events: The Day of the Dead, when everyone visited the graves of the departed, and Good Friday, the night when groups of sharecroppers visited the villa's courtyard to sing Easter songs in exchange for a few coins. But during his months in Brittany, George James devoted much of his energy to improving life for others.

> Where we lived was really in the country; even the chateaux didn't have running water. Near our home we

had a natural spring. It was covered by a large stone to shade it from the sun, so the water was always cool.

We paid a woman to draw water several times a day. She had two pails and I remember Papa ordered a wooden collar, such as the Chinese wear on their shoulders, and the pails hung on each side. It made it easier for her. "

Mimi's father was known for his creativity. Alain Tate said he "lived the life of a gentleman-farmer, writing musical pieces or inventing machines, such as a shoe-brushing machine, which he had patented but was not able to sell."

According to Tate, the patriarch placed emphasis on staying well-informed, too. "He was following world politics very closely, reading from the first to the last page the many papers he used to receive from Britain, namely the *Daily Mail* and the *News of the World*, underlining with a pencil whatever news he felt was noteworthy. His views were clearly conservative."

Certainly one of the most noteworthy events of that time was the death of Queen Victoria, who passed away one year after the turn of the century. Most of her subjects, George James and Queeny included, had never known another monarch.

It was the end of a century, and the end of an era.

8

Unhallowed Ground

England may have passed into the Edwardian era of increasing modernity, but the bucolic life Mimi lived in the countryside of Brittany remained the same. Yet no childhood, even if idyllic, is free of worry.

Despite the beauty and abundance surrounding them, the local priests kept Mimi ever aware of the afterlife and the frightening existence that might follow the serene one they were enjoying on earth.

The Church wielded a strong influence in Brittany, a region known as one of the most devoutly Catholic in all of France. Notwithstanding George James's upbringing in the Church of England—and any personal beliefs to which he may have clung—he was now a Roman Catholic, and there was no question about his children being brought up in that faith.

Queeny, although perhaps a bit more pragmatic than pious, was a committed Catholic who raised Mimi to follow the practices of the Church, whether sitting through Mass or walking the dusty road to Hillion.

"In France there's always been a custom, that wherever there is a fatal accident, where a man might fall off his horse, or have a heart attack and die, that on that place where he fell, there should be erected a memorial, usually a cross with his name on it. Along the road there were several crosses testifying that some man or woman had died there. When you passed the crosses or monuments, it was customary to make the sign of the cross, in honor of the man who died, and to bless him. **"**

More numerous than mishaps along the road, however, were casualties at sea. The ocean provided a livelihood to many, including coastal fisherman and the adventurous deep-sea anglers who regularly crossed the Atlantic to fish as far away as Newfoundland and Iceland. But the sea brought hazards to both those in boats and those closer to home.

The large bay at Hillion, like much of the northern coast of Brittany, was subject to unusually strong tides. The water did not simply rise and fall a few feet in a gradual manner. Instead, from tide in to tide out, it dropped as much as forty feet. In spring and autumn especially, the ocean retreated miles from shore, revealing the seabed and stranding boats that just hours before had been floating above their anchors.

It was a boon for Breton clam diggers, and the mussel growers too, who reaped their harvest from rows of exposed wooden pilings. Farmers pulled their two-wheeled handcarts to the bay to gather kelp for fertilizer.

But they had to be careful. When the water returned, it rushed back at speeds of five miles an hour; during the strongest tides, it raced in as fast as a horse could gallop. Any people unlucky enough to be caught in the surge could find themselves knocked off their feet.

Drownings were common, and the coastal inhabitants grew up with respect for the strong ebb and flow of the sea. But those from other districts, especially after a visit to one of the local pubs, weren't always as cautious. Mimi spoke often of one such man.

" The ocean receded every twelve hours for miles, just as far as your eye could see, and it left the land, where the sea had been, dry enough to walk on. Across the bay there was another village where people used to go occasionally to do errands. But they would always go, of course, when the tide was out, knowing they had several hours in which to get there and back on dry land.

Now, when the tide began to flow back, it was very strong and came in fast. There was a first flow that wasn't as deep, but the second was like a tremendous wave.

One day, my father and mother were sitting on a friend's verandah overlooking the sea and they knew the first flow would be coming very shortly. In the distance, they saw this man weaving home. They could see that he was drunk but trying to get ahead of the water. **"**

Alarmed, George James raced to a boat, but by the time the tide had lifted him and he'd rowed out to the man, it was too late. The ill-fated fellow couldn't be revived.

" Now, nobody had seen this man before. They didn't know who he was. Was he a heretic, or was he a Catholic? If he was a heretic, no one would touch him, and he certainly wouldn't be buried in sacred ground, which was the cemetery.

Beyond the cemetery was another parcel of land where heretics were buried with no crosses, no markings, nothing. Finally, my father, my cousin, and two friends bought a coffin. They had to bury him in that lot, and my father continued to try to find out who this man was.

After a time, they located his mother. She presented her credentials to the Church, which found that she was a good Catholic, as was this young man. So my father, my cousin, and these two friends dug him back up. They got a grave, paid for by the mother, and buried him properly, with the knowledge that he was going to heaven. **"**

Aside from the occasional heretic, almost everyone—rich and poor alike—attended Sunday Mass at *Eglise Saint Jean-Baptiste*. The only church in Hillion, it occupied its rightful place in the middle of the village. The tall stone edifice, part of it dating back to the fourteenth century, dwarfed the surrounding buildings.

The interior was similarly humbling. With its high vaulted ceiling and lofty canopied pulpit, it reminded the congregants of their insignificance.

Some worshipers, however, were more significant than others. The local nobility and Mimi's family enjoyed the relative luxury of reserved seating with privacy sides and doors.

"There were wooden benches, which were most uncomfortable, and three pews that had doors. One was for our family, and the others were for the families that lived in the two old chateaux on the hill. When we got in our pew, we would be ensconced inside with the door shut. No one could come in, and we were really and truly private.

The peasants sat behind us, the women on one side of the aisle and the men on the other. They would never sit together. Never.

A man called *le bedeau*, the bell-ringer, would ring the bells by the ropes hanging from the ceiling. He would ring them during the service, as well as before and after. It was usually the notes CDE—sometimes changing to CED—over and over again.

At Sunday Mass, they passed bread around, which was supposed to be blessed, and everyone took a piece, signed themselves, and ate it, right where they sat. Those of us

> with private benches had our own baskets. The others had great big communal baskets, and everybody put their hands in them.
>
> The priest of this church was himself ancient. I don't believe he even had a tooth left in his head. When he got up in the pulpit, he would start *The Lord's Prayer* as 'Our Father...' and end up just mumbling 'chum-chum-chum-chum.' So he got the name of 'Old Chum-chum.'
>
> But he was nice. He'd come to the house and play chess with my father and drink my father's wine. He was a dear old boy, and we always tried to go to his service.
>
> Of course, we had to go, regardless. It was the only church around, and my mother wanted us to be decently brought up, learn about the Bible and, after all, if we died, we didn't want to be buried in unhallowed ground like that poor man who drowned.

Although the story of the drowning victim's unfortunate end left a strong impression on Mimi, it was not nearly as momentous to her as a later, firsthand experience.

Mimi's interactions with the children of sharecroppers living on land owned by the nobility were supervised. Mimi's parents did not want her going alone into their homes. Still, Mimi occasionally dropped in on neighboring farms with her nanny. Having been born in the vicinity, Adele knew the women well and visited with them while Mimi played with their children.

> Their houses were square and made of stone, with an earthen floor, a door, and a small window. They had one large room with possibly an extra, smaller room leading from it for provisions or even for a setting hen that they didn't want to disturb.

They usually had just one bed, though sometimes two. Several members of the family slept together. They had no choice.

Every family had a chamber pot, too, kept under the bed, but only to be used in case of illness or bad weather. Otherwise, they went out into the yard. **"**

Mimi's parents may have limited her contacts with the farmers to protect her from learning too early in life facts from which well-born English girls were generally sheltered. On one of her visits she learned about local funeral practices.

"The peasants tenaciously followed the customs of their ancestors, oblivious to the fast-changing times. One observance strictly carried out among them concerned death. They never used embalming. The deceased, if a woman, was merely washed and dressed by members of her own sex, and male members of the family followed the same practice.

When the deceased, if a woman, was all prepared and arrayed in her Sunday clothes and lace cap, she would be placed in a half-reclining, half-sitting position either on a bed or a table. She would be left like that, with her folded hands holding a rosary, during the twenty-four hours before burial. A laurel branch would be laid in a nearby basin of holy water, and when family and friends came in to pay their respects, they'd sprinkle some of the water over the body to ward off the devil.

On just such an occasion, my nanny, without my parents' knowledge, took me with her to see a girl, a playmate of mine, who had died the previous day. The shock to my childlike mind when I looked upon my friend, dead and sitting up with her white hands clasped together, left me shaken. I sobbed for hours.

This was the beginning of years of torture, which led me since, many times, to warn mothers against subjecting their children to any form of unnecessary shock. ”

Her exposure to the young girl's death—combined with the Church's dire warnings about Purgatory and Hell—contributed to a growing fear in Mimi. She worried about what lay ahead for those who disobeyed the rules. Especially since she wasn't among the most well-behaved.

9

Making Mischief

Some children who turn out to be very pleasant adults aren't known for being particularly obedient or thoughtful in their early years. And Mimi, despite her church lessons, vigilant nanny, and conscientious parents, was one of them.

The family couldn't seem to take their customary walk to Hillion without Mimi running ahead and scaling the sacred stone cross that dominated the entrance to the village.

> **"**I have a cunning photograph of myself sitting on a memorial I used to climb, much against my elders' wishes. They were very angry. I would climb up the cross and sit there and have a perfectly lovely time.**"**

It was just as hard to keep up with her at home. She could frequently be found at the top of the spiral staircase amusing herself by taking aim and spitting into the entrance hall below.

Next to that third-floor landing was one of Mimi's favorite places, a well-furnished playroom. While playing there, she often removed the door latches so no one else could enter.

> **"**I had everything a little rich girl could want, even a play kitchen and play stove. One day I thought I'd light a real fire in my stove. That was a 'no-no' in the family so I removed the handles from the door so my nanny could not come in.
>
> Well, I set fire to the whole thing! The fire started burning the curtains and wallpaper, too.

I got scared and leaned out the window, which was very high up. By then, smoke was belching out of it. When Nanny and Mummy looked up and saw me, they came rushing to the top floor.

I was so young and scared that I was trembling, and I couldn't put the door handles back. By that time, my brother's nurse, Bobonne, had raced up, so Mummy sent her back down for the hatchet, which she came back with. My brave mother calmly beat the damned door down and dragged me out.

Everything burned. Dolls, doll furniture, dishes. The only thing saved was a small brass saucepan.

That's the kind of brat I was. "

Mimi should have had a younger, faster nanny to keep up with her. Poor Adele was in her sixties and no match for Mimi.

" She was a beautiful person, my nanny. She was lovable, but very severe with me. She brought me up to be a nice, polite little girl. She insisted upon it. I loved her dearly, but I used to play many bad tricks on her.

As I got older, she had a little rheumatism and walked with a cane. When I did something I shouldn't do, she tried to get after me, but I would crawl under the bed or under the table, where she couldn't possibly bend down to reach me. That was always my retreat.

My nanny was very clever, though, and taught me many things. "

Fashioning Mimi into a "nice, polite little girl" took patience and persistence. In the meantime, just about everyone—her mother and father aside—was fair game.

"I was often told by my parents that I was full of tricks as a little girl, always doing things I shouldn't do.

Once I took my mother's discarded perfume bottle and put a little bit of ammonia in it. Then when these peasant women came by in their lovely white caps and sabots, carrying baskets with eggs or what have you, I managed to meet them at the gate, before they entered the courtyard.

I said to one of them, 'Mary, would you like to smell this dear, beautiful perfume in this dear, beautiful bottle?'

She said, 'Oh, yes, Mademoiselle, I would love it.'

'You must take a good, deep breath,' I told her, 'or you won't smell it, you see.'

Well, of course she took a big breath. Then she started to gasp and stagger in a circle around the garden, while I ran off and climbed up a tree.

This didn't mean I was unkind or cruel, but sometimes children do things without realizing how grave or hurtful they might be. I think of it today and realize it was a very childish thing to do in every way."

But as a little girl, Mimi was no more considerate than the mischief-making jackdaws in the willow tree.

Perhaps she didn't have enough to keep her occupied. Her father believed her formal education shouldn't start until eight, a view that limited the social opportunities school provided. And although Mimi mentioned playing with the two girls from the nearby chateau, they didn't seem to be particularly close.

Mimi's constant companion was her brother, George Edward. She spoke little about her three-years older sister, Rita, except to mention that they rarely did things together.

" She was much older than I was, and she had no use for me at all. I couldn't please her no matter, so I never really felt I had a sister. **"**

Rejecting the role of tag-along to Rita, Mimi sought ways to have her own fun.

" Now my sister and her friends collected some tiny, exquisitely dressed dolls. They had clothes and furniture of different periods, like Louis XV, and carriages, doll-houses, cradles, chairs and everything to go with them. Each of the girls had a doll, and they would have christenings for them.

I remember this particular day. It was the day of the christening for Rita's doll. She had a large barrel outside covered with a white cloth. It was to be the altar. Of course, the barrel was empty, and the cloth was just laid over the opening. **"**

Just then, poor old Aunty Harrie, blind in one eye, had the misfortune of making her way across the courtyard.

" Aunt Harrie lived with us at the time, and I was always playing tricks on her, which was not very kind, by the way. But this day I said to Aunty, 'Do you want to be the big priest? Do you want to sit on the altar?'

She thought that was perfectly all right. She said, 'Yes, if you want me to.' So she sat down where the cloth had been spread and, of course, having no bottom to it, she just went right through!

I'll never forget her feet and her nose coming together! I rushed away as usual and climbed up a tree. My poor mother came out and saved her, got her out of the barrel. I don't know how, but she did."

Mimi's mother, who held up the dearly departed Mary Kathleen as an example of a good child, always admonished Mimi that her sister "was looking down from heaven and would be disappointed in her."

In the years since the toddler's death, Mary Kathleen had become more loved than ever. A perfect angel in heaven was hard to compete with though, especially for a less-than-perfect child like Mimi. Her mother's rebukes did little good. Soon Mimi was off on her next escapade.

Mimi's father eventually hired an English governess for her, a young woman named Miss Langlee.

> "Of course, Miss Langlee wasn't allowed to chastise me, or strike me, or anything like that. But we also had a young man, Edward Pine, visiting us with whom she was quite friendly. And so she would just tell him to give me a slap. She'd say, 'Give her a good slap.'"

Not surprisingly, the governess didn't last long. In the end, Mimi was enrolled in the local Catholic girls' school. Queeny, Adele, and Harrie must have welcomed the respite.

As Mimi grew older, she gave up the worst of her misbehavior, but there were still lessons to be learned. One night after she and her family returned from Christmas Eve Mass at the chateau, she came to understand the effects of harsh words—those both given and received.

> "Now my nanny always slept in the same room with me, and I remember once coming back from one of these

wonderful evenings. I got home and she was waiting for me so she could help put me to bed. Nanny never went to bed before I did.

We both went to bed, she in her bed and I in mine. But about an hour later she was complaining about not feeling well. She got up and then went to sit on a chair, but she fell off it in a dead faint!

I was simply terrified because I loved her so. When I finally brought her to—I don't know how I did it—I was so frightened I said to Nanny, 'How dare you faint in my presence!'

And she said, 'Oh, you should never say that to me. Your little sister would never speak to me like that.'

Well my sister had died when she was two, and ever since then all I heard was what a beautiful little girl she was. And I had become very jealous of her. So when my nanny said that to me, it cut me to the quick. "

10

A Different Sensibility

Even if Mimi had been slow to develop sympathy for the feelings of her elders, she'd always adored animals and couldn't stand to see them hurt. She surely acquired this from her mother, Queeny, who bred collies for a select clientele and, according to Alain Tate, had brought the first of the breed to France.

But whereas Mimi's family viewed dogs as pets, the farmers in the surrounding fields had a different sensibility. They kept theirs for hunting birds and guarding property. They treated them on a par with their farm animals.

> A little distance down the road from where we lived was a farm owned by a man who was more or less prosperous, that is, he had a decent herd of cows and four or five pigs. He was considered well-to-do.
>
> Now, my parents were people who adored animals, especially dogs. My mother, in fact, was the first one to start the *Society for the Prevention of Cruelty to Animals* there, and she worked a great deal at it.
>
> One day we were walking down towards the beach to play in the sand, and we passed by the home of this farmer, whose name was Campion, if I remember right.
>
> The farmers would always keep a dog chained to their door. It was the only defense they had. They didn't love animals—they didn't let them in or pet them—they just threw scraps to them. The poor things were tied on a short chain and taught to bark loudly.

> So we were walking by, and my mother stopped to see how the newborn baby was doing and whether the family needed any help. And there was a dog with blood on his ears. My mother said, 'Monsieur Campion, what's wrong with your dog, with his ears?'
>
> He said, 'Ah, Madame, you know he is an obstinate dog, and he constantly yanks the collar over his head and runs away. So now I have found how I can stop him. Every few days I take my jack knife and cut a little piece off his ear so, of course, it's sore, and he doesn't pull his collar over his head because it hurts him.'
>
> Well, you can imagine my mother was ill when she heard a thing like that. Naturally she told him he'd have to stop immediately, but we are quite sure that poor dog led a hard and miserable life.

The farmers also seemed to have no particular love for birds. Large beehive-shaped dovecotes were a common feature of the landscape, but the doves that lived within the ancient stone walls were regarded as food or income rather than a source of songs or feathered friendship.

> Often peasants came to our house with baby birds. Mummy would give them pennies and take the birds in and we'd try to feed them. But they usually died because they needed things we didn't have.
>
> One day my Aunt Harrie was alone in the house, and she didn't speak French. These men came and rang the bell. My aunt opened the door, and they had these birds in a hat. My aunty tried to tell them, in whatever French she could, that *Madame* was not at home and couldn't help them.

The men saw that they were getting nowhere with her, so they took these poor birds and dashed them against the house and killed them that way. That's why we used to take these birds in. **"**

Life may have been fairly grim for the poorest of laborers who sought pennies for fledglings. But the Bretons heartily enjoyed life's celebrations.

"The weddings were always great occasions. Usually the wedding party would walk, sometimes three or four miles, to the church. They walked hand-in-hand, by twos, preceded by a man who played old tunes on a *hurdy gurdy,* a sort of mechanical violin.

Everyone knew the words to the songs. It was a real pageantry. The musician was like the Pied Piper of Hamlin. He led the long procession of people, first the bride and groom, his and her parents, family, and finally friends, all in a line. Then they entered the church and the village priest held the Wedding Mass.

After that, they returned to the bride's home where they danced to the *hurdy gurdy* most of the night and drank, of course, heavily. Or they went to various pubs that had been notified ahead of time and sat at tables at which everyone drank and sang. Each person would sing a song. It was really quite something, for they sang ballads that were, some of them, hundreds of years old, and the peasants had powerful voices.

During the drinking and eating, it was customary to have men say to the groom such things as *You won't sleep much tonight! We hope the bedsprings won't break!* Everyone laughed and was happy.

After leaving the pub, they would dance in front of it, and then they went to another pub and came out and danced the same way. There were many pubs in the little village of Hillion.

I well remember one of our maids was getting married, and my mother was asked to go to her wedding. Of course she didn't want to go, but she didn't want to hurt the maid's feelings. My father abhorred such vulgarity and refused to attend, but she went and I went with her.

Well, they had wonderful food and lots of drinks, which my mother never took. At the fifth or sixth pub most were quite drunk, but well-mannered, and songs were called for at one of the many tables. I remember one song which started with *Sitting at a round table when I have my love near me, from time to time I look at her saying, 'Pretty one, kiss me.'* And of course, the men, to emphasize their point, would bang on the table.

Then, my beautiful blond mother was asked to sing. At first, she said, 'Oh, no, no, no. I don't know your songs,' but after much begging of *la belle dame Anglaise,* finally Mummy stood up and she sang a lovely stanza from the French opera, *Manon*.

It was such a contrast to what they'd been singing, but everyone clapped, and I was so proud to be there and let them all see that she was my mother. They thought my mother was really quite a queen, which is, of course, what we all thought. "

11

Queeny

No one knows how Agnes Mary got the nickname Queeny. It could have been her regal bearing, but she seems to have been called that from her earliest days. The names Agnes and Mary were already overdone in the family; her father's younger sisters, all three of whom died young, each bore one name or the other. After christening his daughter in memory of them, he probably wanted to give her a special name that would be hers alone. Or maybe it was her mother who bestowed it.

The name Queeny was not particularly pretentious or uncommon in the Victorian era and, in any case, it fit her well. She had some aristocratic connections, even if they were more downstairs than upstairs.

Her maternal grandfather, John Bennett, had been the Duke of Norfolk's house steward. It was an important position that put him in charge of paying wages and handling bills for grand homes in London, Suffolk, and the Isle of Wight—estates the duke rotated through during the year. The duke and his entourage also made occasional visits to Arundel Castle, his medieval citadel in West Sussex. Although impressive from the outside, the castle was in sore need of renovation and thus no one's favorite stop.

Queeny's maternal grandmother, Margaret Bennett, was also employed by the duke. Her job title hasn't survived, but as the wife of the head steward, her duties were surely not menial. However, the couple had six children, so she may not have traipsed along with the rest of the staff on their seasonal moves from manor to manor.

Queeny's
Maternal Tree

John Bennett
1781 - 1847

Margaret Rockliff Croft
1785 - 1867

Edward Barnaby Gudgeon
1820 - 1890

Jane Bennett
1819 - 1857

Queeny's Siblings:

Emily Jane
Edward Masters
Robert Ritchie
Henry John Oswald
Rose Mary
Bertram Richard
Charles Erconwald

Agnes Mary (Queeny) Gudgeon
1855 - 1929

The 1841 census shows Margaret living in a flat on London's Jermyn Street, while John resided around the corner at the duke's palatial Norfolk House. Living with Margaret was their twenty-year-old daughter, Jane Bennett, a girl with lustrous brown ringlets, porcelain skin, and wistful blue eyes.

A small painting of Jane attests to her beauty. According to the oft-told story, a few years earlier the sixteen-year-old had gone to Buckingham Palace to visit her uncle, an emissary to King George III. The court artist happened to see Jane and, struck by her beauty, painted her portrait.

The tale is as sweet as the artist's rendering, but the uncle hasn't been confirmed and the Buckingham Palace setting is unlikely, especially since a second painting was discovered. The latter, of Jane's rather average-looking mother, appears to have been done by the same hand. Perhaps the portraits were painted by a resident artist at the duke's palace instead of the king's.

In any case, Jane was a lovely girl who a few years later caught the eye of her Jermyn Street neighbor, Edward Barnaby Gudgeon, the young clerk at the Bank of England. When Jane was twenty-six, she married Edward at the renowned St. James Church. They settled in a narrow terrace house in Peckham, a commercial district popular with those keen to avoid central London's high rents. A year after marrying, Jane had their first child, Emily, and most every following year, produced another.

From all accounts, the Gudgeons lived well. But her youthful beauty, his respectable position at the bank, and their shared devotion to the Catholic Church could not protect them from tragedy. Mimi often told the story of their third child, Robert Ritchie, a baby just past his first birthday. One May evening, his nursemaid took him to bed with her.

In that era, slumbering adults were believed to produce foul air unhealthy for children, so sharing beds was frowned upon in middle-class and upper-class homes. Perhaps the nanny, though, wanted to warm Robert on an unseasonably cool night. Or to comfort him. Maybe he was teething. But such small details—the why of it all—have been lost to time even as the end of the tale has endured. During the night, the nanny reportedly rolled over on Robert, suffocating him.

Jane's grief was overwhelming, but so too was her need for answers. What had happened? How could a healthy thirteen-month-old be smothered without putting up a fight vigorous enough to wake up even the drowsiest nanny? Had she given him one of Victorian England's popular teething medicines—many laced with opiates—that dulled his senses? Or had she taken something that dulled her own? Could it have been anything other than an accident?

An inquest stretched on for four months but provided no further explanation. Robert's death certificate was finally filled out as "Accidentally Suffocated."

His family buried him at Nunhead, a new park-like cemetery on a slight rise that afforded the mourners a view of the city. Robert's grave was near the Dissenters Chapel, an area reserved for non-Anglicans. It was a half-hour walk from the Gudgeons' home, a place now overshadowed with sorrow.

But another boy, Oswald, was born the next year, and even if Jane's heart lingered on thoughts of her departed son, the rhythms of life—including the annual addition of another child—eventually resumed.

Edward was successful at the bank and every few years he moved his family—even if never too far from Robert's grave—at least a little closer to central London.

By now he could afford to include his sons in England's time-honored tradition of boarding schools. Because these institutions served the purpose of child rearing as much as education, he chose a Catholic school. When the boys turned five or six, they were sent to Sedgley Park, a large three-story, brick academy a hundred and fifty miles away.

Six-year-old Oswald was living at the school when he was stricken with typhoid fever. Because the illness was so contagious, Jane was forbidden to see him. Whether her husband forbade it, or the academy itself, is no longer known, but it didn't matter; nothing could stop her from rushing to her son's bedside.

Oswald recovered, but in the course of Jane's caretaking, she contracted the disease. She came home sick.

Jane's widowed mother, Margaret, who lived with them, took care of her daughter. But throughout three weeks of fever and delirium, Jane steadily declined. At the end of November, with her husband by her side, she succumbed to the fever. She was only thirty-eight.

The gravediggers at Nunhead Cemetery dug open the plot of Jane's little boy, Robert, who had been buried ten feet down in anticipation of other family members eventually sharing his grave. After the funeral prayers were recited, Jane's remains were carefully lowered, the ropes let out hand over hand, until her coffin rested upon her son's.

Although the family continued to function with their governess, servants, and boarding schools, the heart of their home was gone. They were plunged into mourning—curtains drawn, clocks stopped, mirrors covered in black cloth—in the same way the Royal Household was two years later when Queen Victoria's beloved Prince Albert died, supposedly of the same illness.

When Jane died, Edward was left with seven children to rear, the oldest eleven and the youngest barely one. Queeny was two, an age that deprived her of clear memories of her mother. But her grandmother Margaret must have done her best to keep Jane's memory alive, surely pointing out the small painting of a bare-shouldered ingénue displaying the hint of a smile. And a sepia photograph, taken two decades later, of a somber woman in a conservative dress, a white rosary draped around her wrist.

If there is anything surprising about Edward remarrying, it is that the forty-one-year-old single father waited four years to do it. But his waiting might not have been entirely by choice. Even with a good income and high standing in the community, a widower with several children not yet old enough for boarding school may have been a poor catch. Moreover, his former mother-in-law still lived with him. But at some point, Margaret moved out and rented a room in the home of a family ten minutes away.

Edward's second wife was twenty-six-year-old Caroline Lydia Smith, an Englishwoman from Paris who was touted in the newspaper announcement as the "grandniece of the late Admiral Lord Collingwood" of Napoleonic War fame.

At the time of her father's marriage, Queeny was six. Not much is known about her adolescence. When she was twelve, her grandmother Margaret died, and by fifteen she was living at a seaside convent school not far from where Henrietta would spend her final days. But Henrietta's stay was still decades into the future.

When Queeny was there in 1871, she was enrolled at St. Mary Magdalene, which housed a hundred girls from ages five to eighteen, many of them the daughters of men serving the British Empire in India. The convent was run by a progressive Catholic woman who promoted a well-rounded education for girls. Aside from the expected academics—including Latin, French and Italian—the students studied music and art, learned needlework, and took lessons in the polka and waltz. They also engaged in "sea-bathing," an early term for swimming in the ocean.

Later, Queeny followed the path of the older Gudgeon girls, Emily and Rose Mary, to the Sacred Heart Convent in the city of Amiens, France. A world apart from St. Mary Magdalene on the quiet English coast, this convent was located near the renowned Amiens Cathedral, a huge gothic structure with a lofty spire, imposing statues, and an astonishingly high ceiling.

In such different surroundings, Queeny may have been lonely for her sisters, who had already finished their French studies and returned to England. But she adjusted to the changes in landscape and language, and it was there at the Sacred Heart Convent that she forged her lifelong bond with the future Countess de Bélizal.

And it was through their friendship that Queeny had first come to Brittany and fallen in love with the countryside. Now, years later, she found herself, an upper-class Englishwoman, living in rural France ... advocating for mistreated dogs, rescuing baby birds, and singing in a pub at her maid's wedding party.

12

Being Helpful

Queeny was well known in the community for aiding mothers and babies. Quick-thinking, decisive, and competent, she was the kind of woman people were thankful to have nearby in an emergency. When expectant mothers had trouble giving birth, she jumped on her bicycle and sped off to assist.

> My mother, I believe, brought every child into the world around there that could not be born normally. Usually the farm women would take care of themselves. But sometimes complications arose, and then someone would come flying to my mother for help.
>
> I can see her now, leaving the house and screaming, 'Bring me a cup of tea!' That's all she wanted. So a cup of tea would be made and brought to her at whatever farm she went to deliver the child.

Even if stiff in appearance, Mimi's father was also a humanitarian. He was deeply touched by suffering and fairly successful at relieving it. His grandfather had been a medical practitioner, perhaps inspiring George James's own interest in medicine. His knowledge, coupled with an innate resourcefulness in problem-solving, allowed him to provide much-needed help to the farmers.

> My father was the only one resembling a physician in the area, though he wasn't a licensed doctor. The peasants were deadly scared of hospitals, so my father decided to

do what he could, with the knowledge he had, to treat the minor injuries these people incurred at home or in the fields. Most often the calls my father received from these people were for burns, and he finally perfected a remedy for them. I believe it was made with oil from hartshorn and limewater. It was very efficacious. "

George James's burn solution was often requested on laundry days. Washing was a labor-intensive task. And hazardous.

"Now the women did their laundry only about three times a year. They wore the same clothes for a long time. In fact, in the winter, they practically sewed themselves into their undergarments, of which they wore many.

There was a public, man-made pool surrounded with flat stones, and the women went there to wash their things. They used wooden paddles to hit the sheets and clothes, and a great deal of bleach to make them white.

They had large cauldrons, under which they made a fire, and in them they put water and soap and wood ashes. After they finished beating the laundry, they put it inside these cauldrons and boiled everything.

Then the women used a long stick to pull out the hot, soapy things and they put them into a sort of vat that they carried back to the pond for rinsing.

But during the washing, there was a lot of smoke and steam, so the mothers couldn't see well, and they didn't have time to watch the little ones that hung onto their petticoats. I can't tell you how many times boiling water was spilt on children, or how often the toddlers, if they stood too close, were scalded by the steam. "

As for the farmers in the fields, cuts they suffered during their work often led to infection and sepsis.

> Another frequent problem was blood poisoning. It's amazing that more of them didn't die of it, but my father used potassium permanganate, diluted and applied regularly to keep the area wet. It nearly always alleviated the pain and healed the sore.
>
> So this was the sort of thing he did, always walking miles to take care of people. When he was at home with us, it was his greatest work. As a child, I remember going with him on these long walks. I often held the babies on my lap while my father, tenderly and with tears in his eyes, took care of these poor little things.
>
> The doctors around there said he was absolutely a nut, an English nut, because he told them about his cures and such. But he's since been proven right.

Despite their best efforts to assist the hardscrabble farmers, George James and Queeny were outsiders . . . and wealthy ones at that. Their presence was resented, and their help, although readily sought during frightful times, was not always appreciated.

> My parents were loving in their actions towards the sharecroppers, yet these people were often ungrateful. And more than once they said things out of cruelty. They hated the English, of course. Sometimes they would run after me or my brother or sister, and throw stones at us, and shout out, 'Old English, go back home where you belong!' But if they were in need, they would come rushing to our house and to my mother and father, and fall on their knees.

> Once my mother was walking across a farmer's field because it had rained and the roads were muddy and deeply rutted. Suddenly this man came rushing over with a pitchfork. He said, 'You dirty English, get off my land or I'll put this in your guts.'
>
> Well, my mother was a proud and brave woman, and she stood her ground. She continued to walk in the field. She took a chance with him.
>
> It was only a few days later that he came for help for his daughter, who suffered complications in childbirth. Mummy said, 'Aren't you the man who threatened to put your fork in me and kill me?' He said, 'Oh, ma'am, I was not right. I'm sure I must have been drinking. Please forgive me, but my daughter is in need of your help.'
>
> So it went, my mother and father continued to take care of these people, ungrateful as they often were.

Perhaps the sharecroppers' lack of gratitude stemmed, at least in part, from an awareness that they weren't held in high regard by the master of the villa. George James's feelings of compassion were often outweighed by his distaste. The poor farmers' earthy lifestyle—especially in matters of proper toileting—offended him.

> Modesty simply did not exist with the Brittany peasants. To see a man walking ahead stop to urinate on the side of the road was nothing.
>
> My father used to be shocked. He was an English gentleman, very reserved and modest. In fact, after I became six years old, my father would never enter my room without knocking. That's the sort of man he was.
>
> So if he and I were walking, as we often did, my father might suddenly say to me, 'Look at that lovely tree up

there!' and he would point in the opposite direction of where a man was relieving himself. He would say, 'Isn't it beautiful. How high it grows!' He would do anything to take my attention away from this person.

My mother accepted it, but my father never could."

Based on the delicate sensibilities of Mimi's father, Queeny may not have told him about their daughter's next prank.

By eleven, she had mostly given up the thoughtless larks of a bored child, but they had been replaced with an adolescent sense of fair play that also got her into trouble. She was intent on exacting justice when a situation called for it, and the actions of Madame Crosson—a well-to-do woman who lived in a towering house at the entrance to Hillion—shouted out for revenge.

"I remember as a child I suffered from awful freckles all over my face. I hated them. Even though I was just a little girl, I thought they were terrible.

One day this friend of my mother, Madame Crosson, came to have tea, and the question of these freckles arose. She said, 'Do you know there is a way to get rid of them? When we have the next rainy day, pick up some mud and rub it on your face, and your freckles will disappear.'

Well, I believed her. She was my mother's friend, and I had no idea she might be lying. So I waited for the rain.

Of course these roads were quite foul. Horses, cows, pigs, and all sorts of animals left their droppings on the road, in the ruts. When it rains, these things get all mixed up together. But nevertheless, I wanted to get rid of my freckles.

So this rainy day I went to the road, and I picked up a handful of this mud and rubbed it all over my face. When

I came in with it on me, Mummy said, 'What on earth have you been doing?'

I said, 'Well, I heard what Madame Crosson said, so I went and rubbed some mud on my face.'

And she said, 'What did you ever do that for? Go up immediately and wash it off!'

It was awful. It didn't take away my freckles, and I gained a thorough dislike for this woman. So much so, in fact, that I was going to play a trick on her.

First, I should explain that my mother would never permit us to drink cows' milk because cows were susceptible to tuberculosis and, of course, they were not as carefully screened as cows are in this country or in England. My mother and father only permitted us to have goats' milk. So in the stables we kept several goats.

Now at this time there was a little candy on the market that looked just like what the goats drop, and I thought, 'I'm going to fix her!' I found a cute box, a small candy box, and I went to the stable and put in three or four of these black things that the goats had dropped.

But when this woman came back for tea, my mother could tell from my eyes that I was up to something. I went up to Madame Crosson and said, 'Madame, would you like a sweet?'

She said, 'Oh yes.'

My mother got right up and said, 'Wait a minute! Wait a minute!' She took the box out of my hand, of course, and she knew what I had done.

But I would have been very glad, believe me, to have the old girl eat one of those!"

13

Zizi, Coco, and Caramel

Although Mimi had not been successful in removing her hated freckles or exacting revenge on Madame Crosson, she had her accomplishments. For one, she raised birds and enjoyed a deep rapport with them.

> I had a remarkable way with birds. They used to come and fly all over me. They would stand on my shoulder or on my head. It was quite a show when we had family from London or friends from Paris or what have you. Mummy would say, 'Why don't you call your birds?'
>
> I'd go out in the middle of the court and call, 'Koko-kokoko,' and all these birds would come out of nowhere. Sparrows, pigeons, doves . . . all sorts of birds would come and hover around me.
>
> Of course, Mummy always gave me some seeds, which I would throw down, and that was one of the attractions, naturally. However, I did have quite a hold on birds.
>
> One thing I learned to do was raise doves, beautiful mourning doves. The farmers would kill the mothers and fathers and eat them. So these poor little things would be left in the nest, and we would go rescue them and bring them home.
>
> I taught the baby birds how to take food from me by putting buckwheat grains in my mouth. In the beginning, I had to force them because the birds weren't used to putting their beaks in my mouth. With my tongue, I'd put a

few little grains in their beaks so they got to know where their food was. After maybe a day, the birds would rush to me as fast as they could to put their beaks in my mouth. And I would raise them like that until they were able to feed themselves.

We had many doves around the house because we had saved so many. **"**

Aside from doves, Mimi had a kitten she liked to dress up and push in a doll carriage. But most of the household pets were dogs. Along with Queeny's stately collies—at one time she had nine, not counting their litters—there was a lap dog named Caramel. The family adored him.

" My parents were devoted to animals, especially dogs, but any animal really that needed love and care. They were marvelous people. Among the dogs I loved deeply was a black and tan pup, much like a Mexican Chihuahua, only he had hair and was slightly fuller and stronger. His name was Caramel.

He was a precious little animal, very intelligent, and he had one privilege. When we ate, he was allowed to sit on the table next to my father's plate. This dog was the most dignified gentleman you can imagine. He would sit there without moving.

When my father finished eating, he would always keep his plate and leave a morsel on the side, which he called a 'bombush.' My father couldn't speak French well, and what he meant to say was *bonne bouchée,* which in French means *a good mouthful.* But we all adopted his expression and still use it when we speak of something good. We'll say 'Bombush!'

Anyway, my father would leave this small piece of food. Then he would converse with us as though Caramel didn't exist. After a few moments, the dog would lift his paw and gently touch my father's hand, as if to remind him. But my father, of course, ignored him and went on talking. A few minutes later, Caramel once more would touch his hand with his paw, and then my father would turn around and say, 'Oh, I beg your pardon, I beg your pardon, please excuse me. I forgot your bombush.' So he would give Caramel the treat and then set him down to run around. **"**

Mimi also acquired a couple of her own pets from one of the local boys who had recently returned from the military. During the farmers' compulsory service, Mimi's parents and nanny served as letter writers for their families, most of whom were illiterate. With the help of writers and readers at each end, the parents and their sons could communicate. Now one of these young men had come to thank Mimi's family.

" One afternoon when I was about eleven, we were all sitting under the tree that I have spoken of, that lovely weeping willow, having crumpets and cakes. Tea means a lot to the English. They just couldn't live without it.

So anyway, we were enjoying our tea, and the big gate opened and this young sailor came in. He had a parrot on one shoulder and a monkey on the other. This young man was one of the boys who had gone into the Navy, and he was coming back now and wanted to pay his respects to my father and mother.

He approached the table and saluted, and I rushed forward to take the animals. I just adored animals. But he pushed me away and said, 'Don't touch them because they are both vicious, and you will be bitten if you do.'

Well, I didn't believe him, so I picked up the parrot and put him on my finger. The parrot calmly bent his head, took my thumb in his beak... and bit me! I'm sure he cracked the bone.

But instead of screaming, I hit him on the head. And, you know, that's what did it. He suddenly realized that I was his master. He let me caress him and straighten his feathers.

Then I went to take the monkey. Again the young man backed away from me, but I picked up the monkey, and she cuddled up to me. The young sailor was amazed. He said, 'I've never seen anyone who could approach them. As long as you have your father's permission to accept them, you may have them.'

So that's how I got my beautiful parrot, Coco, and my darling monkey, Zizi.

I could do anything with that parrot. I could put him on his back and rub his tummy or whatever I wanted. And, of course, he spoke several words. I taught him some, too, but he could imitate anyone.

At that time we had a butler named Francis. Every afternoon about two o'clock, after he had cleaned the kitchen, Francis would go up to his bedroom, which was two high floors above. There he would stay until Mummy would call him for tea. She would say, 'Francis!' That meant Francis had to come down and get the tea ready.

Well, as soon as the man got up into his room, the parrot would call, 'Francis!'

And Francis would stick his head out the window and say, 'Oui, Madame!' and I could hear him coming down the two big stairways, *dun, dun, dun, dun, dun, dun, dun* all the way down to the bottom. Then he would go into the kitchen, and the parrot would laugh at him.

Francis just went wild. The butler couldn't tell the difference between Mummy's voice and the parrot's, so the parrot did this more than once.

The parrot was clever, but my father loathed him. He couldn't stand the bird because he didn't like his language. Once in a while it was far from what it should be."

Not only had the bird picked up some salty talk from the sailors, but he took his cues from the domestic help, too.

"One day my father came to the kitchen, and as he walked in, the bird said, 'Here comes the old goat!'

Of course, we all know the parrot never thought of that. The servants had probably said it on occasion when they heard my father coming, because my father was very strict and wanted everything done just right."

Although Coco had a mischief-making mind of his own, it was the little monkey who served as Mimi's accomplice. Zizi did her mistress's bidding and was rewarded with undying affection.

"Now, my dear little monkey was my defense and my love. I just adored her. When my brother teased me or annoyed me, I tried to retaliate, but he would climb a tree very high, thinking I couldn't reach him. And sometimes I couldn't. But I got into the habit of using my little Zizi. Of course she always had a chain or a leash on her because if she didn't, she would have been up in the tree and taken the jackdaws' nest and torn it to pieces.

Anyway, George would climb a tree, and I'd run to the tree with Zizi and start her up. When she was about two inches from his leg, where she could bite him, he would say, 'Stop, I'll do anything, I'll do anything for you!' "

No matter how annoyed she might be, it's doubtful Mimi ever let Zizi take a bite out of her little brother. She was very fond of him and they were always off on adventures together.

14

Bravo, Mona!

At the age of twelve, Mimi's behavior improved considerably. Perhaps she had finally taken to heart the appeals of her mother and nanny, or maybe she'd simply outgrown her childish antics. Most likely, though, she was responding to a change in the household. Her father had taken up year-round residence in Hillion.

George James hadn't been happy living away from Queeny and his children for such long periods, so when he was in his early fifties, he gave up his auditing career in London.

Seeking work in nearby Saint-Brieuc, he was initially hired as manager of a skating rink. But before long, he found employment at St. Charles Grammar School, where he taught English, a much more suitable profession for a man of his cultured interests.

He was quite the teacher at home, too. Aside from making sure his children's English was faultless, he also instructed them in music. A perfectionist and stern taskmaster, he taught Mimi the piano just as critically as his mother, Henrietta, had taught him. He stood behind Mimi with a wooden ruler and if she made a mistake, he whacked her fingers. She wasn't a musical prodigy and often her fingers were so swollen she couldn't close her hands.

Now that he was home year-round, George James also kept a tighter rein on his children's daily activities. He was strict about rules and proper conduct. Once he made Mimi and her brother go back and replace a few carrots they had pulled out of a field on their way home from school. And Mimi often spoke of the cheerless Christmas when she awoke to find nothing but a lump of coal in her stocking. She didn't say what she'd done to deserve it, but between her exploits and her father's harshness, the sooty surprise was probably surprising only to her.

Her father's influence eventually had the desired effect. Mimi, who longed for his approval, gave up the worst of her mischief.

The family enjoyed a number of special outings. Every year George James took them by buggy to attend the traveling circus, as well as the colorful Breton fairs and the annual summer horse races held on the sand. He even took them to the famous Wild West Show put on by the American folk hero, Buffalo Bill.

After a successful tour of Paris in 1889, Colonel William Cody returned in 1905, bringing his entourage across the Atlantic on sixteen ships. He arrived in Brittany with a convoy of five hundred horses and eight hundred men, traveling on a fifty-car railway train that stretched half a mile.

The big day finally came. Mimi and her siblings, seated under a huge tent, were treated to exhibitions by marksmen and riders, including troops of not just American cowboys and Indians, but Mexican horsemen, Cossacks, and Arabs. They also watched cavalry exercises by French and English detachments.

But most thrilling of all was the grand finale—a recreation of the taming of the West, ending with Colonel Cody's portrayal of General Custer at the Battle of the Little Big Horn.

The Wild West Show was more than just great entertainment. The performances led Mimi to believe America was an exhilarating land still dotted with teepees and populated by fearless cowboys and bareback-riding Indians.

By then, Mimi, although petite, was fit and strong like her mother. She'd also inherited Queeny's bravery and decisiveness in the face of danger.

One summer day after the Wild West Show's display of horsemanship, Mimi and her family were having tea on the beach when a French officer's steed, left unattended, suddenly bolted into the surf. In no time, a strong current swept the struggling animal toward an outcropping of rocks.

When Mimi saw what was happening, she sprinted into the water and swam after the horse. She caught up to him and grasped his bridle. Talking to the equine, she calmed him and pulled him back to shore. As she led him out of the water, she saw her father.

> "My father came running towards me. Tears flowed down his cheeks as he waved and cried, 'Bravo, Mona! Bravo! Bravo!'"

15

Crossings

Aside from receiving visitors at Villa St. George, the Tate family traveled to England each year. It was mostly to visit Queeny's kin, since George James had few close relatives remaining in London. Or, at least, few that he called on.

His nieces and nephews—the children of his deceased sister, Ethel—were being raised by a woman he disliked. A "wretch of a second wife," he wrote of her, "who behaved in a most shocking way to Ethel's kids." He kept in touch with the children through letters but didn't often see them.

His artist sister, Maud, had also suffered a cruel loss. Having waited until thirty-three to marry, she was widowed at forty. Like many women left without means, she was reduced to domestic work. She took a job as a live-in servant seventy-five miles east of London, in the affluent coastal community of Cliftonville. The town was known for its picturesque promenade along the sea, but Maud had little free time to walk it, much less paint it.

Queeny still had family in London, a sister and brother. The four others, however, had gone abroad decades earlier. As part of the natural order of things, children leave their families of origin and make their own way in the world. But Queeny's siblings scattered sooner and farther than most, mainly, it seems, to escape discord that began when their father, Edward Gudgeon, married his second wife, Caroline.

Although Queeny had gotten along with their new mum, her sister, Emily, had not. The eldest and fourteen when their father remarried, Emily steadfastly refused to let her siblings call their stepmother anything other than *Mrs. Gudgeon.*

"My mother often told me about this," Mimi said, "and what a hard life this lovely second wife had."

There is some question as to how lovely this second wife actually was. Alain Tate, who was close to Emily's children, was told the friction was brought on by Caroline's attitude. Whatever the cause, the unhappiness allowed for no family harmony and soon the children ventured even farther away than their boarding schools had taken them in earlier days.

The eldest son, Edward Masters Gudgeon, was the first to seek his fortune on far-off shores. At twenty-one, he sailed to the foreign enclave of Kobe, Japan. It was less than two years since the exotic port had opened to outside trade, which was what brought the young man, said to have been a tea importer, to the storied land of samurai and geisha.

But Japan was going through great political upheaval. A civil war had wrested power from the military leader—the Shogun—and restored it to the Emperor. Embracing change, the new government created the Foreign Concession, a seventy-acre settlement established for British, American, and French traders. Still, many Japanese factions resented the unequal trade agreements foisted upon them by the West, and rogue attacks were not uncommon. International tensions often ran high.

Perhaps it was this backdrop of conflict that inspired the story that one dark night, Edward Masters was murdered on his ship. Mimi was sure he was slain because her father—who preserved what information he could gather about Queeny's family—had told her so. But it turns out the young man's demise was less sensational.

A recently uncovered death certificate and newspaper article reveal he died on February 23, 1870 "after a few days illness, of remittent fever." Although Kobe had no shortage of ailments that could cause remittent fever, at that time the community had been suffering an epidemic of rubella and smallpox.

Edward was buried in the foreigners' cemetery, a paltry piece of land so close to the sea that gravediggers struck water just one meter down. The unavoidably shallow plots kept the foreign community anxious that the coffins might be dug up by foxes and dogs on balmy nights or washed out to sea on stormy ones. It was a miserable place to leave the bones of hoary old sailors, much less those of a fresh-faced youth who had barely entered adulthood.

The next three of Queeny's siblings moved to the East Coast of the United States.

Bertram went to New York in 1876, got work as a clerk, and married an Irish girl. Rose Mary followed him five years later and married a fellow Brit. Neither of those siblings fared well. Bertram succumbed to pneumonia at thirty; Rose Mary had a child who didn't survive, and she herself died at fifty.

Oswald, the poor boy who had been the indirect cause of his mother's passing, was the last to emigrate. By then, he had a well-earned reputation as the black sheep of the family. At thirty, the shipping merchant had defrauded a number of businessmen and was convicted of "obtaining goods by deception."

Reputed to be remorseless at trial, he was sentenced to five years in prison at hard labor. For all that, he didn't learn his lesson, and at forty, the family called a meeting to resolve new problems arising from either gambling or unpaid debts. Shortly thereafter, he sailed with his wife and children across the Atlantic and settled in New Jersey, where he became an accountant.

By the turn of the century, the only siblings Queeny had left in England were Emily and their youngest brother Charles, a successful merchant. Between the two households, however, there were dozens of first and once-removed cousins. Every year, normally in autumn, Queeny took her children and went for a long visit.

While in London, Mimi and her sister and brother attended school with their cousins. Her father was, as always, concerned about them maintaining their British heritage, so the trips served an educational as well as a social purpose.

The only downside to the annual reunion was getting there and back again. The journey required them to cross the English Channel, a twelve-hour run, on a small steamship.

The *SS Hilda,* capable of carrying a few hundred passengers, ferried wealthy British residents to and from Brittany's fashionable coast. It also provided passage for Frenchmen doing business in England. Twice a year, *Onion Johnnies* were on board, or more accurately, in steerage. These were the well-known Breton farmers who brought their region's luscious pink onions to England, hung braids of them on their bicycle handles, and sold them door to door to waiting housewives.

But whether traveling for pleasure or business, the passage between England's Southampton and Brittany's Saint-Malo was hard on almost everyone.

> "We'd go back and forth, traveling over the channel, which was an awful crossing. The boat was small and the sea was very bad. It is noted even today as one of the worse crossings anyone could take."

Mimi and her family were accustomed to the voyage and although they found it unpleasant, were rarely concerned about their safety. In November of 1905, however, that changed. George James, who had stayed at Villa St. George while the others went to London, had misgivings about their return trip. Mimi was twelve at the time.

> "My father, who had the gift of precognition, did something quite extraordinary. We were in London, my mother was there with us children, and we were supposed

to come home on a Tuesday. But as Uncle Charles's birthday was on Wednesday, Mummy changed the tickets to come home later, and she wrote my father to tell him.

Well, my father would have none of it, and he wrote to her to return as planned. Mummy thought he was being selfish to want her and us back home, so she waited. But finally, he sent a telegram saying that my nurse, Adele, was very ill and to return at once.

So she exchanged the tickets again and we came home. Then, when we arrived, we found out my nurse was not ill after all. It was just a ruse my father had used to get us back. My mother was not pleased. "

However, days after they returned to Villa St. George, the crossing Queeny had hoped to return on encountered trouble. The *SS Hilda,* after its late-night departure from England, got caught in heavy fog. The captain, a seasoned sailor who had commanded the ship for twenty years, had to anchor off the Isle of Wight until morning, delaying their arrival in Brittany. Then, as he finally neared the French coast at six o'clock in the evening, he faced a snow squall.

The crew could see the lights of Saint-Malo, and over the next five hours—each time the visibility cleared—the captain tried to maneuver into the rock-rimmed harbor. But each time, the storm forced him to retreat. On his last attempt, at eleven o'clock, he slammed into the jagged reef.

Dozens of the 131 people on the ship were thrown overboard. Others were swept off their feet by waves and flung into the churning sea. The crew set off flares that weren't seen in the storm and lowered lifeboats that shattered against the rocks. Thirty people climbed the rigging of the mast. Then, after fifteen terror-filled minutes, the battered ship broke in two.

It wasn't until nine the next morning that the captain of an outbound steamer discovered the splintered wreck caught in the surf between the rocks. Throughout the night of wind-whipped snow, sleet, and hail, only six people had been able to maintain their frigid grip on the listing mast. They were the sole survivors.

Of those who lived, one was a British crewman and five were *Onion Johnnies*.

At the time, the sinking of the *SS Hilda* was the worst disaster to hit the northern coast of Brittany, and it was felt hard on both sides of the channel. Seventy of the dead, more than half of all on board, were the hard-working onion sellers. The other victims were mostly wealthy Englishmen who perished with their once well-coiffed wives, bright-eyed children, and dedicated nannies. For days, the roiling sea, which made no distinction between first class and steerage, cast their bodies ashore.

> " My father was terribly upset and told us then that the reason he begged us to come home on Tuesday was because he had known it would happen. He had seen it—a ship going down, and all of us in it. We often talked about that, how my father was the reason why we all didn't drown. "

16

First Beau

In the same way that George James was determined to protect his family, so was Queeny, especially in regards to the virtue of her now adolescent daughters.

Although the Victorian Era had given way to the Edwardian by the time Mimi reached puberty, prevailing views on sex education had not changed. Sex was not discussed with children, particularly girls, and young women were to be kept ignorant of "the needs of men" until marriage. This made it hard for girls to protect themselves from men who might take advantage of them, and required their parents to be extra vigilant.

Growing up surrounded by farms, one would think Mimi had figured out for herself the facts of life. Like many children, however, she never made the leap from the reproductive behavior of animals to those of people.

> **“**One time, coming home from the village, my brother and I met this farm woman with a tremendous stomach. I said to my brother, 'Why is Mary Louise so fat? Why do these women around here get so fat?'
>
> My brother said, 'Why, don't you know? She's going to have a baby.'
>
> I think I was probably about eleven then, and I should have known better, but my brother said, 'That's the milk. The milk forms in the tummy, and when the baby is brought to her, the milk goes into the mother's breast so she can feed him.'

"I believed it because I was completely innocent. Yet we had animals, and I knew how they came and how the mother fed them and so forth, but it never occurred to me that human beings did the same thing. I was so completely surprised, but I never spoke to my mother about it."

Given the times and Mimi's naiveté, it's understandable her first love would elicit a protective response from her parents. Even if they believed it was an innocent romance—on her part and the boy's—Mimi's history of testing the limits throughout childhood surely left her parents worried.

"When I reached twelve or thirteen, I became rather sensitive to the attention of boys.

At that time my family casually knew another family living in a village called Saint-René. The mother, Madame Brushen, had a private school. She had two sons and two daughters, about our ages. One of the boys was named Guy. He was some years older than I was.

We all used to play games together at the house. I was small and shy but when I became thirteen or fourteen and Guy was going away to college, he told me he loved me. He fell in love with me, and I fell in love with him.

But what could we do about it? My father and mother would have never tolerated anything of the kind, and his mother was very severe, too. So we arranged that he'd write to me through one of our maids, Marie. She was a new acquisition to the house, but I knew she would pass me his letters.

Now, when my father was away it was always a joy for me to spend the night with my mother in her bed because we would talk, and I was permitted to sit up later. So one night when he was out, we were in her room undressing. Well earlier, I had tucked a letter from Guy in my waist, my blouse. When I unbuttoned my blouse, the letter fell out. I picked it up quickly, but Mummy saw it and said, 'Oh, what is that?'

I said, 'Oh, it's really nothing.'

But she said, 'If it really isn't anything, why are you so anxious to pick it up? Let me see it.'

Of course, I couldn't argue with my mother. I never did in all my life. Nor with my father, either. I let her see the letter.

It was a perfectly innocent letter. Nothing was ever wrong between us. Guy told me he loved me and that when I grew older, he wanted to marry me.

Well, Mummy was a person of few words, and because of that I always knew when she was angry. We went to bed but I don't think I slept at all because I was so upset by the whole thing.

The next morning Mummy jumped on her bike and rode over to Saint-René to see Madame Brushen. They talked it over and it was arranged that Guy wouldn't see me again until I was of age and my parents permitted it.

In the meantime, I was absolutely heartbroken. I had done no wrong except to love and be loved. He was my first beau.

Guy's sister, Helen, was the closest to my age and my best friend. She kept me informed. One day she told me Guy had left college and joined his uncle, who was the captain of his own ship. He had sailed to America. Well, of course, America was so far from my consciousness at that time that to me it was the end of the world. "

17

The Mexican Railroad

At about the same time that Mimi was enduring the anguish of lost love, her parents were facing challenges of their own. The family's financial position had become precarious. It was just a few years earlier that Mimi's father had left his job in London, and teaching English in France was not as lucrative.

Mimi attributed the greatest change in their finances, however, to a disastrous business venture. Her father knew the stock market and made profitable investments for a number of French aristocrats. But while he was successful at managing other people's money, he was not as good at handling his own.

> " My father invested most of his fortune in a railroad with two of my uncles. It was supposed to be a marvelous opportunity and make millions, but the whole thing went down the gutter. They lost every penny.
>
> His loss was catastrophic, and our income dwindled to interest from my mother's marriage settlement—which in those days was always made by the bride's father. That interest was small compared to the dividends which had come from the money my father had invested. "

Perhaps the first George Tate's success with railroads made his son overconfident about the financial strength of the iron horses and their lengthening tracks. Or perhaps George James simply picked the wrong country. Whereas the elder George appears to have mostly invested in the British-backed railways of Canada, the younger George put his money in the railroads of Mexico, a country not nearly as stable politically or economically. But whatever the cause of the financial collapse, George James had, as in his youth, lost his inheritance.

Mimi, who aspired to the life of those in the chateaux rather than those on the farms, feared they might end up poor.

> "My father and mother were now living on a small income compared to what they used to have. Though they never discussed business affairs with us children, nevertheless we heard things here and there. We saw people coming and asking that their bills be paid, and it troubled me. I always worried about things like that."

Soon eighteen-year-old Rita became a nurse in Saint-Brieuc. Then fourteen-year-old George Edward, without the resources to continue his education, left school to take up a trade. It was arranged that he'd learn mechanical dentistry—the construction of dentures—from Dr. Millard, an American friend living in the resort town of Dinard.

But the training didn't turn out as planned. The teenager was more interested in the mechanics of the dentist's two automobiles than in the workings of false teeth. Eventually another friend, Viscount Alain de Lorgeril, introduced the boy to the owner of a motorcar garage in Saint-Brieuc. In short order, George Edward started a three-year apprenticeship in the exciting new field of auto mechanics.

By the early summer of 1909, fifteen-year-old Mimi was the only child left at home. Although inexperienced in work and money matters, she'd been strong-willed since her days in the cotton-lined box by the stove and was now determined to solve the family's financial crisis. Moreover, she felt perfectly capable of doing so. She had an innate faith in herself, along with a firm belief that the world at large would provide her with whatever she needed to succeed.

> "I decided within myself to run away from home and become rich and do what I could for my parents. I made up my mind to leave without telling anyone.
>
> I got ready the night before and left the house about four in the morning. It was sort of a dull day, not exactly raining, but it wasn't a nice day. I had to leave Zizi—I'm sorry to say that—but I did take my parrot and the cage. I tied it to the front of my bike. And I took my violin because I played the violin then. I couldn't do without the parrot, and I couldn't do without my violin.
>
> I had no money, of course, because if I dared ask anyone for money they would have wanted to know why."

Mimi set off on the thirty-five-mile ride to the home of their friend, Dr. Millard, a practical person known for his sage advice as well as his ability to make things happen.

> "I knew I could confide in him. Dr. Millard believed in everyone earning his own living. He was a man who believed that all young people should be thrown out like birds from a nest and just learn to become independent, which, of course, is good.
>
> So I started out and it began to drizzle. The roads were muddy and slippery. When I was hungry, I stopped at farms and asked them for a glass of milk, which they would kindly give me, and I would go on.
>
> While I was pedaling along, that darn parrot would get excited—he hated the wind—and stick his head out

between the bars and squawk. So I would bat him in the snoot and put him back. He really slowed me up. Dinard was far away and it took me one whole day. I didn't get there until nine o'clock that night.

When I rang Dr. Millard's doorbell, I was wet and muddy and exhausted. Felix, who had been employed by Dr. Millard for many years, opened the door. He was surprised to see me, of course. He knew my whole family. He said, 'Do come in, Mademoiselle. You look just dead.'

And I was. He took my parrot and ushered me upstairs to Dr. Millard, who was in the library reading.

When he looked up and saw me, he asked, 'What on earth has happened? Why are you here?'

I said, 'I've come to ask you to help me earn a living.'

'Good gracious,' he said, 'you have to finish school.'

I told him I wanted to work and asked him please not to stop me, but to help me. Seeing I was exhausted, he insisted I take a bath and get right to bed. So I had a cup of tea and something to eat, bathed, and went to bed.

Dr. Millard contacted my father and mother and let them know I was at his house. My mother, of course, was quite frantic.

I naturally knew my mother would come, and she did, and I had some explaining to do. I said that I wanted to earn my own living. She said it was perfectly silly, that we had enough money.

'No,' I said, 'I want to help you, and this is the way I want to do it.' It was the first time ever in my life that I went against my mother. But Dr. Millard thought the right thing was to let me have my way.

He knew of a lady and her daughter, lovely people, who had a little tearoom not far from there. The daughter

> played the piano, and they wanted an accompanist and someone who could be an extra waitress, especially during the tourist season. Of course, I played the violin, so they took me in for a fair salary.

As brave as Mimi had been at the start of her venture, it was mere weeks before the sheltered teen—now alone in unfamiliar surroundings—developed homesickness.

> I had never been away like that. I was terribly lonely, and I didn't know anyone. I would hide in my room and cry at night, and this went on for some time.
>
> Finally one day I went down into the kitchen to the cook, who asked me what was wrong. I told her I was so lonely I couldn't bear it. She said I should get a hold of my mother immediately. 'Tell your mummy,' she said. 'Write to her and tell her. She'll understand.'
>
> So I sat down and wrote Mummy a letter saying I was very lonely and would like to go home. The next thing I knew, my mother replied that she was on her way and told me to meet her train.
>
> When she came, I felt I had let her down. I had broken my work agreement and I was a bit ashamed. But Mummy was so wonderful. She was so dear and said she was glad I had gotten in touch with her.
>
> From there we stopped at Dr. Millard's. He said he knew some fine Americans, the Reverend George Paine and his wife, Clara. He had invited them for dinner that night and said it was just perfect that we were there so we could meet them. Then he said they had two sons, who were not good in French, and he thought they would love to be tutored, and perhaps I could do it.

They were charming people, but I was terribly shy. At the dining table, Dr. Millard seemed to take a certain joy in trying to make me express myself. He asked me, 'Who discovered America?'

Well, I had no idea because in France, and certainly in England, you don't learn much about American history. It wasn't taught. So I fell down on that.

Then he told them, 'You know, she's a marvelous cook, and I want you to taste her wonderful omelet.'

So he said to me, 'You go into the kitchen and ask the cook to show you where all the things are to prepare the omelet because I want these friends to taste it.'

Well, I was just panic-stricken. I didn't even know how to warm water. I walked into the kitchen and began to cry. Felix said, 'Now don't cry. We're going to show you how to do it.'

And that's where I learned to make my first omelet. So this glorious French omelet was made, and Felix brought it in. Of course, Dr. Millard and Mummy knew I hadn't done it, but everyone loved it.

Then they began speaking about someone to tutor the boys. Mr. and Mrs. Paine said, 'We'd love to have you stay with us this summer.'

They had a beautiful little house near Saint-Malo, and they thought I could teach the boys French. "

This new job worked out better for Mimi. She was happy as a live-in French teacher for seven-year-old Lyman and six-year-old Alfred. With Mimi's refined manners and serious attention to her charges, she fit in well and quickly became a part of this upper-class Boston family.

> "Mrs. Paine, whom I called Aunty Clara, became very fond of me, and I of her. When it got time for them to go back to America, she said she couldn't bear to go and leave me in Brittany. She asked me to go with them.
>
> The Paines wrote my parents, but my father said no, absolutely not. Finally, however, they wore him down. My mother was more willing than my father because he was an educator and worried about my education. But Aunty Clara suggested that I could try it for three months, and she promised him that I would attend school."

Even if more agreeable to it than her husband, Queeny must have had misgivings about letting her daughter go to America, where both Rose Mary and Bertram had died. Only Queeny's disgraced brother Oswald was still there, alive and well.

But despite family tragedies on foreign soil, Queeny seemed mostly untroubled about sending her children out at a young age. Mimi's brother had spent a year in England with Aunt Emily and Uncle John before he was even twelve. And, although the United States was much farther away, Queeny was probably relieved to see Mimi settled in a respectable position with a good family. She may have already sensed that Brittany was too small to contain Mimi's boundless energy for long.

> "I went back to Villa St. George to get my trousseau ready for the trip to America. The seamstress was there, sewing day after day so I would have decent clothes. I was to meet George and Clara Paine in Paris."

Back in Hillion, Mimi called on her friends to say goodbye. She rode her bike to Saint-René to see Helen, whose brother, Guy, had stayed in touch with Mimi through postcards.

"Guy managed to send me a card for Christmas. He was allowed to write me postcards because they could be read by anyone. I told Helen about my going to America and she wrote a letter to Guy and told him.

Now every year there was a dance on the green in the city of Saint-Brieuc. It was beautiful. Lights were strung up, with lanterns and decorations for the night. Dancing was held from the afternoon all through the evening. It was a great event and we always attended. That year, I don't know where my sister and brother were, but I went with my father and mother and Dr. Millard.

Then, through the crowd, who should I see walking towards me but Guy!

He came and he bowed to my mother and father. He kissed my hand, which was the custom in France, then he turned to my father and asked him, 'Would you permit me to dance the first dance with Mona?'

My father gave him permission, and we headed the dance. We were at the front of the marches. That whole afternoon Guy and I danced.

He was heartbroken about my going to Boston."

Through conflicting emotions of excitement and sorrow, Mimi said goodbye to her family at Villa St. George. Nanny Adele gave Mimi, who was the closest thing she had to a child of her own, her most prized possession.

"Adele's father had been a soldier in Napoleon's army and had fought at Waterloo. He was wounded in a battle, but he was proud and very much in love with Napoleon, as were all his soldiers. No matter what he put them through, his men were loyal beyond words. They suffered hell and death because of this selfish emperor, but in 1812, Adele's father had received the Legion of Honor. She gave his medal to me.

My poor, old nurse—my nanny—said, 'You're going to the end of the world and I will never see you again.'"

Although Mimi was unhappy to bid farewell to her home in Europe, she never expressed misgivings about going to America. Perhaps she didn't realize how completely it would change her life. Or perhaps she did and welcomed it. She had just turned sixteen, an age when young people know everything and nothing. In any case, she'd set her course, and once Mimi made a decision, it was made. Even as a teenager, she was never one to second-guess herself.

18

The Lusitania

On the morning of September 10, 1909, Queeny took Mimi to the old domed train station in Saint-Brieuc, bought her a ticket for the 10:55 train to Paris, and waited with her on the platform.

> "In France all trains have compartments, like little rooms. You're not in one long passageway the way you are in this country. Anyway, Mummy saw two nuns in one of these compartments and thought I would be safe with them, which of course was true. So she got me settled in there and told them I was going to Paris and asked if they would take care of me. They said they were glad to do it.
>
> Well, this was a Friday. I lived in a Catholic country and on Fridays they never ate meat, but I had sandwiches made of meat . . . roast beef. When it became lunchtime, I didn't dare open mine because the nuns had egg salad and things of that kind.
>
> Finally, I was so hungry I had to open it. I explained to them both that I was able to eat meat because the priest said when you were traveling you had this dispensation. Of course they concluded that I was Catholic, but they thought the lunch was quite all right.
>
> I arrived in Paris that night, excited and rather tired."

Perhaps in her eagerness to meet up with the Paines she took leave of the nuns too quickly, or maybe they perceived their duties to her discharged when the train reached its destination. In any case, she was soon alone.

"I looked all over the station for Uncle George, but there wasn't a sign of him or Aunty Clara anywhere. I was completely lost. I'd never been to Paris, and I didn't know where to go. A truck had been sent on with most of my things; I just had a suitcase and my violin with me.

Then one man after another came up to me and asked:
'Are you lost?'
'Are you looking for friends?'
'Could I help you?'
I had never heard of the destructive things these men could have done to me. But something told me not to have anything to do with them, and I didn't. I just turned away and waited.

The only ones I knew in Paris were old family friends, Dr. and Mrs. Austin, and I had the address of Uncle George's bank. I decided to take a taxi to the bank.

I rang the bell, and knocked on the door, but of course the bank was closed. Finally a man came down. I told him the situation, that I couldn't find my friends, and asked would he please give me their address.

Well, he was a kind man and took me upstairs to his private apartment. He and another man looked through their books and different ledgers, but they couldn't find the name of Paine.

In the meantime I had enough sense to have the taxi wait for me. I never knew how I was going to pay the driver because I didn't have a lot of money, but I did feel he'd better wait. So I came downstairs again, got in the taxi, and told him to drive me to Mrs. Austin's home.

It was about nine o'clock at night when I rang the doorbell. Mrs. Austin came down, very much surprised to see me. She paid the driver, took me in, and made me dinner. Then I took a bath and went to bed. I had been in bed about ten minutes when Mrs. Austin knocked at my door and said Aunty Clara had called. They were staying at a hotel and wanted me to come there immediately. So I got out of bed and dressed, and Mrs. Austin put me in another taxi.

I don't know how we missed each other at the train station. Uncle George said he looked all over for me.

That night I felt bewildered and lonely for my parents, especially my mother. And for my brother. But I finally got to bed again.

My stay in Paris was short because the Paines had already been visiting there several weeks and were starting the next day for London. So it was only time enough to unpack the clothes I needed and repack them.

We left France, crossing the channel by boat, and went to London. We stayed at a grand hotel, Morley's, right off Trafalgar Square. "

Mimi was familiar with London, but Morley's was a luxury she had not experienced. The imposing building, fronted with soaring Greek columns, took up one whole side of the square.

The Reverend George Paine came from an old-money family and although his calling may have been humble, he and his household traveled first class.

They also had a first-class sense of fashion. Despite all the work the Brittany seamstress had put into Mimi's new wardrobe, Aunty Clara thought she should have clothes that weren't quite so countrified.

"I was still wearing little girls' clothes, short dresses, and my hair hung down my back. Aunty Clara said it wasn't at all fitting for a young lady of sixteen to be dressed like that. So she took me to Harrods and bought a grown-up suit for me, and a pretty hat. I wore it while I was in London. **"**

A week later, the family—which on this trip included Clara's spinster sister, Louise—traveled to Liverpool, where Mimi got her first look at the *Lusitania*.

A marvel of its time, the 2,200-passenger ship had made its maiden voyage only two years earlier and was immediately hailed as the world's largest and fastest luxury liner. Size and speed aside, it was stunning. As Mimi made her way up the first-class gangplank and along the promenade, she saw how luxurious it was—at least for its top-paying passengers.

It boasted an ornate dining room called the "grandest room afloat" that extended up the height of two decks. And the lounge featured a barrel-vaulted skylight with twelve stained glass windows, each depicting a different month of the year. In keeping with the times, the ship also had a smoking room for men, as well as a pink-carpeted retreat where the gentler sex could write letters or read in front of the fireplace.

Second-class passengers had their own dining facilities and a deck on the stern. But the bulk of the travelers, over a thousand, were third-class ticket holders housed in the bowels of the ship. Since the lower classes were restricted to their own areas, Mimi was unaware of them as she followed the Paines down the hall to their cabins.

" We boarded the *Lusitania,* a gorgeous ship, for our voyage to America. Aunty Clara, Aunty Louise, and I shared one bedroom, and Uncle George and the two boys were in another.

> I remember that first day, when we arrived on the boat. There were letters waiting for us, one of which was from my family. When I read it, I broke down and wept. Not that I didn't want to come to America. I really did, but just the same, I felt lonely for my parents, who had written farewell to me.
> Aunty Clara, who was always a strong-willed woman, thought I was stupid to cry like that, but her sister was more tender. She said, 'The poor young girl. She's lonely. It's natural that she should cry.'
> So then I was sat down and told that my hair must go up. I had very long, curly hair. In fact I could sit on it. Aunty Clara was on one side of me, and Aunty Louise on the other, and they braided my hair into these great long braids, which they wrapped around my head in a sort of little cap. It looked rather nice, but I hated it. I told them that Mummy said I couldn't put my hair up until I had my coming-out party. Well, of course, they both laughed because I guess my coming-out party was gone forever.
> It took me a pretty long time to get accustomed to the motion of the ship. I spent several days very seasick and miserable.

After passing the first half of the voyage in a deckchair on the promenade, she got her sea legs and took Lyman and Alfred to explore the ship.

> The *Lusitania* was a magnificent floating hotel. The boys and I had a great deal of fun. We wanted to see everything and talk to everybody, as all young people do. One day after the other was perfectly beautiful on this wonderful ship.

> I liked talking to one of the elevator boys, who was probably fifteen or sixteen, because he spoke with an English cockney accent, which amused me. One day he asked if I liked to read, and he loaned me a magazine. I brought it down to our room, and Aunty Clara asked what I was reading. When I said that the elevator boy lent it to me, she said I had to take it back immediately, and never to borrow anything from strangers, especially an elevator boy. So I began to learn the things that a young lady had to do.

Aside from shuffleboard, quoits, and other deck games, the ship offered a number of activities. And, since the lowest-paying passengers' privacy was less important than the highest-paying passengers' curiosity, affluent ladies and gentlemen were routinely escorted below to view the lower-class quarters.

> On the *Lusitania,* as on all large ships, there were hundreds of immigrants down in steerage. There was a ship's tour of the engine room, and, of course, we were taken to steerage. As a young girl, my heart just ached to see these poor people in these stuffy rooms with so little space. The babies were crying, and some of the women and men were eating things they had brought from their native countries—Czechoslovakia, Germany, France, or what have you. They were all herded together and looked very unhappy and very dirty.

Six days after setting out from England, the Lusitania sailed into New York Harbor. Mimi was below in her room when those on deck caught the first glimpse of the skyline.

> As we arrived in New York and came alongside the Statute of Liberty, Aunty Clara came rushing down to get me, saying, 'Come quickly. I want you to see the beautiful New York buildings.'
>
> I rushed up, and there were all these tall structures. Even then New York had many high buildings. I remember how dismayed I was. We were standing at the rail with friends we had met on the boat, and I said, 'Well, I know, but... where are all the Indians and the wigwams?'
>
> They simply screamed with laughter. They couldn't get over it, and I couldn't understand why. I assure you when I first came to the United States, I expected to find Indians waiting for me on the shore. I had learned history that way. It was impossible for me to think that there was such a metropolis like New York. It was funny and everybody laughed at me. I suppose I did sound ridiculous.

The initial stop for most foreigners was Ellis Island, but Mimi never set foot on it. First-class passengers weren't considered at risk of becoming dependent on government assistance and were therefore only subjected to a cursory interview aboard ship. She avoided the routine immigrant experience of crowding onto the barge, waiting in long lines, and submitting to probing questions and physicals.

> When we arrived in America, after we got off the ship, the steerage passengers were taken to Ellis Island. All I could think of was a herd of cattle. They were pushed off the ship... herded out. It was miserably sad. I couldn't get over it.
>
> Then we had to wait for our luggage. And the Negroes were all around... all these black men carrying packages

and trunks and bags. I'd never seen a Negro in my life. I sat there in absolute surprise, watching them.

Aunty Clara came up to me and said, 'If you don't stop staring at those people you're going to get into trouble.' I suppose she was right.

After that we went to a restaurant to have our lunch. It was fall, and they served ears of corn. I had never before seen corn, but I thought it was very bad manners to eat it off the cob. I said, 'The Americans don't have any table manners whatsoever. They eat food with their hands.'

Of course, you must realize that I was quite young, and everything to me was a mystery. My eyes were everywhere looking at things.

We boarded a train for Boston, riding in a first-class car. In those days they called it a parlor car. We even had our own armchairs. Upon our arrival, we took a taxi to Dorchester, a little town outside Boston. The Paines lived at 38 Sumner Street in an attractive house.

We were met by the two servants who had worked for them for many years. They had everything in readiness for us. I was taken upstairs to my own room, which was very pretty, and I even had my own bath. In Brittany we lived in the country, which was, of course, beautiful, but we didn't have all these latest conveniences. To me it was all out of this world . . . a fairyland. "

BOOK III

New England
1909–1923

MIMI

AUNTY CLARA—Clara Paine, who brought Mimi to America.
UNCLE GEORGE—Clara's husband, Reverend George Paine.
HERBERT HAYFORD—Mimi's husband.
GWEN—Mimi and Herbert's first child, Gwendolyn Clara.
JANE—Mimi and Herbert's second child, Jane Rosemary.
WILDER HAYFORD—Mimi's father-in-law.
ROSE HAYFORD—Mimi's mother-in-law.
FRANCES BEAN—Herbert's cousin, also known as Tish.

19

A Redcoat in New England

The Reverend Paine was tall and, even as a young man, distinguished looking. He knew how to carry himself, having inherited it through generations of proper bearing. A direct descendant of one of the signers of the Declaration of Independence, he was also the son of a governor known for social reforms. Educated at Harvard, he had served his first ministry in New York's Bowery before accepting the position of rector at St. Mary's Episcopal Church in Dorchester.

Clara Paine was born in Brooklyn, but her father's business took the family to France, where she spent her first dozen years. Her upbringing made it easy for her to relate to Mimi; they'd both experienced French girlhoods, even if a generation apart.

Possessing a classical profile and stately beauty, twenty years earlier Clara had been a favorite model for the artist A.H. Thayer, who often depicted her as an angel with wings and flowing gowns. She had acted on stage, too, in college productions during her Radcliffe years. A professor for ten years before marrying, she now wore pince-nez eyeglasses that gave her an authoritative demeanor. Like Mimi's mother, she was a couple of years older than her husband and uncommonly independent.

Clara's reverence for education ensured that Mimi's duties as governess and French teacher didn't interfere with her schooling.

❝We arrived in the fall, in time for school, so I was registered at a high school outside Dorchester. I walked there every morning and back every afternoon.

I was an English girl and there was no doubt about it. When I first enrolled, a boy turned to me and said, 'Oh, you're a redcoat, aren't you?'

I had no idea what he meant. I didn't know if he meant that I *might* have a red coat, or *should* have a red coat. I couldn't understand it, but a girl came forward and said, 'Oh, leave her alone. Why do you tease her like that?'

Then she explained to me that during the war between England and America, the English wore red coats.

The schoolwork was delightful. In Europe we really studied hard, so in most subjects I was two or three years ahead of these other students. I enjoyed school and met many lovely girls and lovely young men.

Boys wanted, of course, to walk me home and pick me up in the morning and carry my books, but Aunty Clara forbade it. What happened, of course, was that the boys would simply meet me behind a house, so they carried my books after all.

Aunty Clara was also strict about clothes. I had a little sailor suit that I loved dearly, but it was open in the front. So Aunty Clara said, 'No, no, we can't have that. You'll have to wear a little dickey [a false shirt front].'

But when I met the boys, I'd take the darn dickey out and be without it until I got home again. One fine day, however, we were told a photograph was going to be taken of the whole class, so we went, *hurry, hurry, hurry,* and I forgot my dickey. I rushed out with the rest of the students and stood in line.

Well, when Aunty Clara saw the picture, naturally she said, 'What happened to your dickey?'

So I got it, just for that. "

Although Mimi may have occasionally spread her teenaged wings, she mostly abided by the rules. And she took Clara's lessons to heart, too, including one on the importance of financial security.

> She said I should start setting aside money every time I received my allowance, which I did. I began to save by taking it to the post office, where I had a little account, and I saved until I got quite a bit of money.

The Paines also had an influence on her religious thinking. In spite of having been raised a Catholic, she quickly became an Episcopalian. Given Uncle George's work, as well as her father's upbringing in the Church of England—the predecessor to the Episcopal Church in America—this wasn't surprising. But there was more than theology behind Mimi's decision.

Unlike in France, where Catholicism was the majority religion, most Catholics in Boston were the less affluent Italians and Irish, with whom Mimi had little in common. Sitting in St. Mary's front pew with Aunty Clara and the boys while Uncle George delivered his Sunday sermons was surely more enjoyable than going to weekly confession and Mass with the servants.

> Aunty Clara had two servants. There was Maggie, who was the second girl, and Angela, the cook. Both were staunch Catholics and very hateful to me. They were Irish and they hated the English, of course. I had an unhappy life with them. I spent hours weeping and feeling terribly lonely away from my mother, especially because Aunty Clara was so very severe with me. But I stayed. Although Mummy and my father had agreed we would try this position for three months, nevertheless, I was very proud and didn't want to go back unless I absolutely had to.

When young people settle into a foreign country, they usually focus on their new surroundings, expecting that everything will stay the same at home. But it rarely does. Letters from Villa St. George during Mimi's first year abroad brought two heartaches.

As the elderly Nanny Adele had feared, she did not live to see Mimi again. She died nine months after Mimi's departure.

> She was with our family until she passed away in 1910. I was absolutely heartbroken. She was honored, not only by our family, but by all the people in the village. They buried her in my sister's grave.

But it was to her pets—who loved her without measure—that Mimi had always given herself completely. Soon she learned that the small family dog, Caramel, had also succumbed to old age.

> By then he was blind and he didn't have a tooth in his head, but we adored him. Whenever we took him out, someone always stayed with him for fear he would knock up against trees and things. When I heard the news that the dear little thing died, I was frankly unashamed as I wept bitterly for my little dog.

Despite the difficulties of the first year, Mimi adjusted to her new life in Boston. Aunty Clara came to love her like a daughter and Mimi felt the same kinship. Finding a surrogate family outside the home was not new to the Tate women. Just as Queeny had been more a friend than a lady companion to the Countess de Bélizal, Mimi was more a member of the family than a governess in the Paine household.

The second year—which continued her routine of going to school and teaching the boys French—was easier.

" Then Uncle George accepted a call from St. Paul's, the largest Episcopal Church in New Haven, so we all moved down to Connecticut. Later, the boys started going to a more rigorous school, and I didn't have much to do. So it was arranged that I would teach someone else. "

At one point, Mimi trained under the popular Maria Montessori, where she honed her skills. Demanding excellence without using the harsh methods of her father and equally strict grandmother, she brought out the best in her young charges.

By the time Mimi was eighteen, she was a vivacious young woman. Five feet, four inches tall, she was petite like her mother and had the same fair complexion and regal bearing. Gracious and charming, she possessed an upper-class, European hauteur that made her popular at schools for older girls, too.

" For quite some time I taught in Mrs. Glendenning's School on Edwards Street. It was a beautiful school that all the young society ladies attended. "

But Mimi mostly educated younger children. At twenty, she was working as a live-in governess for four-year-old Arnold, the son of Mr. and Mrs. Norcross of New Haven. Mr. Norcross, treasurer of the gas company, was from Maine and every summer he took his wife and child north to escape the city heat and visit relatives. They had a waterfront cottage on the edge of a glacier-carved lake called Sebec Lake by most but referred to by Mimi as the more European-sounding Lake Sebec.

On their summer sojourn of 1914—as Mimi was turning twenty-one and Germany was declaring what was expected to be a brief war with France—she met Herbert Hayford.

20

Herbert Hayford

Twenty-four-year-old Herbert Hayford and his father, Wilder, were close to finishing construction of their family's lakeside vacation home. Residents of nearby Dover, they had spent several summers camping along the shore to find the best location and were now pleased with how their vision was finally becoming a reality.

Herbert, a sinewy five feet, nine inches tall, cut a slight but manly figure as he sawed boards, straddled beams, and drove nails into joists. And up close you couldn't miss his devilish smile, soulful hazel eyes, and soft brown hair.

But he wasn't just another good-looking guy with a tool belt. He was on summer break from the University of Maine, where he was securing a bright future as well as enjoying college life. A member of Delta Tau Delta, Herbert was the all-American fraternity boy. He swam, sailed, played the mandolin, and could hold his own on the ballroom floor. A popular storyteller, he kept others amused for hours with his tales.

Soon he was spinning those tales for Mimi.

> "Herbert Hayford was handsome and in demand with the girls, but he fell in love with me. We used to play tennis together, go bicycling, and so forth. We'd meet at the lake, and he'd spend the evenings with me. By the fall, we were very much in love."

An outdoorsy, fun-loving couple with similar interests—she working as a governess and he studying to be an educator—they seemed to be a good match by the standards of young romance. According to Mimi, it was Herbert, ardent and sentimental by nature, who wanted to tie the knot.

> "He prevailed on me to promise that when I got to Maine the next summer, we would marry. I really didn't want to, but he urged me so strongly I finally consented.
>
> Well, I returned to Connecticut, and Herbert went back to the University of Maine. In New Haven, I continued to teach Arnold and also joined a school run by a Mrs. Modd. She had a refined class of wealthy youngsters and I taught them, too."

The following spring, after graduating cum laude, Herbert started teaching on Indian Island, a Penobscot reservation forty miles southeast of Dover. It turned out to be a brief career. He had a run-in with the men of the tribe and, fearing for his life, grabbed a rowboat, hightailed it to the opposite shore, and made his way back to his parents' home.

Because of the distance between New Haven and Maine, the betrothed couple hadn't seen each other since the end of the previous summer. They communicated through letters. If Mimi was dismayed to read her fiancé was now unemployed, she was likely reassured by his clear potential. Aside from a good education, he possessed a fine lineage.

Herbert was born July 7, 1890 to an influential family with prominent members who traced their roots back to the decks of the Mayflower—three brave men and their families—and the battlefields of the Revolutionary War.

His grandfather, Otis Hayford, Jr., had served as a captain in the Civil War and went on to become a state senator. Like Mimi's own grandfather, in later years Otis made his living through the railroads, but at some point, his financial investments failed to deliver, and what he'd gained, he lost. His latest and most lasting contribution was a book he'd published in 1901 titled *History of the Hayford Family 1100-1900*.

This shared experience of success and failure from the railway industry—and a common reverence for family history—probably made it easy for Mimi to relate to the Hayfords. She particularly liked Herbert's father.

Wilder Hayford was six feet, four inches tall with a deep voice and kind face. Like Mimi's own father, he was a man of numbers, working as paymaster at the nearby American Woolen Mills. True to his Hayford heritage, he was a civic-minded Freemason and a consummate gentleman.

Mimi was less sure of her feelings about Herbert's mother, Rose Bean Hayford, who descended from Maine farmers. Rose's father had left the family grange to become a town carpenter, and when Rose was a teenager, she learned the millinery trade. At twenty, she turned her attention from hats to dresses, and found a seamstress job a half-day's wagon ride away in the little town of Canton. She worked as a trimmer for Wilder's spinster cousin and it wasn't long before Rose met the tall young man.

There was no doubt—on either the Hayford or Bean side—that Rose married up when she tied the knot with Wilder. But she was equal to the challenge. Out of five sisters, she was the only one to survive to adulthood. Whether she was coddled as a girl or, conversely, too tough to succumb to the ills of the 1800s, she was strong-willed. And used to getting her own way.

Now that she was married to Wilder, that didn't change. Outside the home, she ran civic organizations and the local chapter of the Order of the Eastern Star, an association for Masons' wives. Inside the home, she ran the house and her husband. Although a foot and a half shorter, she was the boss.

Herbert's
Paternal Tree

Otis
Hayford, Jr.
1834 - 1921

Amanda
Phinney
1835 - 1915

Wilder Otis
Hayford
1860 - 1943

Rose Alice
Bean
1863 - 1958

Herbert Wilder Hayford

Mona (Mimi) Tate

Wilder and Rose lived in a white, two-story clapboard house in Dover, which seven years later would join Foxcroft to become Dover-Foxcroft. But even with two names, it was a small dirt-road town in the middle of Maine. The Piscataquis River, which ran through it, provided energy for a number of mills and factories.

The couple had four children. Herbert, nicknamed Kracker for his post-Independence Day arrival, had an older sister, Mildred, and two younger sisters, Dorothy and Celestia.

Rose raised their children in the Christian Science Church. A devout follower who had met Mary Baker Eddy, she believed in healing through prayer. Wilder, despite being at least a third-generation Universalist, dutifully went with his wife and children to her church on Lincoln Street.

Even if Mimi wasn't completely at ease with her soon-to-be mother-in-law, she was attracted to her religion, particularly the belief that the world was God's perfect creation. Mimi was intrigued by the metaphysical view that sin, disease, and death—the mainstays of most Christian denominations—were not God's work. The Scientists' all-powerful but loving Father-Mother God was a far cry from the judgmental, testosterone-laden Heavenly Father who regularly assigned congregants to purgatory or hell, if Catholic, or simply straight to hell, if Protestant.

Mimi had embraced the Paines' orderly, cultured Episcopal community, but Christian Science's emphasis on the power of the mind quickly drew her in. She was, after all, a confident young woman with great faith in her own abilities. Mimi eventually became a Christian Scientist. She didn't always adhere to their tenets in matters of medical care, but the religion soon provided the core of her beliefs. It's doubtful, however, that she converted before marriage, given that the Reverend Paine came to officiate.

The nuptials were held in the early summer of 1915 at the Hayfords' large house in Dover. It was mid-week, a Wednesday, but Herbert wanted to be married on his birthday. He turned twenty-five that day; Mimi was almost twenty-two.

> On the evening of July 7th we were married. It was a quiet wedding because Father Hayford's mother had died three days before, and we didn't want to make a big showing. But we didn't want to put it off either.
>
> We were married in the Hayford home, and Father Hayford gave me away. Of course, Uncle George and Aunty Clara and the two boys came from New Haven because Uncle George wanted to perform the ceremony. In fact, he was one of two ministers. Because he was not recognized as a minister in Maine, I had to have a minister from that state to certify that we were husband and wife. But Uncle George was able to do everything except the final words. We were married that evening at seven.
>
> I wore my Aunty Clara's veil. And instead of roses, I had peonies, beautiful white peonies with delicate pink centers. They were very becoming and quite unusual.
>
> After the wedding we had a short reception with just a few friends, not a great many of them. For refreshments we had ice cream and cake ... a real English wedding cake that my aunty made for me. It was all very lovely.

It was a day filled with personal and traditional touches. Even the frosted fruitcake—like the one served at Queen Victoria's marriage and still popular with the royal family—had been carefully chosen to make the event perfect. In her wedding photo, seated with the armful of peonies, Mimi was as polished a bride as had ever graced the town of Dover. But small-towners don't necessarily enjoy being graced by an outsider. The wedding was romantic and promising. The honeymoon ... not so much.

> "After the reception I went upstairs with Aunty Clara and changed into my traveling clothes. Herbert and I were going to go by car to Lake Sebec to spend our honeymoon.
>
> We came downstairs, everybody said goodbye, and we went outside. I walked out first, and then, suddenly, three or four of the young people grabbed me and threw me, rather violently, into another car.
>
> They grabbed Herbert and held him while the driver of the car I was in drove off madly. I didn't know where they were taking me. They didn't tell me. I was awfully upset. We went way into the country to a hotel and into the lobby where they presented me to everyone as a bride who had been taken away from her husband. It was a miserable experience."

Mimi was the victim of a mean-spirited rural custom called *shivaree,* which generally doesn't go beyond banging pots and pans under the newlyweds' bedroom window. But sometimes the revelers, particularly those with a callous streak, kidnap the bride, a practice for which Mimi was totally unprepared.

Herbert, looking forward to the grand gesture of carrying his bride over the threshold of the cottage he'd helped build, was equally caught off guard. This, in spite of the fact that his older sister, Mildred, was in on the abduction.

> "Then they took me to an empty farm, where they sat and played cards for hours. I was in terror because there were spiders everywhere. Finally, however, they drove me back to the Hayford house at about three o'clock in the morning. Herbert's sister, Mildred, said, 'You think you're going to go inside now? Indeed you're not! We're going to keep you out all night.'

I was so exhausted and disappointed I began to cry. So one of the boys said, 'Oh, let her go in.'

So I went in and everything was silent. I went upstairs to Herbert's room. He was in bed when I came in. I sat on the bed and spoke to him, and he broke into tears. He said, 'This entire thing's been a farce. It's all been ruined.'

We had a pretty awful time of it. Neither of us, I think, ever got over it.

The next morning, we went up to the cabin by the lake with Aunty Clara and Uncle George and the two boys. They were going to spend a few days with us. We didn't mind that, even though it was our honeymoon. We were so happy to have them. "

21

A Hard, Hard Life

Mimi and Herbert spent the rest of the summer at Sebec Lake. His future employment had by then been decided; he was to be given a desk job at the woolen mill where his father worked. So the newlyweds took their time, dipping into Mimi's post-office savings for daily expenses.

At the end of the season, when the lakeside turned chilly, they returned to Dover and moved into the Hayford family home. It was a well-kept house with a generous porch spanning the front, a large living room, dining room, kitchen, and a big New England pantry. Upstairs were four bedrooms and a bathroom with modern plumbing, although their two-seater out in the barn was kept clean for those times when the indoor facilities were in use. All in all, it was a pleasant home, but Mimi, who was already a couple of months pregnant and suffering from morning sickness, was not prepared for what awaited her there.

> "We came back to the village to stay with his parents. When I walked in, his mother said, 'Well now, I have dismissed the maid, and you have to work to pay for your lodging and Herbert's. We can't keep you for nothing. So here is the apron and you'll have to take care of the house and do the cooking and the general cleaning that the maid did.' That's what I was told."

The demanding work was one thing, but Mimi's diminished status was equally hard to take. Rose insisted to others that her son could have done better for himself than a nanny. Even if Rose was only a seamstress when she married Wilder, the recent death of her mother-in-law had made her the new family matriarch, a role that added to her already considerable sense of authority. She may have been several inches shorter than her daughter-in-law, but it was clear from the beginning she expected to be looked up to. Mimi had a strong will, but in fortitude and determination, Rose could match her grit for grit.

Herbert worked for his father in the office at the mill, which sat directly on the other side of the river. It was a two-minute walk from their front door, across the bridge, and into the prominent five-story brick building visible from their bedroom window. When the noon bell rang, father and son came home for a hot lunch.

Even with Herbert now gainfully employed, Mimi's position in the family didn't change. After her privileged upbringing in France and refined life as a governess and French teacher for the well-to-do in Boston and New Haven, Mimi had a hard time adjusting to the role of maid to her husband's family.

> It should be understood that I was a delicate girl. I had never done heavy work in my life. I had been a student. I had taught French. My mother and father had servants who took care of me and took care of everything. So, this heavy work was new to me and my health really felt it.

As the Maine cold deepened, Mimi contracted pertussis, or whooping cough. The highly infectious disease spread through the mill town, causing uncontrollable fits of coughing that persisted so long it was also referred to as "the hundred-day cough."

> My mother-in-law would knock on our door at six every morning, and say, 'Daughter, time to get up!'

> Now at the time I had whooping cough while carrying my baby, and sometimes I would cough and be nauseated all night long. Finally, towards the early dawn, I would fall into an exhausted sleep. So, when that knock came at the door, it was a terrible thing.
>
> But I had to get up. Mother Hayford returned to bed while I went downstairs to shake up the furnace, build a new fire, and cook the breakfast for the entire family. I'll tell you, for a young lady who had never done any work of that kind, it was a hard, hard life.

Mimi never said how Herbert reacted to his mother's expectations of her. As the only son, he was likely accustomed to the women of the house taking care of the endless domestic chores. And, like most Maine men, he was working long hours himself. Mill hands worked from 6:45 in the morning to 5:30 at night and until noon on Saturdays. These hours no doubt applied to the mill office as well, since most of the town followed a fifty-four-hour workweek schedule. Still, Herbert may have protested on his pregnant bride's behalf... but probably not very strenuously.

Even without Mimi's trials at home, everyday life in this small community was difficult due to her connection to France.

Maine had long experienced tension between its Protestant English-speaking New Englanders and the immigrant Catholics from the French-speaking areas of Canada. From the mid-1800s, an increasing number of French-Canadians had migrated south in search of jobs in the newly industrialized towns of Maine. By the time Mimi arrived, the outsiders had settled around the mills and factories, where they turned out essentials from shirts to shoes, and buttons to brass tacks. In Dover and Foxcroft, they took jobs in the two woolen mills, or toiled in the dye works, sawmill, spool factory, corn cannery, creamery, or the cider mill.

The growing presence of these Francophones tended to inflame anti-French sentiment. Low on the social ladder, the foreign workers were not welcomed by the townspeople, who didn't like the French, and especially didn't like Catholics. Unfortunately, these were both attributes they associated with Mimi, despite the fact that she was of British ancestry and two conversions removed from Roman Catholicism. She must have tired of explaining to those curious about her accent that, although she was raised in France, she was indeed English.

The final straw for Mimi, however, was closer to home. It came the day Rose and her daughter, Mildred, saw in the mail a personal letter to Mimi from her mother... and opened it.

Seething, Mimi went to see Mrs. Brown, the elderly mother of Mimi's former employer, Mrs. Norcross. The kindly woman interceded on Mimi's behalf by having a heart-to-heart with Herbert and insisting he find them an apartment of their own.

> "We did find an apartment, very small, just a bedroom, dining room and kitchen. But we had to go outside to the toilet, so it wasn't a pleasant place, and it was cold that winter. I wasn't a bit well either. At least, though, I was free. But the conditions got so bad finally, I didn't know how we were going to have a baby in that place, and I was getting worried."

As the bone-chilling snows set in, the drafty apartment walls provided little comfort from Maine's nor'easter storms, and with Herbert's meager paycheck, there was no chance of getting better housing. Mimi's relationship with Rose and Mildred was still uneasy too, and she wanted to put even more space between her and them. Not one to sit back and wait for weather, finances, or relations to improve, she decided it was time to take charge.

Inherently resourceful, Mimi wrote to an influential friend back in New Haven who owned a fairly large foundry. He offered Herbert a position as a clerk.

Midwinter, they moved to Connecticut and found a place in a boarding house. Mimi was happy to be back in the less insular, and slightly warmer, New Haven. But they still had little money, and when they weren't eating dinner with Uncle George and Aunty Clara, they subsisted on canned soup heated on the single burner in their room. Then spring arrived and at the end of April, Mimi went into labor.

> One Sunday at midnight I began to have labor pains, and as we had no money for a taxi, I knew that I had to go by trolley car, which didn't start until six o'clock in the morning. So, I labored as best I could all that night, and at six o'clock Herbert and I got on the trolley and traveled down to the New Haven hospital.

In that era, most women gave birth at home, and based on Herbert's religion, it would be expected that Mimi would too. But Aunty Clara, concerned about Mimi's frail health—and most notably her small frame and large belly—had arranged for her care in a modern hospital.

Even with the medical help, she endured a long labor due to what her doctor called a funnel-shaped pelvis. After three days of unproductive contractions, the nurses wheeled her to the operating room where the doctor administered ether and used forceps to pull out her ten-pound baby girl.

Employing the metal tongs in an already tight space, however, tore Mimi open all the way through her rectum. In those days, such injuries—not uncommon with forceps deliveries—usually took months to heal, with some women never fully recovering.

But on that Thursday, April 27, 1916, Mimi was just relieved to have the ordeal over with and know her newborn was healthy.

She and Herbert named their fair-haired, blue-eyed daughter Gwendolyn Clara. Although Mimi's parents and siblings had all been named after family members, this was the first Gwendolyn on both Mimi's and Herbert's side. There's no record of where the name came from, but it's interesting to note that Mimi often called her Gweny, which sounds remarkably like Queeny.

Mother and daughter remained in the hospital for six weeks. Mimi, already thin, lost even more weight. Before they were discharged, Herbert found a better, albeit temporary, place to live. He arranged for them to stay in the home of a family that was away for the summer.

Mimi made the best of their new living situation, but she couldn't regain her health. Aside from her poorly healing wounds, she was exhausted by the physical and emotional stress of the previous year. And new motherhood was demanding, too. She had no reserves—physical, spiritual, or emotional—on which to draw. Autumn approached with its looming task of once again finding housing.

Regardless of the war engulfing France, Mimi wanted to take Gwen and convalesce at her childhood home. Her doctor concurred. "A visit to her parents is advisable from the standpoint of her health," he wrote. "She has lost weight and strength over the summer and is in urgent need of change and rest."

A United States citizen since her marriage, Mimi submitted the doctor's letter with her passport application, and Aunty Clara bought her a second-class ticket.

Herbert may not have looked forward to being left alone in a new city just fifteen months after his wedding, but a man could hardly argue with an ailing wife needing her mother. Rose, on the other hand, had no problem expressing disapproval. She made her opinion clear to the Hayford family that her daughter-in-law's planned departure was nothing short of spousal abandonment.

Mimi wouldn't be sailing on the *Lusitania* this time. On a transatlantic crossing the previous year, a German U-boat had torpedoed it. The grand luxury liner—that "magnificent floating hotel" that brought Mimi to the United States six years earlier—sank in eighteen minutes, killing 1,198 people, including ninety-four children.

Among the dead were 128 Americans. This provoked outrage in the United States and became a rallying cry for those urging the U.S. to join the fight. President Wilson responded by demanding Germany put an end to its submarine warfare against commercial vessels. In fear that the U.S. would enter the war, Germany called off its campaign. The crossings seemed safe for now.

Mimi bundled up five-month-old Gwen and boarded the *SS St. Louis,* a Spanish-American war veteran that would soon be returned to service in "the war to end all wars."

> "The crossing was very, very bad. We had rough seas and storms. I finally arrived in London, where I was met by my aunt, who took me in for two or three days. Then I got on the ship that would take me to France. It was also a bad crossing and I was desperately ill, but my mother and my brother met me in Saint-Malo, where the boat landed, and from there we took the train and traveled to Villa St. George in Brittany."

22

Farewell to Villa St. George

By now, Mimi's brother, George Edward, was a handsome young man, even more so in his military uniform. A few years earlier, he had worked in Paris as a private chauffeur for a retired American businessman and eventually moved with him to England. Then war broke out. When the Germans threatened to invade Paris, George Edward enlisted in Britain's Red Cross ambulance corps, which was soon incorporated into the Royal Army.

He was sent to the Western Front where his automotive skills came in handy. Keeping his vehicle in working order, he drove it behind the dangerous and often muddy battlefields of northern France to ferry the wounded to safety.

Mimi's sister, Rita, had also supported the war effort, working as a nurse in the Saint-Brieuc military hospital. A year before Mimi returned to Brittany, Rita fell in love with one of her patients, a French soldier named Adolphe Cantor. He had sparkling eyes and a thick handlebar mustache set on a broad face. They were wed in the old Hillion church, in a ceremony attended by the Countess de Bélizal and prominent families from the local chateaux. The couple settled near Dolphe's family in Le Havre.

Mimi's first love, Guy, was off fighting in the war. His sister, Helen, told Mimi he had sworn he'd never marry if he couldn't have her. Despite the changes brought by marriage—or perhaps heightened by them—Mimi treasured his words of devotion.

Although the war was on everyone's minds, the battles were not near Hillion, and Mimi was happy to be there.

> "It seemed so good to be back home, where I'd been brought up... to see old friends, to see the peasants and their farms, the golden gorse flowers on the hill, the beautiful old chateaux, the sea, and the dogs, and my mother and father. It was just heavenly.
>
> I missed my husband, naturally. I was in love with him, but I was so delicate and so ill that I was willing to accept almost anything to regain my health."

Under the capable care of Queeny, who had seen so many women through childbirth and postpartum recovery, Mimi began to improve. Her life in Brittany, however, wasn't as easy as it had been in the past. With the war raging, goods normally available in the region were now in short supply. Chief among them was coal. Even if the winter temperature rarely fell to freezing, the chilly air was damp and the winds sharp, often forcing the family to huddle around the hearth.

> "Sometimes we had hardships, because it was cold and we only had heat in the chimneys, by the fireside. Then Gwen came down with pneumonia and I was quite worried. One morning, she seemed so ill that I left her with my parents and went to get medicine. I started out for the doctor, which was a five-mile walk. I ran all the way and made it in less than an hour. But he was busy himself and couldn't see me for quite a while. Finally he gave me some medicine to give her, and I came back.
>
> I was met partway by my father, and when I saw him coming, I almost died because I thought he was going to tell me that Gwen had gotten worse. But he pacified me immediately and said she was feeling better and that she had taken a turn for the best, so I was relieved."

Despite the bitter winter and food shortages, Gwen got well. She thrived on goats' milk—sometimes suckled directly from the teat—and grew plump. Mimi, who had regained her strength, was healthy now, too, and took comfort in the company of her family. But she longed for Herbert.

> " That whole winter passed in joy... and yet in loneliness. I was getting more and more homesick for America and my husband. I could hardly bear it. "

Mimi's stay in Brittany stretched out longer than she had planned. By the beginning of January 1917, Germany figured the U.S. would enter the war whether the empire revived its submarine campaign or not, so it vowed to torpedo any and all ships. It was no longer safe to pass through the English Channel. Mimi's return to America had to wait.

During this time, on the other side of the ocean, Herbert published a letter in his college alumni magazine. In it, he referred to the U-boat blockade that kept his wife from joining him.

"I suppose your little book wants to know what I am doing. To be perfectly frank with you, I am waiting for the Germans to get 'licked' so my wife can come home. She wasn't very well last summer, and in the fall she went to England for a visit home and then over to Southern France to spend the winter months. She was to have come home last month and, of course, the submarine war made it too dangerous. So I am just dangling around waiting for peace to be declared or war to be declared, and then I can go over myself and help kill off what remains of the German empire.

"I must not forget to tell you that I have a little girl now, Jim. And she is a corker. Best that ever was made, and the image of her mother. I was sorry that it was not a boy, but you will find out that you won't have much to say about it when you get married, so it is no use kicking. I don't think I shall send her down to Maine to coach the Freshman team, as we used to sing in the Maine Y.M.C.A. song. But you can just bet your life that if ever I have a boy it will be the joy of my heart to send him down to Maine to 'yell to H--- with Bowdoin,' as his daddy used to do.

"Business is good, and I am still with the old concern. I have a little bungalow that sits up on a bluff and overlooks the sea. I am keeping bachelor's hall and would welcome any and all my old classmates who can spare the time to make me a call. You will find the latchstring still out.

"Well, I guess this trash will fit all the space you will want to allot to me, so I will ring off. Let me hear from you again sometime, Jim, when you don't want a check. This is an expensive letter and I am not rich yet. I am saving my money for a car, a real car, understand. I bought two last summer, but they both push.

Yours in [class of] 1915

Herbert W. Hayford, But Better Known as 'Kracker.'

Ansonia, Connecticut"

It's curious that he implied his wife's home was in England. And why did Herbert say she was passing the winter in southern France, rather than in her home on the northern coast? It's hard to believe Mimi didn't have him well versed in her family history. Perhaps he wanted to downplay anything that made her sound French. Or possibly—as is often the case when communicating with fellow alumni—vacationing in Southern France just had a classier ring to it.

As for his bravado regarding what he'd do to the Germans, Herbert didn't jump at the chance to join when the U.S. geared up to enter the war. In a February 1917 Connecticut military census, he claimed he had dysentery and poor teeth. When asked if he was a "good swimmer" or could "handle a boat—power or sail," the man who spent his summers on the lake wrote "no" to both questions. Four months later, when he filled out his draft card, he claimed an exemption due to "weight + family."

But his I'll-kill-them-off-myself routine was popular, and he was, at heart, a pleasing raconteur. He had charmed the girls with his stories, and then Mimi, too. Yet, as their separation lengthened, he sought her audience less and less. His letters to her, never frequent, had all but stopped.

To a young wife who missed her husband, his inattention was painful. To a proud daughter who wanted to show her parents she had a devoted husband, it was mortifying. His protracted silence also delayed her return.

> **"** During my year in Brittany, he had only written a few times and only sent eleven dollars. He was not sending me money to buy a ticket to come back, so my mother simply bought my ticket. **"**

Since traveling by ship from England was out of the question, Mimi decided to go to Bordeaux and board a French ocean liner. Despite adding five days to the voyage, it was the safest route.

This farewell was hard for Mimi, who knew it was the last time she would ever enjoy the idyllic days at Villa St. George. As glorious as life had been in Hillion, it lacked job opportunities and the Tate children were all long gone. Changing circumstances were prodding the others out, too. Years earlier, old Aunt Harrie had been sent to live in the London Nazareth House for the Poor. And George James and Queeny, both in their early sixties, were making plans for their own future. They had decided to sell their Brittany home and move close to Rita and Dolphe, who resided 200 miles east in the bustling port of Le Havre.

Before Mimi left, her father placed a few mementos of childhood in her steamer trunk, including a volume of fairy tales and her very first book, an 1894 edition of *Mavor's Spelling*. It covered not only language arts but science, morals, poetry, and prayers. Soon Mimi would be reading these to her own daughter.

Queeny boarded the train with Mimi and seventeen-month-old Gwen to accompany them on the long ride to the Bordeaux port, where they climbed the gangway of the *SS Rochambeau*. The ship had already gained fame for ferrying people to safety. When the war in Europe first broke out, it was used to repatriate U.S. citizens to America. Now, three years and many sailings later, the reliable liner was still carrying travelers more interested in safe passage than luxury.

It was no-frills travel, but Queeny made sure her daughter and granddaughter were comfortable on board. When the *All Ashore!* was announced, she hurried back down to the dock while Mimi, toddler in arms, stood at the railing to wave goodbye.

> I hated to leave, and we both cried, but it had to be.

Mimi accepted the inevitability of certain life changes. Children move on and their parents move on. Still, as the ship steamed out into the open sea, she must have hoped that another relationship—her marriage—hadn't changed.

23

Dresses in the Closet

The year of recuperation had been good for Mimi. With her parents to care for her and share the constant work of tending a baby, she was returning home in October 1917 with her health and strength restored. Morning and afternoon strolls on the deck of the *SS Rochambeau* revived her self-assurance, too... the ship was packed with admiring soldiers.

Six months earlier, when the United States had declared war on Germany, American men who had enlisted in the French or British forces began to return stateside to join their own military. It was on Mimi's New York-bound ship, which carried a large number of these troops, that she met a clean-cut chap in a uniform much like her brother's.

This young man's insignia, however, indicated he drove an ambulance for the American Red Cross rather than the British. His name was Fred Kramer and he'd spent the last six months on the front lines. Mimi was particularly interested in him since her brother, George Edward, served in the same area.

Fred was as much a mechanic as a driver, and had been proud of his ambulance. As soon as he'd arrived in France, he helped assemble it, fitting the large wooden body on the imported Buick chassis. His open-air cab afforded him little protection, but he no doubt assured Mimi that none of the drivers, American or British, ran willy-nilly over the battlefields. They stayed on roads—if the wheel ruts could be called that—pulling up as close as they could to the trenches. From there they loaded the wounded and rushed them to dressing stations. It was dangerous work, but not so bad if you kept your head down. Certainly, he held back the harrowing parts—the shells bursting overhead, the injuries he'd seen, the fear in the soldiers' eyes, the boys who were alive when he put them in the rear compartment but dead when he opened the door to bring them out. The endless loss of life. And the times he thought he might lose his own.

Like many soldiers of adventure, Fred had been eager to sign up, even adding three years to his age to do so. Now he was just as eager to get home and enlist in the U.S. Army, the flight division, and fly this time instead of drive.

Although still only seventeen—which he surely didn't tell twenty-four-year-old Mimi upon their first meeting—he had a breadth of experience that matured him beyond his years. His mother had died when he was eleven, and by fourteen he left his Philadelphia home for a job stoking the furnace in the engine room of an Italian ship. He visited Italy, Spain, and France before returning stateside where he found work as a machinist. Then the volunteer ambulance service was formed.

The corps was made up of about two hundred drivers, mostly elite students recruited from Ivy League colleges. But despite Fred's lack of high school, he was bright and well read. He fit in.

No matter how grim his work had been, it hadn't dampened his good humor, and over the following days he played with baby Gwen whenever he saw her pattering on deck with her winsome mother. Mimi took a liking to Fred and told him that after the war, if he should need lodging or help getting resettled, to get in touch. He was welcome to stay with her and her family.

The chance meeting with that attentive young man may have only accentuated Mimi's disappointment when she disembarked. Her reunion with Herbert—who worked outside New Haven as an accountant for the Farrel Foundry & Machine Company—was not the storybook event for which she'd yearned.

"I had written to Herbert telling him when I would arrive in New York. Then while I was on the ship, I sent him a wire telling him when I would arrive in New Haven if he missed me in New York. By the time we docked, I had just a few dollars. But there was a darling person on the boat, and she said she would lend me any money I wanted. Which she did ... enough to take the train up to New Haven. But Herbert wasn't in New York and not in New Haven either.

I didn't have enough money to take a taxi so, with all of my luggage and with this little baby, I took a trolley car and went to Aunty Clara's once again. She wasn't there, but they took me in and I will never forget the peace and joy I felt when I got in her lovely kitchen."

Her happiness, however, was short-lived. Where was Herbert? Why hadn't he met her? His lack of letters during her year abroad had been bad enough, but his failure to pick her up upon her return was humiliating. And worrisome. What was wrong?

"I telephoned to Herbert. It was the middle of the afternoon, and he said he'd come to fetch me when he got through with the office, which he said was about five.

And he did. He wasn't overly excited on the telephone, but when he came, he seemed to be glad to see us both. We got in his car and he drove us home.

Since I'd been away, he'd got a one-room cottage. I arrived there joyful to be back with my husband, but I went to hang up my clothes, and in the closet were six or seven dresses. I asked him, 'What on earth are those?'

He said his cousin, Frances, had sent those clothes for me because she thought I could wear them when I came back. I was so grateful that I wrote to her and thanked her for the dresses.

Well, I learned to live there. There were farms around, so we had milk and eggs and everything that was good for a baby. And I tried not to think about the dresses."

Regardless of the lukewarm reception, Mimi had her energy and enthusiasm back. Throughout the fall, winter, and spring, she set about making a proper home for the three of them, and added a Collie that reminded her of the friendly dogs her mother raised. They named him Bob.

Then twenty-one-year-old Frances, Mother Rose's niece and the donor of dresses, sent a letter from her home in New York. She had a vacation proposal that delighted Mimi.

"The summer after I got back, Herbert's cousin wrote to him saying she hoped we planned to visit Maine on vacation, and that she would love to come and spend time with us there. She said she could take care of Gwen while Herbert and I went out canoeing on Lake Sebec, which sounded lovely. So it was arranged that she would meet us in Maine and we would spend two weeks together at the Hayford camp by the lake.

Because Herbert had only two weeks of vacation, it was decided that I should go to his parents' home ahead of him by a week or two, and then stay with them again after he left. So altogether I arranged to spend four weeks in Maine with baby Gwen."

The Hayford home in Dover routinely held extended family, and—aside from Mimi's earlier residence—a bona fide servant as well. In the summer of 1918, Herbert's sister, Dorothy, lived there with her husband and two toddlers. So the house was already full, but there was always room for more... and more inevitably came, especially in the warm months when the lake beckoned.

Rose, who prided herself on keeping an attractive home in town, made sure the summer cottage was fashionable, too. She'd painted the bedroom furniture—dresser, bed table and chair—a different color for each of the four upstairs rooms: one set pink, one yellow, one lavender, and one pale green. With their matching pastel bed linens and knotty pine walls, the bedrooms were simple but chic.

Wilder and Herbert, for their part, had chosen and built well. At Sebec Lake, most people entered their vacation homes, which they referred to as camps, via the back porch or kitchen and made their way through to the living and dining area. The Hayfords had constructed theirs the same way, with the most important rooms, upstairs and down, overlooking the water.

The rustic front porch—facing the lake—was the length of the cottage and built directly on the boulder-lined shore. In the evening, if the mosquitos weren't out, it was the ideal place to watch the loons glide by and listen to them call to one another in their mournful tones. By day, it provided an unobstructed view of the large lake and a shaded refuge from which to wave at passing boaters while reading or sipping lemonade. The gentle sound of wavelets lapping against the lakeside rocks competed only with the laughter of vacationers.

The wooden dock, mere feet from the porch, was used for tying up the rowboat, jumping into the lake, or sunbathing—as much as one could in heavy knit swimsuits that covered more skin than they revealed. On the far side of the dock was a pebbly inlet for teaching children to swim, or for bringing the canoe ashore after paddling out on the pristine lake... perhaps to one of the secluded coves.

Mimi, waiting at her in-laws' home in Dover, looked forward to revisiting the camp where she and Herbert had honeymooned.

"When the time came for Herbert to arrive, I walked down to the station in Dover to meet him. I waited for the train, and he got off, but to my surprise his cousin was with him. They picked Gwen up, and there was only one car there, a cab, so Herbert, with Gwen in his arms, and Frances drove off in it, leaving me standing on the platform to walk home. I had quite a distance to walk, at least a mile, but what could I do?

I walked home and when I got there the family was rejoicing and he and Frances were saying hello to everybody. I was like a stranger, and heartbroken. I hadn't seen him for two weeks and that he could do such a thing to me, forgetting entirely about me and going back to his parents' with his cousin...

Well, I let that pass. The next day we went to the camp by Lake Sebec and Frances came with us. Then I found that it wasn't *I* who was going to canoe while she took care of the baby. Instead, *I* took care of Gwen and *she and he* went out in the canoe. Day after day. And, somehow they were beginning to be very intimate with each other. I felt like I didn't count at all. I became worried and thought I'd better find out what was going on.

So one afternoon, I put Gwen to bed for her nap and said that I was going to the postbox to mail a letter. They said, 'Fine.'

It was about a mile away, but I only went a certain distance, less than half, and then came back. I entered the house quietly and went upstairs. And as I did, they heard me. They were in our bedroom... together.

Frances came rushing out of the room, absolutely stripped naked!

I couldn't speak. I was so ill from what I'd seen that I ran downstairs. At first, I didn't know whether I wanted to live. I thought I wanted to die. But I had Gwen and I knew she needed me. So I sat down and wrote Aunty Clara a long letter telling her exactly what had happened from the moment I came back from Europe—what I had found, what I had heard, what I had seen. The Paines were then at Sutton Island, near Bar Harbor. I wrote, 'I'm coming to you to decide what to do about a divorce.'

Then I handed the letter to Herbert. I said, 'I'll let you read it.' So he read it, and he felt awful. He said, 'Please don't send the letter, and if you don't send it, she'll leave immediately. I'll see that she goes back to New York.'

Which she did. But of course he was going home the following week, before I had to go back. Later I heard, from people who found out, that she had left and waited for him in Bangor, Maine, where they spent a weekend and then traveled home together."

At the time, Mimi didn't know about their Bangor meeting. It was crushing enough that she'd caught Herbert with Frances, and she wanted to believe it wouldn't happen again. She returned to Connecticut, woefully disillusioned about their marriage but still determined to make it work.

24

Chestnut Ridge

At about that time, Herbert changed jobs again, hiring on as an accountant at an electric company. It isn't clear whether it was the position that brought them to Orange, Connecticut—five miles west of New Haven—or the lovely countryside that prompted the change in employment, but Herbert and Mimi purchased an old two-story farmhouse at 473 Chestnut Ridge.

Rumored to have been visited by George Washington in his later years, the house had been built in 1780 and lacked modern conveniences. Mimi, however, was no longer the delicate bride unused to hard work. With the same vitality and passion that her Tate grandfather had brought to his engineering projects, she set about making home improvements.

> "There was no heat, no running water, and no lights. A big well in the back had a chain going down, and I used to pull up a pail or two of water several times a day, which I would heat on the stove. For lighting, of course, we had oil lamps until I studied something about electricity, so much so that I electrified the whole house. We finally had electric lights."

Utility companies had begun extending service to rural areas, and adding electricity to homes was becoming so common that even Sears, Roebuck and Company sold electrical kits. The earliest installation was usually limited to fixed lighting on the walls or ceilings, accomplished by stringing the wires along the framing and then running them through the beams. It was a notable feat for a housewife in a society that didn't expect such things from a well-bred woman, and Mimi was rightfully proud of the electric light bulb hanging down in each room.

She went on to have the heating system upgraded from fireplace to stove—which could burn both wood and coal—and ran a flume through the upstairs bedrooms. It provided a bit more heat, but her daughter, Gwen, later recalled that it was still difficult to keep the place warm.

"We never lived in the front part of the house—the parlor, which was a large room—because it was hard to heat," Gwen said. "When people came, we visited in the kitchen."

However Mimi, like her mother, Queeny, was rejuvenated by the country life. While Herbert spent his days working with numbers and ledgers, she worked the soil.

> It was a beautiful old place with lots of ground and, as I was enthusiastic and young, I had many chickens and geese, and a great big garden. I used to borrow the horse and a plow from the farmer next door, and I'd put the reins around my neck and plow the ground. I sowed all sorts of things . . . corn, beans, and peas. And we had lots of trees with fruit. I used to put them up in the old cellar, which was cool all winter long. I had shelves upon shelves of canned goods.

Mimi also raised three pigs, which she sent out to be slaughtered when they grew into large hogs. With the help of a Swedish neighbor, she learned how to cut bacon, and make sausage and head cheese. Pleased with her farming abilities, Mimi took a snapshot of Gwen posing tentatively next to a hog carcass hanging down from the porch beams.

The nearby city of New Haven allowed Mimi to enjoy cultural pursuits as well. Like Aunty Clara had in her youth, Mimi modeled for artists. One day in an oil painting class, a student turned her attention from Mimi to Gwen, who was playing in a chair while she waited for her mother. The result was a primitive but charming portrait. Mimi framed it.

When Gwen was two or three, Mimi became pregnant again but suffered a miscarriage. Years later, Gwen relayed the story she'd been told. "It seems that I had very carefully placed a row of milk bottles across the side door steps," wrote Gwen, "and she tripped over them."

The not-to-be child was a boy. Mimi placed his tiny body in a good-sized matchbox she'd lined with cloth. Then she buried him under a pine tree in their front yard. It was a difficult time, but with her busy little girl to look after, she eventually rallied and refocused on the living.

In spite of their rural surroundings, Mimi made sure Gwen learned the things she'd need to know in polite society.

"I'm four years old," Gwen recounted. "We're living out in the country, and it's very primitive, but my mother is training me how to answer the door. We go through a routine. There's a knock and I go to the door and my mother, impersonating a man, says, 'Good afternoon. Is your mother at home?' or 'Is Mrs. Hayford at home?'

"And I would say, 'She's not home right now.'

"Then he would present me with his card, and I would take it, and he would say, 'Thank you,' and walk away.

"So here we are, out in the country, and my mother is teaching me what they did in London in Queen Victoria's time."

Mimi, however, having been raised in provincial Brittany, did not see pastoral living as a reason for neglecting proper etiquette. Besides, she knew first-hand that people didn't always end up where they had started.

While Mimi and Herbert were facing their triumphs and sorrows at home, her family in France was celebrating the end of The Great War. In October 1918, Germany, reeling under the latest Allied offensive, signed an armistice. On the eleventh hour of the eleventh day of the eleventh month, it went into effect.

By this time, Mimi's parents were living in Sanvic, a suburb of Le Havre, and were relieved when their son, George Edward, was discharged and joined them. He'd spent three years on the battlefields, been gassed, and suffered a severe wound to his knee. But he was safe and eventually recovered from his injuries.

Early in the war, he had distinguished himself on the frontlines and was the first British soldier to receive France's 'Croix de Guerre.' An article in *The London Gazette*, however, later gave that distinction to the Prince of Wales. Queeny, by then an older woman best described as indomitable, would have none of that. According to George Edward's son Anthony, who recalled the story, Queeny immediately contacted the paper.

"Dear Grandma Tate wrote back that the Prince of Wales may have been the *first officer* to receive the medal, but that her son, George Tate, was the *first private* to receive the decoration, giving date, details, etc. An amended article was duly published in *The London Gazette*, putting matters right!!!"

Fred Kramer, Mimi's shipmate, also survived the war with limbs intact. After serving six months as an aerial photographer for the flight division of the U.S. Army, he returned to America. Not having much in the way of family, he contacted Mimi and asked if he could board at their Chestnut Ridge home. He was a quiet, polite man with a shy smile and an appreciation for her homeland. She was happy to have him move in.

Mimi encouraged him to apply for a position at New Haven's Seamless Rubber Company, which produced hospital supplies.

His medical experience in the war—as well as his pleasing personality—made him a successful salesman. He traveled for work most of the time, but always kept a room with the Hayfords, where he was known to Gwen as Uncle Fred.

It was into this large old house on September 4, 1920, that Mimi and Herbert welcomed their second daughter. Mimi was much healthier this time around and the delivery, though still difficult, was not the ordeal the first one had been.

This baby, with hair as dark as Gwen's was fair, was named Jane, after Mimi's grandmother, Jane Bennett. However, the girl was called by her middle name, Rosemary, bestowed to please Herbert—who called her Rosebud—and his mother, Rose, who was no longer as troublesome since Mimi had put four hundred miles between them.

Yet even without his mother around, the couple's relationship was increasingly strained. Herbert tended to tune her out, which frustrated her to no end. She was a woman who liked to work out conflicts before saying goodnight. For her, it was a matter of wifely pride that they never retire on an angry note. But Herbert preferred to leave things well enough alone. With such differing approaches to problems—tackling versus side-stepping them—their marital bed became a verbal battleground.

Little Gwen, whose temperament was more like her father's than her mother's, felt sorry for him when she overheard them in the evenings.

"Father and Mother are in their bed and Father is saying, 'For the love of God, Mona, I've got to sleep.'

"And she'd say, 'But, Herbert, you've got to . . .' and here she'd say the things he'd have to do.

"Then he'd say, 'Please, Mona, stop talking. I've got to sleep.'

"And she'd say, 'Herbert, you're not listening to me.'

"It would go on all night."

25

A Wife's Curse

In September 1922, as the New England air began to chill, Mimi told Herbert she wanted to take six-year-old Gwen and two-year-old Jane Rosemary to France. It had been five years since she had seen her family, and they had never met her youngest. Herbert agreed to the trip, although it may not have been without a number of late-night discussions, since Aunty Clara ended up buying their tickets. Ever generous, Clara also paid for the passage of the girls' young nurse, Pauline. The foursome sailed on the French steamship, *La Savoie*, directly into the port of Le Havre.

By now Mimi's parents were well-established in Sanvic at 41 rue Gambetta. It was a large house with a courtyard in front and sufficient room indoors for the elder George to conduct private English lessons. The younger George, now an assistant manager of a garage, lived with them, while Rita and Dolphe resided a few miles away in Le Havre proper with their two little boys, Maurice and Georges Cantor.

> **"** When we arrived, my parents were disappointed that I had brought over an American nurse because, as Mummy said, 'If you want the children to learn French, it's no good having an English-speaking nurse for them.' **"**

Mimi, who planned a long visit, agreed. They recruited the aid of Dr. Austin—whose wife had helped Mimi years earlier when she was lost in Paris—to find a training position for Pauline at an American hospital just outside the French capital.

> "My mother got a French nurse to teach the children, and it wasn't long before they were chatting away. Not Jane, because she couldn't speak yet, but Gwen could.
>
> We'd settled in for a nice holiday when a letter came from the woman who was taking care of our house with her husband. She said I should come back because things were taking place that would displease me.
>
> I discussed it with my father and mother. They wanted me to leave both children and go and see for myself what was taking place. But I would not leave Jane because she was a tiny little thing and, anyway, I wanted one of my children with me. So I left Gwen with her Grandpa and Grandma, and without saying a word to anyone, not to a living soul, I boarded this big ship and came back to the United States."

She'd been gone six weeks. The autumn leaves had already turned their brilliant colors and by now lay dirty on the ground beneath the bare trees. Mimi let herself inside the house, and as before, discovered women's clothing. Not just dresses that a good storyteller might be able to argue away, but a nightgown, too.

Herbert's cousin, Frances, was once again staying with him. Later it was whispered among friends and family that she "wanted him so bad she left her nighty there on purpose." But whether it was Frances's designs on Herbert, or his pursuit of her, didn't much matter to Mimi.

No longer a young, starry-eyed wife with love enough to forgive a husband's infidelity, this time she didn't hesitate. Every photo of Herbert she could lay her hands on, she tore up. Then she packed up her belongings, took Jane—who was never again referred to as Rosemary, Rosebud, or anything with Rose in it—and checked into a rural inn.

Righteous anger stoked Mimi's creative side, and taking up the hotel stationery, she composed a curse that was as poetic as it was fearsome.

> Memories are sweet, and thoughts of the past
> Surge in our hearts for a spell
> When the leaves have fallen, the hair turned gray
> And we bid our friends farewell
>
> To you who have brought me my pain and woe
> To you who have proved unfair
> I bid adieu, and wherever you go
> My curse and my tears are there
>
> They will follow you home where you hope for mirth
> They will mar your pleasure and sleep
> They will follow you far, to the ends of the earth
> Where the lost souls sadly weep.
>
> In the smile of a child you will find my tear
> From her heart you will hear my moan
> Tho you curse and you weep in your grief and fear
> My sorrow will be your own
>
> You will live to know the curse of a wife
> You may wring your hands in vain
> But I and my curse are there thru life
> Thru cloud, and sunshine and rain!
>
> To you, dear ones, who have played me fair
> I say goodbye for a time
> Thoughts and words like yours have stayed
> To be mixed with the gall of mine!

> In all of my anguish your faith came true
> As the light in a dark, sad hour
> You filled my soul and my heart anew
> With the thought of Godly power
>
> And I felt a strength in my soul arise
> And I smiled at my foes anew
> As I raised my eyes to the bright blue skies
> And I knew that God was true!

She signed it with her maiden name, *Mona Tate.*

Not one to think unshared words carried much power—and she believed in the power of a spoken curse just as Grandmother Henrietta had—Mimi returned to their residence to give voice to her message.

She walked by the field she had plowed, stood before the historic old building she'd filled with electric light and canned fruit, and stared up at the window of the bedroom she'd shared with Herbert. Next, rhythmically chanting her poetic curse, she circled three times . . . step by step . . . the house that had been their home.

Then she was done with him.

Mimi boarded the train to Aunty Clara's, where she set about reordering her life. She filed papers to divorce Herbert. Their marriage ended as miserably as it had started, with Mimi accusing him of adultery, and he referring to her long trips abroad as abandonment. It didn't stop there. Later Herbert's court-ordered ten-dollars-a-week child support also came into dispute. Mimi told her friends he didn't pay it. He said he did. Whatever the truth, it lost out to the issue of pride. Mimi had put her heart and soul into her marriage. That she could then be seen as anything less than the wronged party infuriated her.

26

Starting Over

With Gwen safe in Queeny's care, Mimi focused on securing living arrangements for herself and Jane. She didn't have financial resources to fall back on, but she had a network of influential friends. It wasn't long before she found a position as live-in nurse for an aging woman in the Elliot family. They resided in a two-story house in a well-off suburb of Boston and said Mimi was welcome to bring Jane with her.

Although taking care of a two-year-old while performing her duties was a challenge, Mimi was up to it. Little Jane was, in fact, much easier than Mimi's elderly charge. The cantankerous old woman had gone through several nurses, but she met her match in Mimi.

> "Of course I used to dress the *Grandma*, as we called her. Every morning I'd bathe her in bed, fix her hair and put a nice little nightgown on her and a ribbon in her hair.
>
> And this I had done, this particular morning, and left her comfortably in bed. But as I was leaving, she called to me that she wanted the bedpan. So I gave it to her and went in to see what Jane was doing and stayed there a few minutes. Then I went back to *Grandma*.
>
> You will never in your life guess what I found. She had put her hand in the bedpan—and of course she'd had a bowel movement—and she had taken everything out of the pan and had plastered it on her hair, her nightgown, her body, her sheets . . . everything.

> Well, first of all, I went into the bathroom and ran the tub with warm water. Then I came back and I picked her up. I was young and strong, so I simply picked her up and plunked her into the bathtub. She was yelling bloody murder, so Mrs. Elliot came rushing up. She opened the door, said 'Oh, my gosh!' and ran back downstairs.
>
> I washed her and she was screaming the whole time. Then I let the water out and started another bathtub full. I did that two or three times. Then I dried her, changed the bed, and carried her back to her room.
>
> I never said a word. I put a clean nightgown on her and combed her hair, but I assure you I did not put a lovely ribbon in it this time. And when I had her all settled, I looked at her and said, 'You listen to me right now. Did you like that?'
>
> 'No, no, no, no!'
>
> 'Did you like my putting your hair down to rinse it?'
>
> 'No, no, no, no!"
>
> 'Okay, well the next time you do that to me, I shall not hold your *hair* down, I shall hold your *head* down.'
>
> That was the turning point. She realized she couldn't play those tricks on me, and that I was not going to leave if she did. I was going to stay there, I was going to take care of her, and in spite of all, I was going to love her.

As sure of herself as the day in her childhood when she'd met her pet parrot—who bit her before she hit him on the head to tame him—Mimi knew *Grandma* just needed to understand who was in charge.

> The result was she absolutely loved me more than any member of her family. I was the one that counted.

I did something else for her, too. All the other nurses had kept her in bed, but a big armchair was by the window and I thought how lovely if she could watch people going by. Sort of give her something to think about. So I lifted her up and put her in this armchair. She loved it.

Every afternoon I had two hours off. Most of the time, I stayed there with Jane, but once in a while Mrs. Elliot would take care of Jane and I would go to the store to buy something. As soon as I came in the door *Grandma* began to go, 'Oh, oh, oh.'

That's the way she would call me, and I would run upstairs, and she had to see everything I bought. She had to open every bundle. And she would say, in her own way, what she thought of each item. She would go into ecstasy about a little dress or maybe a scarf or something. But her whole life started over again. "

Twenty-nine-year-old Mimi was starting over, too. She played tennis with a few eligible men, but in New England in 1922, a divorced woman—no matter how blameless—was not considered wife material. Especially not one with children.

What, though, were her alternatives? Even if decent paying jobs—something more substantial than live-in nurse—had been available, there was a stigma to raising children without a father. Her options were limited by finances and society, not to mention her own belief that marriage represented fulfillment.

There was one man, however, she could count on for support and respectability. Fred Kramer. He seemed to have no qualms about courting a divorcee with two children, both of whom he was very fond. As for Mimi, he loved her.

He had been enamored of her from their first meeting on the deck of the *SS Rochambeau,* and his feelings had only grown over time. Living in the Hayford home, he'd witnessed Mimi's growing discontent with Herbert, and Fred surely saw this as his chance to prove he could do better by her. Whenever he was near Boston, he visited Mimi and Jane. The Elliots liked him and Aunty Clara did, too.

> " Aunty Clara used to call me almost every day to find out how I was, and what I was doing, and did I need anything. She was so generous and a real second mother to me. One day she talked to me about Fred, and said, 'You know, I think that man is in love with you.'
>
> I laughed because Fred and I used to fight constantly. He didn't like the English and I didn't like the Germans, and of course his background was German. So I put him off all the time because I was a little bit afraid. "

As a salesman, Fred traveled throughout Pennsylvania, New York, Connecticut, and Massachusetts, so Mimi only saw him every couple of weeks, leaving her time to consider what a future with him might be like. Their differences—cultural and age—surely gave her pause. But he was a hard worker and made a good living.

He didn't wholly arouse the epic love she sought—the great passion that led to her grandparents' impetuous Paris wedding—but she'd always been attracted to him. He was nice looking with attentive eyes. Moreover, he was steadfast and devoted to her in a way Herbert never had been.

> " Finally, after seeing his kindness and thoughtfulness, I, too, felt he was a worthwhile man. "

However, it had been a half-year of momentous changes and only two months since her divorce was final. As worthwhile as Fred was, she still wasn't sure. Then she received a letter from him.

“One day he wrote and told me he was feeling poorly, and he wished I would come to see him. At the time, he was in Rochester, New York.

He also mentioned he'd like to talk about marriage, but I didn't want to. So I wrote right back and told him, no, that I wouldn't go, that I couldn't leave my patient and I couldn't leave Jane.”

When Fred got Mimi's reply, he called her long-distance.

“He said, 'I don't feel well and I'm wondering if you'd come, even though I know you feel that you should stay.'

Well, I talked it over with Mrs. Elliot, and she said, 'I'll take care of Jane and Mother. You go along and see what it's all about.' So that evening I left on the night train and arrived the next morning in Rochester about eight. Fred met my train and we had breakfast.”

Sitting across from her at the station diner, Fred said he was doing better, just suffering a case of the nerves, but he'd be okay. Especially now that she had arrived.

When they finished eating, Fred reached into his pocket.

“Suddenly, he produced a wedding ring and an engagement ring. He said, 'Please stay, and let us be married.'”

Although Mimi may have wanted more time to think about it, the occasion for making a decision had come. She said yes.

After calling the Elliots to say she'd be gone for a few days, Mimi and Fred went downtown to the old Brick Presbyterian Church. At two o'clock on the afternoon of June 2, 1923, Mimi and Fred married.

Mimi's second honeymoon, however, wasn't much better than her first. That night she realized what Fred had meant by "a case of the nerves."

> We went to bed, and the next morning, very early, I realized that Fred was having a complete nervous breakdown. I knew that I could not go back to the Elliots'. I had to stay with him and travel with him.

Mimi called Mrs. Elliot to let her know she would need to find a new nurse... and to ask her to take Jane to a home managed by a Mrs. Dumphy, who took in orphaned and foster children.

Having left Gwen, now seven, in France, it must have been doubly hard to leave little Jane with a caretaker. Or maybe it had become easier. In any case, Mimi was raised to put the needs of her husband before those of her children. In this retelling of her wedding story—which Mimi wrote to Jane late in life—she may have inflated the situation to justify why she'd left her not-yet-three-year-old in foster care, but she made no apologies for it.

> I stayed with Fred quite a while. But every night when I went to bed, I had to tie his pajama's cord to my arm because I didn't know whether he was going to jump out the window, or what would happen. Often I had to put him in a tub of lukewarm water to make him quiet. He was so depressed he would cry. We'd go to the [Christian Science] Wednesday evening meeting, or even to church on Sunday, and he would cry through the whole service. It was pathetic.
>
> But little by little, with my patience and courage, he became better.

It's unclear why Fred was so depressed, but not surprising. Like many veterans, he may have been suffering from the aftereffects of war. And aside from the horrors he saw during his two tours of service, he had endured a raw childhood, making him all the more susceptible to post-traumatic stress.

He was born in Philadelphia to a stoic German-American photographer. Father and son never developed much of a relationship, and Fred looked to his mother, as warm-hearted as his father was cold, for nurturing. But she was frail, and her years of mothering him were short-lived after she contracted tuberculosis. It fell to Fred to take care of her. According to the story he later told Jane, his father found another woman to spend his evenings with, and Fred, who made his bed in the closet, passed his nights listening for his mother's call.

When he was eleven, he awoke early one morning to find her coughing up blood. Despite his efforts to save her, she died in his arms. His last glimpse of her was when his father returned, put her body—still clad in the bloodstained nightgown—in a burial box and dragged it out the door.

Later, Fred's younger sister, Eva, also came down with TB and was admitted to a sanitarium in the Catskill Mountains. When Fred, by then sixteen, returned from his work on the Italian ship, he asked his just-remarried father for the train fare to visit Eva. She was fifteen and her health was failing. His father said no.

Secreting out one of his father's professional cameras, Fred hopped a freight train and rode the rails to Liberty, New York. Before the train entered the village, he jumped off and stopped at a farm to wash his sooty hands and put on a clean collar.

Eva's bed had been moved out to the building's sleeping porch so she could take in the cleansing autumn air. She sat up for Fred, clasping her quilt-covered knees while he took a photo. It was the last smile he would coax out of her. Within days she was gone.

Four months later—after Fred's father signed an affidavit swearing his son was nineteen—he left for France with the ambulance corps.

Whether the ordeals of his youth, combined with the trials of war, precipitated his depression is not known. Perhaps the sheer relief of securing his future with the woman he loved—finding safe harbor in her arms—opened an emotional gate through which the years of hardship burst forth.

But whatever the cause, for the next couple of months Mimi traveled with Fred while he called on clients. He regained his equilibrium and didn't suffer any more breakdowns.

When they returned from their working honeymoon, Mimi and Fred picked up Jane at the group home and sent for Gwen.

27

When is That Child Going Home?

During the year that Mimi was divorcing and remarrying, Gwen had been living with her grandparents in the hilltop suburb of Sanvic, overlooking Le Havre.

Although Mimi spoke of Queeny hiring a French nanny upon their arrival, she doesn't seem to have stayed on after Mimi and little Jane left. Perhaps a nursemaid was no longer considered necessary for a six-year-old. But, as children usually do, Gwen quickly picked up the language on her own as she ran errands and played with neighborhood kids. She spoke English at home, however, with her grandparents and her uncle, George Edward.

Years later, Gwen described her grandparents' home and her life with them.

"They had a three-story brick house set on a small enclosed lot. The windows were few, but very large. The rooms were large, too, with the hall and staircases in the center. The kitchen was small, dark and dank, and I always had the impression of puddles of water on the floor. The back door led out to the outhouse, which was serviced by the local 'honey wagon' business.

"It seems funny now. The front garden was beautiful, the house looked wealthy, inside were beautiful crystals, china, silver, nice furniture, and objects of art. Then there were chamber pots in the bedroom, and an outhouse in back.

"When I first lived with them, my bedroom was on the third story and the bed was so high I needed a footstool and a boost to get into it. It was far away from any comforting sounds, but I was never afraid or lonesome. The burden of bedding and an extra flight up was hard on the grandparents, though, and I was moved into a large closet off their bedroom.

"In the early morning Grandpa would bring me a bowl of café au lait and a slice of buttered bread, and I would fall back to sleep or just daydream as they read the morning paper and had their own little breakfast.

"Grandma's dressing table was placed against the south window, with a green glass toilette set arranged on the lace. Every morning, fully dressed, she would carefully put on her make-up. Her eyebrows and eyelashes were as white as her skin, so she'd color her brows and lashes, and perhaps put on a touch of powder and lipstick. Above their bed was a large wooden carved rosary given to her by her friend, the Countess de Bélizal. The green bottles and rosary are my inside memories of Grandma.

"My outside memories are of her love of animals, especially little dogs. And there was a small building housing canaries. She raised, sold, and loved them. They owned a field too, on which they grew vegetables and also kept a goat and her yearly offspring. They milked her, and the kids were butchered for meat.

"Every Thursday (on Thursdays and Sundays stores and schools were closed) we spent the afternoon down at Aunty Rita's and had supper there. They lived on the top, the thirteenth floor of an apartment building, and after supper we would start back and catch the funicular [cable car] before it closed. Each way was probably three miles. No wonder we were healthy!"

Le Havre had served as an important base throughout the war. It had only been four years since the end of the fighting, and the reminders of it were inescapable. Gwen recalled a veteran's observance they attended, presumably on Armistice Day.

"When I was six, we went down to a parade, and that was a real parade. There were soldiers who marched with all the glitter. They carried their swords and they carried their guns and they carried their flags. But it was terrible. They paraded out all the wounded, all the amputees, and all the hurt persons. There were whole contingents of people on stretchers, amputees being pulled in wagons because wheelchairs were expensive and they just didn't have them. And many of them still had bandages on wounds that had never quite healed. So, when the French saw the results of the war, it wasn't with drums and bugles and a sense of patriotism. It was with a sense of great loss."

Mimi's brother, twenty-eight-year-old George Edward, had lived at home since returning from the war. Gwen liked him and they often made mischief together at the dining table.

"We'd take pieces of French bread and roll them into little balls and throw them back and forth," said Gwen. "That would annoy Grandma terribly because in the end she had to get up and pick up all these pieces. We didn't realize it then. Uncle George was just a happy young man and I was just a six-year-old kid."

Gwen turned seven in April, and the following month served as flower girl when her uncle married a gentle-faced schoolteacher named Marthe. The bride and groom, to thank Gwen for her participation, presented her with a sterling silver powder box. They had possibly noticed Gwen's fascination with her grandmother's green toilette set and thought that—as a budding young lady—she'd like a nice piece for the dressing table she'd someday have. Gwen, who loved boxes and containers, cherished it.

While Gwen's Uncle George was an open-hearted young man and as French as he was British, her Grandpa George was another matter. He had not embraced France at all. Despite having lived there for almost thirty years, he was a proud Englishman of the era when the British Empire was so vast it was said that the sun never set upon it.

"Grandpa had an uncomfortable relationship with the French," said Gwen. "One day we were walking to some small shop (all shops were small and a bit dingy) and a man approached us on the same cobbled walkway. The man lifted his hat and politely said, 'Bonjour, Monsieur.'

"And Grandpa lifted his hat and grunted.

"Having passed, Grandpa snapped his cane on the stones and muttered, 'Damn foreigners! Can't speak a word of English!'

"They were very good to me but Grandfather kept to himself. I never knew him to hug me or kiss me. Not because those feelings weren't there, but because they weren't expressed."

What was expressed to Gwen, on more than one occasion, was his belief that "children must be seen and not heard."

Toward the end of Gwen's stay—which included all the usual childhood illnesses—she recalls her aging grandparents tiring of the living arrangement.

"I remember Grandfather saying, 'My God, Queeny, when is that child going home?'

"And Grandmother's helpless, 'I don't know. You know Mona as well as I do. We simply will have to wait and see.'

Ten months after leaving Gwen in France, Mimi wrote and asked her parents to send her back to the States. Regardless of the long voyage and Gwen's young age, Mimi didn't express much concern about her daughter traveling across the Atlantic alone. It seems to have once been a fairly common practice among far-flung English families, especially those in British colonies with children at boarding schools in England. Besides, the luxury liners provided nannies for hire on board.

> **"** We arranged to have Gwen return on this big ship. We had her come back alone, although she was only a little girl. But we knew that there was always a nurse on the boat and that she would be taken care of. **"**

Queeny packed Gwen's things and put them, along with her granddaughter's powder box, into a steamer trunk. Uncle Dolphe, who had a good position in the steamship business, paid for his niece's passage on the *SS Paris,* a two-year-old ship Mimi had returned on the year before.

This luxurious liner—designed in the Art Nouveau style—featured a ballroom with a twenty-piece orchestra, a gymnasium for fencing, and a fountain that was lit in the evenings. First-class rooms included private telephones, square windows rather than round portholes, and adjacent rooms for the valets or maids so they could be summoned more quickly than from second-class quarters. The food was said to be so good that, in hopes of grabbing jettisoned scraps of the haute cuisine, more seagulls followed the *Paris* than any other ship.

Sporting bobbed hair with bangs, and gaps where her baby teeth had fallen out, Gwen boarded the steamer in Le Havre on August 4, 1923. During the weeklong voyage, in which she remembered having the run of the ship, she became the darling of some of the first-class passengers, including the popular American Ambassador to France, Myron Herrick. Perhaps to provide her with companionship, the diplomat—who was returning to the U.S. after the sudden death of President Harding—bought Gwen a curly-haired doll from the onboard gift shop. She named her new friend Bernadette.

Gwen was excited when the ship finally arrived in New York. Gripping her doll, she leaned over the railing and saw her mother waving on the dock below. In the sea of faces, she also saw the man she'd always known as Uncle Fred, with Jane hoisted up on his shoulders. But she couldn't find her father.

No one had told her about her parents' divorce, much less her mother's remarriage.

> "When Gwen arrived, she asked, 'Where is Father?' And I said, 'Well, he is not with us today.' I didn't want to go into detail, but she insisted. She said, 'Well, where is he? Why isn't he here?' I told her he couldn't come with us because he had gone somewhere else. Anyway, she was quite upset that he wasn't there, but we quieted her.
>
> Eventually we made our way down to the dock where Ambassador Herrick was surrounded by newspapermen. And Gwen just scooted from me and went up to him and pulled on his sleeve and said, 'You must meet my mother. She's here.'
>
> So he left all the newspapermen and came to me and shook hands with Fred and me, and talked about what a lovely little girl Gwen had been and how he had enjoyed spending time with her."

When they left the hubbub of the dock and were out of the public eye, Mimi told Gwen the truth about her father, or as much of it as she believed a child should be told—which was probably both too much and too little. Gwen was instructed that Herbert's name was not to be mentioned again.

For the next few years, the ambassador sent Gwen Christmas cards, a thoughtful gesture that reminded her of how much fun that voyage had been, and of how miserably it had ended.

But Uncle Fred, now known as Dad, was kind to Gwen and Jane, and three years later legally adopted them. Mimi took that opportunity to change the girls' middle names along with their surnames. To honor their British grandparents, Gwendolyn Clara Hayford then became Gwendolyn Clara Tate Kramer and Jane Rosemary Hayford became Jane Gudgeon Kramer. Mimi, who had dropped Maud in favor of Mona on her first United States passport application, was Mona Tate Kramer.

That day back on the dock, though, when they first became a family, Mimi had just turned thirty, Gwen was seven, Jane was almost three, and Fred—now responsible for all of them—was a shaky twenty-three.

As for Mimi's ex-husband, he'd started over, too. Back when he was only ten, Herbert, upon first meeting his three-year-old, red-haired cousin, had said he was going to marry her. And now he'd done just that. Two months before Mimi married Fred, Herbert married his childhood love, Frances.

BOOK IV

Upstate New York
1923–1929

Mimi, Fred, Gwen, and Jane in 1923.

28

The Kramers of Albany

Mimi and Fred took the girls and moved to Albany, New York. They settled into the bottom floor of a two-story wood-framed house at 127 Grove Avenue.

When Mimi decreed that Herbert Hayford should never be referred to again, it was for social as much as personal reasons. She didn't want her family tainted with the scandal of divorce.

"We were never, ever, ever to discuss any other father," said Gwen. "This was the only father we ever had. But I let it slip to Mother that I'd told some neighbor boy that I had another father. They were so upset about having this revealed that they picked up and moved across town. Within a week we were in another neighborhood. In those days, women just didn't get divorced and a man didn't marry a woman with children. And Dad sincerely wanted to be our father."

Fred, who had recovered from his depression, made sure their first yuletide together was special.

"He wanted it to be the most beautiful Christmas," recalled Gwen, "and it was. We heard noises on the roof that were supposed to be reindeer and Santa Claus, and there were jingle bells. The next morning I got a carriage and several beautiful dolls."

Mimi received a gift of silver serving pieces from her parents. Her father had written earlier telling her to expect it.

"I beg to advise you of our having handed to Adolphe to be forwarded to you, by the first available ship captained by one of his friends, a strong box containing the following, meant as a sort of wedding and Christmas present. It may not reach you for some weeks—but there is no other way, save at great expense (I tried American Express), so it means a little patience and you will get them by post as from, probably New Orleans."

The list showed he had packed a carving set with horn handles, a meat skewer, a cheese scoop with an ivory handle, a bread fork, grape scissors and Mimi's baby knife and fork. "I hope they will reach you in due course, and as old friends—having been in our use when you were a kiddie—give you pleasure and put you in mind of the old folks at home."

Mimi was thrilled with them. They brought back fond memories for Gwen, too, who recalled Queeny sitting at the dining table snipping grapes with the ornate scissors.

Gwen was becoming a lot like her grandmother, and her mother, too... women who, when they saw a wrong, did what they could to right it. Gwen later wrote about an incident during her first winter back in America.

"I was seven, a little new to this country, and especially new to this town of Albany and a new stepfather. It was a cold day, with a bit of ice on the walk and the blacktop road. I was walking and came to a junk man who was whipping his horse because the very thin, poor thing couldn't get the wagon up the slight incline.

"I told the junk man to stop whipping his horse, and he told me to mind my own business. I told him again, same response. Then I threatened him with a policeman, same response.

"I walked around and found a policeman, brought him back to the still whipping man and struggling horse. The policeman made him unhitch the horse and leave his junk wagon there."

Jane would also come to resemble Queeny in her fearless way of championing those in need, but at this time, she was seen as being most like her great-grandmother, Henrietta. One day Mimi was cutting up green apples for a pie when three-year-old Jane, playing under the kitchen table, began recounting how she had once been Mimi's grandmother. She described how Mimi—a toddler in a white dress and bonnet—had held her hand as they walked down a dirt road lined with big trees.

Mimi was so startled she dropped the paring knife.

She didn't brush off the words as a child's wild imaginings. Jane was already showing signs of the musical talent for which Henrietta was known. Although Mimi rarely spoke about reincarnation to nonbelievers—and never discussed how it squared with Christian Science—she took her daughter's pronouncement seriously. Decades later she would write about it to Jane.

> You assured me you had been my grandmother once upon a time 'long ago' and had held *my* hand and led *my* feet. I knew this was so, and I know it well today.... I did indeed live many times, but it took a little child to awaken me to this lovely reality.

Henrietta was said to have had paranormal abilities, as indicated in a 1923 letter from George James. Although Mimi doesn't seem to have mentioned Jane's claim of reincarnation—her father would have responded directly to words as surprising as those—she must have referred to similarities between them.

"Yes, I should say little Jane takes after my darling Mother," George James wrote. "My Father always called my Mother his little gypsy, not only for her eyes and long lashes and looks, but her foresight. She was a woman of second sight."

Mimi herself spoke of having an ability to see past the mortal realm. She often told the story of how, on her walk home from the store one day, she stopped to speak to a neighbor, Mr. Alling, who was splitting firewood with an axe. Then, moments after she arrived at her house, this same man appeared at the kitchen door. Surprised, she said, "Why, Mr. Alling, what are you doing here?"

He told her he had come to say goodbye. And then, right before her eyes, he disappeared.

Confused, she hurried back to where he'd been working. She saw him lying on the ground and people gathered around. They told her that when he'd split a large piece of wood, it shot straight up and struck him in the head, killing him instantly.

Even if Mimi's older girl, Gwen, didn't speak of past lives or newly departed spirits, she exhibited early religious leanings. She and Jane had both been baptized in the Episcopal Church by George Paine and, like Mimi, followed the teachings of Mary Baker Eddy. Raised in an environment rich in faiths and eclectic beliefs, it's perhaps not surprising that at seven Gwen decided to minister to others.

The first recipient of her help was a boy who lived with his widowed grandmother in the upper duplex of their home.

"Harold was a mess, plump, always a bit disarrayed, with a forever dripping nose. And timid," wrote Gwen. "I found him sniffling one day, half hidden by the back steps. He was afraid that the bears would get him. Bears in 1923 were a fact, but pretty iffy in the large commercial town of Albany, and certainly not interested in a bad seven-year-old mouthful like Harold.

"So I sat us down on the lawn by the corner of the house, and with my arm around his shoulders, I cuddled him and explained that God created bears, just like us kids, and God wasn't going to allow any bears to eat his kids."

Gwen had a bigger audience when she was staying in the local hospital after surgery to remove her tonsils and adenoids.

"Naturally I had a private room, but when Mother and my new dad came to visit in the morning, I was nowhere to be found. I was in the large children's ward, going from bed to bed, telling each child that they were safe, God loved them, God was healing them, and soon they would be well again!"

But their home life, headed by a man not inclined to spiritual pursuits, was usually focused on the temporal—work, chores, and paying bills. Fred didn't make a lot of money, but his income was decent. With him out on the road so often, though, Mimi was as independent as Queeny had been when George James worked half of each year in London.

A modern wife and mother, Mimi embraced the changes won by women after the war, including the right to vote. She proudly registered as a Republican, a popular choice among northern Protestants who still thought of the GOP as Lincoln's party.

She soon tackled driving a car. Hand cranks, which required strength to turn, had by then mostly been replaced by electric starters. But there were still the myriad buttons and levers and pedals a driver had to operate while keeping the car on the road. A bit nervous behind the wheel, she jumped some curbs, ran into yards, and once took out a sapling—to Jane's excited delight—but that didn't slow down her determination to drive.

In clothing trends, too, she was a woman of the times. Fashionably attired in her straight-waist dresses, she had the perfect figure for the popular slim styles. She'd given up long hair with her first marriage, and in the twenties kept her curls short to fit neatly under her bell-shaped cloche hats. With her stylish clothes and confident stride, she rarely failed to garner attention on her outings with Jane.

"As a very little girl, I recall our walks in the park," wrote Jane. "Mother's regal bearing, her stately posture, and exquisite grace turned the heads of passers-by, especially men. I remember wondering one day why some stupid man didn't turn around and look, as did everyone else. Perhaps he was blind."

But beneath Mimi's modern pluck and well-groomed style, she was coping with heartache. She and Fred had not been able to conceive a child.

She shared her disappointment with her parents, and in a return letter her father—as emotional and caring on the inside as he was stiff on the outside—encouraged her to think positively.

"I pray for you *night* and *morning—I never omit you and yours.* If it pleases God to answer my prayers, you will have another little one yet." He wrote that "care and prudence and God's help, with your *true belief* and *trust,* will bring about wonders."

Despite his prayers and Mimi's trust, another child was not to be. A year after her marriage, the doctor told Mimi she needed a hysterectomy, putting an end to her and Fred's hopes.

After the surgery, the family went to the Paines' secluded summer home on a private island near Bar Harbor, Maine.

"In early summer," wrote Gwen, "we went to Sutton Island, owned by Aunty Clara and Uncle George. I went with Aunty Clara first, and opened up the large old house. Mother, Dad and Jane followed. Dad left for the summer for work, and Mother rested a lot. She really was fragile that year."

When they returned to the city in the fall, Fred made sure Mimi had help around the house. "We always had a cleaning lady of sorts for washing and ironing and such," remembered Gwen.

One of them was Mamie, a big-bosomed, brown-skinned woman who also took care of the girls. She laid out Gwen's school uniform each morning: Apple green poplin in the warm months and dark green wool in the winter. After Gwen ran out the door for school—the historic Albany Academy for Girls—Mamie did the housework and kept an eye on Jane.

The four-year-old grew especially fond of Mamie and spent as much time as she could on her lap. That is, when she wasn't romping on all fours with their German Shepherd called Wolf. The grandson of Strongheart—the first canine star of silent films—Wolf was protective of Jane. He let her chew on one end of his dinner bones while he gnawed on the other.

That winter, Mimi continued to focus her energies on recuperating. Most Christian Scientists feel they have betrayed their faith when using medical intervention, but Mimi followed a fairly liberal interpretation of Mary Baker Eddy's words. Her views on physicians can be summed up in a letter she wrote years later to a friend facing disapproval at The Benevolent, a stately Christian Science nursing home outside Boston. They employed spiritual practitioners rather than doctors.

> Ma Cherie, I will write this in English, as I can go much faster.
>
> Please remember that Mrs. Eddy cautioned us about not judging and *not being influenced.* The people at The Benevolent are judging, and *you* are allowing yourself to be influenced.
>
> They are judging you to be an unfit Christian Scientist because you see a doctor, consequently not worthy to remain at The Benevolent. You're not listening to your own conscience. You are worried, which is natural, and want to please everyone, even D., who says you should remain where you are.
>
> Who knows best, you who are the burdened one, or those who fail to bear the heavy load?
>
> Mrs. Eddy definitely *commands* that we respect and love doctors for their care of those who cannot find help any other way. She speaks of those who need love with their 'pitiful' search of understanding and healing—*not* judgment and condemnation, but love.
>
> You need care for your *material* eyes, your *material* hearing. One of our most faithful members, a true worker, has worn a hearing aid for years. He did not get it from a practitioner, he went to a doctor. We wear glasses, why

not a hearing aid? Your leg *must* be taken care of or you will lose it. Can your practitioner heal your leg? No. Jesus could—he was the first Christian Scientist. His absolute understanding of our nearness to God gave him the patience, love, and proof of this power, which few have. Are we, you and millions, to suffer and die because we are not willing to admit our inability to see this healing power? I am willing to admit my frailty, and thank God for that which I have, knowing to seek thru a simple prayer that God's love rests confident in the hand and knowledge of a mortal man. "

She closed by urging her friend to find another nursing home.

Back in 1924, Mimi may not yet have developed the strong sense of moral authority evident in that letter, but her views were likely the same. Raised by a father who proudly concocted medicinal cures, and married to a man who had provided aid on the battlefield and now sold medical supplies, her beliefs could hardly have been otherwise.

But faith and modern medicine combined did only so much to hasten the healing of the young woman who had prayed so fervently for a baby.

The following summer, Fred found his wife and daughters a place to stay outside the village of Altamont. Fifteen miles west of Albany, the old farmhouse was located in green rolling hills at the foot of the Helderberg Mountains. The rustic landscape provided hiking trails along ancient escarpments, cold streams, and fresh country air. As before, the idyllic rural life did Mimi good, and she finally regained her health and joie de vivre.

One of the most beneficial things Mimi did for herself was join the Albany branch of *Alliance Française,* an organization that promoted French culture.

After her experiences in Maine of trying to explain or defend her connection to France, Mimi was now free to openly embrace it. She started teaching French again. Soon she was counting members of the French Consulate among her friends. With her growing social set—and Gwen remembering enough of the language to impress guests—their home took on a wonderfully cultured air.

Even if Mimi's sphere of influence was relatively limited, she once again enjoyed a position of expertise and authority. Back in that element, she thrived.

It was a couple of years later, in May 1927, that the aviator Charles Lindbergh became an instant celebrity by flying solo from New York to Paris. Like most in America and France, Mimi and Fred were awed by his courage. Jane was crazy about him. The family had a chance to see him in July.

"Mother and Dad loved Lindbergh," said Gwen, "and there was a big parade for him in Albany. Jane was six years old and she really wanted to touch him, but the cordon of policemen would not let my mother through. My mother, being British, was highly insulted. She talked for days, absolutely days, about how she and her little girl hadn't been allowed through to shake hands with Colonel Lindbergh."

In all fairness to the Brits, Mimi's indignation probably stemmed less from her country of origin and more from her perceived place within it. She was, after all, descended from a woman who had received a medal from Prince Albert, and from men who had been knighted. Needlepoint renderings of the coats of arms of the Tate and Gudgeon families graced her living room walls. And her father's letters lauding their ancestors' accomplishments further fueled her sense of self-importance. She was never just another mother in the crowd.

Moreover, she was not a mother to let her child be disappointed. Six months later, she helped her still-hopeful daughter write to the famed pilot.

January 28, 1928

Dear Colonel Lindbergh,

I am a little girl named Jane Kramer. Mother is writing this for me because I cannot write well enough yet.

Please come here, and if you look down from your plane and see 174 Warren St. Albany, New York, that is my house. I saw you in the paper so I know what you look like. Could I marry you when I grow up? Please let me know soon. Ring the top bell as we live upstairs.

With love from Jane Kramer

29

Left on the Farm

At the time of Lindbergh's visit to Albany in the summer of 1927, Mimi and Fred were getting ready to visit her family, which had continued to grow. Like Rita, her brother, George Edward, now also had two boys. In keeping with family tradition, the first was named George. The second was Anthony and another baby was due in a month. Mimi was eager to meet her new nephews. And, of course, she wanted her family to meet Fred.

George and Queeny had been a bit displeased when Mimi announced she'd married a man of German descent, even if he had served with the Allies in France. But when they met him, they found him rather charming.

Looking as much at home in a beret as a fedora, Fred had a cosmopolitan manner and could put people at ease even when languages or customs differed. Inheriting the one decent thing his father had to offer, Fred possessed a particularly good eye for photography. He brought his latest acquisition, a movie camera, to record the family reunion.

Not everyone, however, was there for it.

Mimi and Fred had decided to leave Jane with a farm family by the last name of Stewart. The reasoning behind their decision isn't known. Eleven-year-old Gwen's ticket was paid for by Mrs. Rice, wife of the French Consul, so perhaps the family didn't have enough money for all of them to go.

More likely, Mimi worried that bringing both girls might be an imposition on her aging parents, who would be caring for Gwen while Mimi and Fred traveled through France. The couple planned to visit Paris, and Mimi was excited about taking Fred to see where she'd grown up in Brittany. Fred, for his part, was drawn to the bunkers and battlefields left from the war. He wanted to revisit them—make a pilgrimage of sorts—and see the rebuilding progress at Reims Cathedral with its newly restored façade.

Or maybe Mimi left her younger daughter home because she thought the whole experience would be too trying for Jane, a sensitive, creative child who didn't speak French and was, somehow, a little different from others her age.

"Backward" was the word they commonly used then. In first grade, the principal told Mimi that Jane was retarded and would have to go to a special school. Mimi, however, wouldn't hear of it and found a physician who identified her daughter as having a neurosis with "a heart disorder and infantilism," a popular 1920s diagnosis for developmental delays in girls.

Mimi was unusually supportive of Jane's educational needs and interests, even making cages for Jane's pet rats, complete with elaborate runs and exercise wheels. But Mimi wasn't a particularly empathetic mother. Having been raised by an aged nanny in a once-removed parenting environment, she hadn't developed a warm style of child rearing. Her role models, even Aunty Clara, were women more inclined to rational rather than responsive mothering. Mimi was protective, conscientious, and practical, but the emotional needs of her girls rarely influenced her decisions.

In the end, it was decided that Jane would be better off staying in upstate New York. Almost seven, she was older than Gwen had been when she spent close to a year away from her mother. What would be the harm in four months?

Jane, however, was not like self-sufficient Gwen, who showed no outward effects from the separation. Mimi's second child was more deeply attached to her. Mimi probably didn't realize how vulnerable Jane was when she dropped her off at the Stewarts' farm. She was concerned enough, however, to try to soften the blow by saying she would only be gone a week or two.

Jane played with the farmer's dog and made pets of field mice and a garter snake—bringing the latter into her bed to the dismay of Mrs. Stewart. She also comforted herself with an array of imaginary creatures. But when a few weeks passed and her mother still hadn't returned, Jane became increasingly anxious.

One day she saw a dead chicken in the barnyard and, face-to-face with death, her mind made the leap to her mother's absence. She somehow concluded her mother had died. Why else wouldn't she have come to get her as promised? Not long after, on a visit into town, Jane spotted a mounted policeman in the park. She went up to him and politely asked him to shoot her.

Mrs. Stewart called Fred, who had returned to the States earlier than Mimi and Gwen in order to resume work. Alarmed, he picked up Jane from the farm. Having to get back on his salesman's route, he was unable to take care of her, so he took her to the home of a kindhearted widow he knew in Albany. But the change in environment did little good. Whether she was with the farm woman or the widow woman, she was not with her mother. Jane was inconsolable. She stopped eating.

Fred sent a telegram to Mimi, who quickly exchanged her ticket and set sail for New York. During the long voyage back, she knitted a bathing suit for Jane, perhaps as a birthday present. She arrived two days before Jane's seventh birthday.

Mimi left Gwen in Le Havre to return home by herself a month later. It's not clear whether there was a problem exchanging both tickets or if Gwen or her grandparents simply wanted more time together. But being an independent-minded child and fond of her grandmother, Gwen seemed happy to remain behind.

A few weeks later, Queeny wrote to Mimi, whom she called Mo, short for Mona.

Saturday, 17 September 1927

Dear Little Mo,

I was so pleased to get your nice long letter written on the boat, but so sorry you had such a bad passage...

I read and gave Gwen the rules you sent for her, so I presume she will obey them. Tomorrow morning Gwen and I will go shopping for those shoes for Jane, poor little darling. You must have had a shock. I should so love to see her, but she is not like Gwen and would never come over alone...

I am washing Gwen's hair again on Monday. Tuesday she spends the day at Marthe's, who curls her hair and makes her more conceited (if possible) than she already is. We all went to the cinéma last Thursday and enjoyed it. She will go again next Thursday for the last time.

We have secured the passport and Adolphe has her ticket, so all is in order. I will see to her clean clothes for the journey. Did you see Uncle Oswald and family on arriving? Well, darling, I don't want to miss another day or post, so with my best love to old Fred and thousands of kisses to you

I remain,
Your loving old Mummy,
Q. Tate
Gwen sends love and is going to write.

Addressing her mother as *Ma Chere Mother Dear,* Gwen penciled a few lines in French and included news about visiting Aunty Marthe and seeing her six-week-old cousin, Alain, being given his bath. On the envelope, her grandfather had shown her how to draw the Tate coat of arms where, in British tradition, the seal would have been stamped. George James, a prolific letter writer, also taught her the importance of keeping the tools of correspondence organized.

"One day he led me to his desk," Gwen recalled. "He opened it and said, 'I want you to see this. This is where the ruler is, this is where the pencils are, this is where the paper is, this is where the ink is kept and, if you always know where everything in your desk is, you can find it even in the dark of night.'"

Gwen liked getting reacquainted with her grandparents, particularly her grandmother, with whom she felt a kinship. "I think she was a lot like me," said Gwen. "She was a no-nonsense person. She wasn't fussy. She didn't fuss with me. We had certain rules and regulations. She was mostly a watcher. She watched me."

Reveling in her role as older cousin of five boys, Gwen played with them on the beach, and at Aunty Rita's she crafted books and hats for Maurice and Georges, whom she called Momo and Jojo.

In her next letter home, she assured her parents she had written to Mrs. Rice in French, proudly noting she could spell some words on her own. She also asked if they would send a dollar or two, "because I have about 10 sous to my name!"

Evidently, she didn't receive any money, because she referred to it in her following letter, and indicated her displeasure about another matter. It seems Gwen had wanted to travel back to the States in the company of some fellow named Howard, but Mimi and Fred thought better of it. Gwen, who felt entirely grown-up, was indignant.

> *Dear Mother and Daddy,*
> *When I get my money, I will send you a real letter.*
> *Daddy, I hope this is not too painful for you and Mother Dear. I found out (from a friend) why I am not going home with Howard, and why you took no effort to let me go home with him. You told this friend of mine it was because I only knew him eight days (even so, I found he was a gentle, quiet gentleman. You and Mother Dear found that out, too). You*

said I was with him too much (but that's friendship). You said I thought too much about him (and I will truthfully and gladly say I like him very much).

I hope Jane had a lovely Birthday, and liked the toys. I read my lesson every day, and brush my teeth morning and night, Mother Dear.

All are well and fine.

Closing her letter with circles for kisses (ten for *Daddy,* eight for *Mother Dear,* eleven for *Jane,* nine for *Mrs. Rice,* and twelve for *Others),* she signed off as *Gwendolyn Tate Clara Kramer.*

In the end, Gwen made the return crossing on the *Tuscania,* a Cunard Line steamer, with an English stewardess, forty-one-year-old Beatrice Crowden, paid to keep an eye on her.

30

A Lovely Strand of Golden Hair

With Mimi and her parents separated by the Atlantic Ocean, letter writing kept the family together. Queeny wrote sweet notes to Jane, who upon hearing Mimi read them, thought of her grandmother as a fairy godmother. Aside from those, and equally softhearted cards to Gwen, Queeny's correspondence tended to the mundane business of the day.

George James's letters fluctuated between sentimental and professorial. Mimi regularly inquired about family history, and he responded with genealogies and material on the Tate and Neville coats of arms. He tucked in greetings to his granddaughters on postcards featuring popular characters and bug-eyed puppies.

After one Christmas with his grandsons, he wrote a wistful note to Mimi. "I've had a happy Christmas and the kiddies received a cart-load of things. They never forget those times, nor should they be allowed to. Time flies rapidly and though looking forward now, they will soon be reversing the position, as we all do, and looking upon the past; so let them be merry while they can, as time is ever fleeting."

Soon there were even more grandchildren in Le Havre to partake in the holidays. In 1928, George Edward and Marthe had a fourth boy, Gerald. And in 1929, Rita and Dolphe had their third boy, André. Gwen recounted the story of André's birth.

"Aunty Rita was a good woman. She had her children at home because she didn't want anything to happen to them. The older boys, Maurice and Georges, were six or seven when André was born. He was born in the middle of the night. The next morning the bell rang and someone said, 'Oh, Momo, Jojo, open the door. Find out who is there.'

"So they open the door and there in a basket is a baby.

"'Oh,' said Aunt Dedell. 'Look what the Baby Jesus left us! A new baby brother!'"

Queeny and George James now had seven grandsons living within easy visiting distance, and two granddaughters in America.

Sometime after their visit to France, the Kramers moved from Albany to nearby Altamont. Before then they had spent only their summers in the country, but by the spring of 1929 they lived there year-round. Twelve-year-old Gwen continued at the Albany Girl's Academy, commuting one hour each way by bus and trolley. She had the attic bedroom, and enjoyed the privacy it afforded, while eight-year-old Jane preferred the room downstairs, closer to her mother. Fred, as always, traveled for work, usually on the road five days at a time.

One rainy night in early April, Mimi put the girls to bed and sat up reading while she waited for Fred to return from a business trip. It was his birthday the next day and she had made plans for a family celebration.

> **"** The rain was pouring and I was reading, never realizing how fast the time was going. Suddenly I happened to look at the clock and saw it was one o'clock in the morning. At the same time there came a torrential rain against the window. The wind was so fierce I looked out. And then I saw the most extraordinary thing.
>
> I saw a small delicate hammock, sort of a veil, floating in the room in front of the window. I looked at it and couldn't believe what was happening. I wasn't frightened. But it came towards me. It floated through the room and

came right by my side, and I said to myself, 'What is holding this thing up?'

It wasn't fright, just curiosity. So I looked down into it and there was a beautiful strand of blond-brown hair. I was looking at it when suddenly it disappeared, and I was looking at the wall.

Then, of course, I became concerned. Because of the weather, I thought something extraordinary had happened, that perhaps Fred had been in an accident and this was some way of my finding out. I was very much upset.

But just then, I heard him pull up into the driveway. I ran to the back door and opened it wide because the rain was coming down fast and I thought he'd better run in, which he did. **"**

Fred said the vision was probably her imagination, but Mimi was adamant that something had happened. The next morning, while she was in the kitchen making a cake for his birthday, they received a phone call.

" I went to the phone and the telephone man—whom Fred knew and did not like—was on the other end. He asked if he might talk to Fred. I said, 'Well, he's shaving now in the bathroom. Can't I take the message?'

And he said 'No, I prefer to speak to your husband personally.'

I called Fred, who reluctantly came to talk to this man, and I heard him say, 'Yes, go on. Go on.'

So I whispered to him, I said, 'Oh, dear, do be nice to him, really.'

Then he got through talking, and he turned to me and said it was a telegram from France. **"**

It was Queeny. After tending the birth of a litter of puppies, she got a chill and became sick. Soon it turned into pneumonia and, at the age of seventy-three, she died.

For Mimi it was a devastating loss. She loved her mother more than anyone else in the world. Even though she had gone long periods without seeing her—and it had been a year and a half since they were together—Queeny was never far from her mind.

> It was a terrible thing for me because I just adored my mother. I remember sort of wrenching myself away from Fred's arms and running into the front room. I took hold of Mummy's picture when she was a little girl of about four and I held it close. I practically collapsed.
>
> What made it particularly difficult was that the day before, I'd received a long letter from my mother telling me she had ridden on her bicycle twenty-five miles that day and picked a big bunch of lovely spring flowers that she knows I love dearly. So it came as a tremendous shock.
>
> Well, I got in touch with my brother immediately, and he wrote and said that Mummy had died exactly at one o'clock in the morning our time. And that was the time that I had seen this little hammock floating through the room coming to my side with a lovely strand of golden-brown hair. That was the color of my mother's hair, so it was possibly a way of her trying to show me that she was so unhappy that she was going on.

This otherworldly visit, which might comfort some mourners as a confirmation of life after death, brought little solace to Mimi. She had embraced the Christian Science view that sickness and death are illusions: that those who seem to die simply adjust to another level of consciousness, inaccessible to the living. Perhaps that was what drew her to Christian Science in the first place . . . an assurance that what the priests of her childhood had said about heaven and hell and purgatory wasn't true.

But religious precepts are easier to accept on a spiritual level than an emotional one. Her mother was, on the physical plane, dead. And someday she would be, too.

Mimi, like most people, had struggled with a fear of death—for her not so much the fear of what lies beyond, but of the dying itself. Once, she submitted an article, "How I Overcame My Fear of Death," to *Liberty*, a popular weekly magazine of the day. She wrote openly of her dread.

> I had always feared death. I had a horror of it and trembled at the realization of having to go through it. I would lie awake at night with terror in my heart thinking about it; and through the day this thought would hamper my happiness.

She went on to write about a dream she had of her own death. She was at the undertaker's, watching him embalming her, and was upset at his rough treatment until she realized she couldn't feel it; he wasn't hurting her at all. At that point, she understood that "the body there on the slab was not I, but merely what I had been." It filled her with a serenity that stayed with her long after the dream was over.

But a comforting faith, reassuring dream, and parting visit could only do so much to assuage the grief she now felt knowing that her mother was beyond her reach. Mimi was heartbroken.

She was also concerned about her father's well-being. Queeny had always been the stronger of the two. She was the heart of the family, and in many ways, the head, too. Her sudden passing left George James devastated.

31

Route 66

Six months after Queeny's passing, Mimi went to visit her father. This time she and Fred took both girls with them but sailed on different ships. Mimi and her daughters crossed on a traditional liner, while Fred wanted to travel aboard the *Minnekahda*, a former American troopship and the first "all tourist class" vessel.

Jane, on the *SS de Grasse*, finally got to experience the girlhood fun and tedium of ocean travel. She and Gwen scanned the sea for whales, played deck tennis—tossing a rubber ring back and forth to each other over a net—and partook of the bouillon and saltine crackers offered by the deck stewards. They celebrated Jane's ninth birthday on board, and at dinner that night she was surprised with a cake from the ship's captain. Around it was a wide gold ribbon imprinted *Happy Birthday Miss Jane Kremer*. Even with the name misspelled, she was delighted, and tucked the souvenir away in her bags.

In France, they stayed with Mimi's father. He no longer lived in the three-story home on rue Gambetta—the one Gwen lived in for a year—but rather in a one-story corner house at 105 rue de St. Quentin, less than a mile away.

Gwen and Jane, wearing old Brittany sabots, clattered around on the brick floor and amused themselves with their grandfather's white cockatoo. They spent most of their time, however, playing with their cousins at Aunty Rita's or Aunty Marthe's.

Mimi's sister and brother both lived well. Rita's husband, Dolphe, had a good-paying job with Cunard Line, and George Edward, who also worked in Le Havre's most important industry, was employed by a respected shipping agency. They enjoyed the prosperity of the growing white-collar class.

The whole family made frequent visits to the pebbly Le Havre Beach. They would rent a hut with a canopy and drapes so the older folks in their proper suits and dresses—and the baby boys in their white lace gowns—could be shaded from the sun while the others splashed in the sea foam. But in spite of such outings, it was, overall, a sad time.

"When staying with Grandfather," Jane recalled, "I'd often awaken at night and hear him walking the floor and weeping, 'Oh, Queeny darling. Oh, come back to me.'"

Gwen, who felt a close bond with her grandmother, was asked if there was anything of Queeny's she might like to remember her by. She was thirteen and a half by then and had matured into a restrained young lady. Not surprisingly, she asked for Queeny's green glass dresser set—the familiar scent bottles, powder jar, and ring holder.

With the house full of family, George James settled into new daily patterns. The Kramers' visit provided a diversion, and Mimi drew her father into discussions of his and Queeny's ancestry—the who, when, and where of oft-told stories.

Planning an extended stay, Mimi enrolled Jane and Gwen in the local girls' Catholic School. Although Mimi was not enamored of Catholicism, she trusted the nuns—who turned out to be especially patient with Jane—and knew this would be a good opportunity for the girls to improve their French while keeping up their studies. It was part of the old routine for Gwen, but Jane found it all new and curious, especially the spare midday meal. "For lunch we had bitter chocolate and French bread," she said. "That's all."

Mimi and Fred left the girls with Aunty Rita and went sightseeing. They visited the island abbey of Mont Saint-Michel and the glittering Palace of Versailles. Fred, a war buff despite his youth, led Mimi on another visit to old battlefields and bunkers. Then the two went to Paris where, at the Arc de Triomphe, Mimi took the camera and immortalized him, standing in solemn tribute with beret in hand, at the Tomb of the Unknown Soldier.

As before, Fred had to return early for work. He had done quite well as a salesman. He wasn't fast-talking or glad-handing, but he had a decided talent for match-making between Seamless Rubber and the companies that needed its products. However, he had long wanted to move to Southern California—the land of warm winters and sunny beaches—so this time when he got back to America, he planned to start looking for a new job that would take them there.

Mimi, Gwen, and Jane saw Fred off in mid-October, waving goodbye from the dock. Then, just days later, Mimi read news of the Wall Street panic. Fred sailed into New York on October 25, 1929, four days before the stock market made its most disastrous dive. The Kramers had no investments to lose, but national anxiety was high, new employment opportunities limited, and current positions precarious.

Given the crumbling economy, Fred was hesitant to make a career move that might jeopardize his family's financial security. So rather than striking out on his own, he approached his boss with an offer to open a West Coast sales office. The head of the company, who trusted Fred's abilities, decided to take a risk on expanding, but with the stipulation that the office be up and running by the new year, less than two months away. Fred telegraphed Mimi and asked her to return immediately to prepare for their move to Los Angeles.

She rushed to exchange their travel tickets, and she and the girls started a last round of visits with George Edward's and Rita's families. Before Mimi boarded the ship, her father presented her with Queeny's silver teapot and caddies so she could serve proper afternoon teas in their new out-West home.

The urgency of their leave-taking may have blunted Mimi's sense that she might not see her father again. But soon the journey would be almost twice as far, and the awareness of this being a forever farewell was not lost on George James. "We said goodbye to Grandfather," recalled Jane, "and the last thing I saw of him was his weeping. 'I'll never see you again,' he cried."

Arriving back in New York on November 30th, they hurried to Altamont to pack. They boxed up their belongings for shipping and loaded their late-model Buick with provisions for the cross-country trip.

It was a thirteen-day drive if they didn't encounter any bad weather, mechanical failure, or other mishaps. Even with the best of luck, the journey would hardly be easy. The motorways were rough and roadside accommodations unreliable. Fred's experience as a traveling salesman, however, served them well; he had a good sense of where to stop and how to keep everyone comfortable. The new under-dash automobile heaters failed to provide much warmth to the back seat, so before dawn every morning he filled a couple of his company's hot water bottles and put them at the girls' feet as he tucked them into wool lap blankets.

First heading south to avoid the worst of the approaching winter weather, they eventually met up with the three-year-old—and not yet completely paved—U.S. Route 66. Known colloquially as the Mother Road, it led them through Oklahoma, Texas, New Mexico, and Arizona. They finally crossed into California.

Despite Fred's motoring expertise, he knew little about the challenges of driving in the sunbaked desert between Needles and Barstow. One day shortly before Christmas, they pulled off the two-lane road to stretch their legs.

"It looked like a wide road where we could turn off, eat our lunch and rest," remembered Gwen. "We saw a train trestle we could go under, out of the sun, and be cool. So we had our lunch and got back in the car. But it had sunk down in the sand, and no matter how we pushed or pulled, nothing happened.

"Then, along the railroad tracks came a cart, one of those two-man pumper carts. The men saw the problem, got off, helped us turn our car around and get it started.

"They took Dad to the back of the car, though, and just gave him hell. They said, 'Don't ever drive into the desert again! This is a wash, a sand wash. You could have been stuck here forever. No one would find you. Don't ever do that to your family again.'"

Properly chastised, he quietly got back on the highway and made no more off-road excursions.

They followed Route 66 all the way to its terminus in Santa Monica. Entering the city's palm-lined streets on a seventy-five-degree Christmas Day, they went directly to the beach. Fred, less than two weeks from the snow and ice of upstate New York, changed into his bathing trunks, strode across the fine-grained sand, and dove into the surf of the Pacific Ocean.

Mimi wanted to live by the sea, so they found a place in Santa Monica, not far from the water. But Fred, who promptly opened the sales office in Los Angeles, discovered he was facing the sun both during his drive into the city in the morning and out again in the afternoon. Soon they moved inland.

BOOK V

Southern California
1929–2002

MIMI—Known in 1929 as Mona Tate Kramer.

FRED KRAMER—Mimi's husband, also known as Papá.

FRITZ—Called Uncle Fritz by the family, he was Fred's boss.

GWEN—Mimi's first daughter, who later went by Scottie.

SAM BAER—First husband of Gwen, then known as Scottie.

RAY DOLE—Second husband of Scottie.

MIKE—Ray and Scottie's first child.

BIDDY—Ray and Scottie's second child.

TIM—Ray and Scottie's third child.

JANE—Mimi's second daughter, who later went by Jay.

BOB ANDERSON—Jay's husband.

SUSAN—Bob and Jay's first child.

MONA—Bob and Jay's second child.

WENDY—Bob and Jay's third child.

HAROLD FRIEDMAN—Mimi's late-in-life love.

32

West Coast

Mimi and Fred rented a few different places in Los Angeles before settling on the Westside, an area they both liked. They moved into a two-bedroom home on Fairfax Avenue near Pico Boulevard. Given the cash-strapped times, they lived decently. Mimi kept Rhode Island Reds in the backyard so they could have fresh eggs every morning, but most of their food and groceries came from a local neighborhood market.

"We went to a small mom and pop store a couple of blocks from the house," said Gwen. "We'd simply get what we needed and at the end of the week, when Dad came home with money, we'd go and pay for it."

Fred worked very hard and, as on the East Coast, traveled for business throughout the week. When he was at home, however, he and Mimi—as she had feared before their wedding—often argued. They shared similar views on the major issues of life but battled regularly on the daily ones. Mostly they disagreed on who was going to run things... Mimi wanted him to do things her way, and he didn't want to. They each vied for control and, as Mimi had the stronger personality, she usually won. But they had by then grown accustomed to an adversarial marriage and—since their passionate arguments led to passionate make-ups—were not altogether unhappy.

The discord was a bit hard, however, on the girls. Gwen tuned it out, but it made Jane nervous. If Mimi and Fred were on the argument end of their emotional seesaw, Jane would retreat to the relative quiet of the backyard. Not far from the chicken coop was a fishpond and, next to that, a large pepper tree with graceful branches that skimmed the ground. A solitary child, she played for hours on end within the leaf-enclosed shelter.

"I was given two little play cars, and I made a virtual town under the tree," said Jane. "I would hunker down close to the earth and take boxes to make houses, and with a spoon, I'd make a roadway branching from one to another. For bushes and trees, I'd pick twigs and sometimes get a hold of the ends of celery."

Jane often lived in a world of make-believe and expressed it in her writing, too, which may have been an outlet for her fears. One story, in the form of a letter to her parents, was about bear-like creatures clad in paisley coats. She called them Krowis animals.

"I married a Krowis animal," she wrote, "and he is very cruel to me. Oh help! He is looking at my letter. He is looking over my shoulder. Please stop, let me go!"

Jane and Gwen were enrolled in public school, where they were teased for their accents—an East Coast dialect overlaid with the King's English—and mocked for their habit of pronouncing Americanized French words *à la française*.

Mimi didn't worry much about their adjustment. She had been an outsider all her life, albeit always on the higher end of the equation—a well-bred member of the ruling class, whether the commoners surrounding her were the Brittany peasants or Maine mill workers. She expected her daughters would feel that same spirit of nobility.

Gwen did on one level—the one that gave her an innate confidence in life—and it helped her adjust to a new school and make friends. But she chose middle-class playmates who hardly met Mimi's social aspirations. Her best chum was a tall, horsey-faced neighbor named Biddy, with whom she rode bikes in the afternoon. Her other close companions were Jewish and Filipino boys she met at the school's chess club.

She wasn't terribly concerned about what others thought of her or her accent. If anything, she enjoyed being distinct. Gwen ached to claim an identity apart from her proper mother. A classmate who couldn't tell one British accent from another called her Scottie, a nickname she relished. It was so much more daring than her medieval-sounding Gwendolyn.

Jane, who had been ostracized on the East Coast for being "different," merely wanted to fit in. Learning disabilities, though, held her at the bottom of her class. Always serious and sensitive, the prospect of failing kept her in a perpetual state of anxiety until one night when she heard a voice she believed to be Queeny's.

"You can do it," said her grandmother.

Whether this was heavenly intervention or just a girl's imagination, it gave her the hope she needed. Having good memorization skills, she enlisted Gwen in reading the textbooks to her and explaining what she didn't understand. Then Jane committed the lessons to memory. She still struggled in math, but she started making As in English and history, and soon earned a place on the honor roll.

Fred liked the Golden State as much as he had imagined he would. Aside from Santa Monica's balmy beach he was drawn to the airports.

"Dad loved airplanes," said Gwen. "We would go out to what is now Los Angeles International Airport, and there was nothing but acres and acres of grass and fields. There would be four or five airplanes tied down, and we'd watch others come in or go out. One time he took us to see the Goodyear blimp and we toured L.A. from above."

Los Angeles was exciting for Mimi, too, and a world apart from her first home in America. Staid New England had provided a good transition from her upbringing in a proper British home, but there was something liberating about Southern California. Especially Hollywood.

Mimi fancied the movies; she always had. A few years earlier, her Uncle Oswald's sons, Bill and Bert Gudgeon, had made names for themselves as silent film actors in New Jersey, once a center of film production. Before the industry moved west, Bert had performed as a stuntman and acted in dozens of motion pictures, including the *Perils of Pauline* and the *Iron Claw* series.

But the world was changing and movies were starting to be produced with soundtracks. Gwen recalled the first time she and Jane saw a talkie, not long before they left New York.

"Mother took us to the movies in downtown Albany, on Pearl Street," she said, "to see a picture acceptable for youngsters. Then, the amazing, dazzling, new thing... Fanny Brice standing on a bridge singing *I've Got a Feeling I'm Falling*. And we could hear her! It was the beginning of talkies. Up until then, picture shows were silent and accompanied by a piano, an organ or, if really big-time, a full orchestra."

With more and more talking pictures being produced, the early thirties were a bustling time in Hollywood, and Mimi had a much-needed skill.

After the war, France—the birthplace of cinema—had a hard time rebuilding its once-booming film industry. American companies took advantage of this opening by exporting movies to them. French audiences, however, naturally wanted motion pictures in French. What was the sense of going to the talkies if you still had to read subtitles? So Hollywood studios dubbed their pictures into French and further produced—strictly for export—French-language films.

Mimi worked as a voice actor in American productions reformatted for France. She also coached actors in proper diction, *en français*, for films created directly for the export market.

Even if their glow wasn't shining directly on her, Mimi loved the bright lights. She was taken by the glamour of the era and the thrill of running into stars at local restaurants and L.A.'s Farmers Market. Fred's boss, Fritz, a competitive skeet shooter, occasionally took them to the popular Santa Monica Gun Club, frequented by avid shooters Clark Gable, Robert Stack, and Gary Cooper.

One summer Sunday, Jane—then a thirteen-year-old in the midst of a spat with her sister—made an entry in her journal giving a snapshot of their oh-so-close-to-show-biz life.

> *This morning I was rather sleepy and felt lazy indeed, but soon I got up and went about my daily duties. Gwen, having had a free lecture from Mother, was rather on edge, and I had a small scrape with her, for she seemed ungrateful to, and for, everything.*
>
> *You see, dear diary, Uncle Fritz had given her $10 to get a bow and arrow and I received nothing, not as I care much because I am satisfied with the gift I have from my creator that is far more important than all the money and bows and arrows in the world...*
>
> *We went down to the skeet shooting range, and there saw Arthur McGoobry and Billy Bob. Of course, I really and truly think that Arthur is the cats, if I may express it that way, and to make a long story short, I was especially glad to see him.*
>
> *Gary Cooper was there and Mother whispered over to Arthur and told him who he was, and he was elated to think that he should be by this actor. My! Of all people!*
>
> *I then went over to see Gwen shoot her bow and arrow, but seeing that she would not let me shoot, I came back and saw Arthur and Billy leaving. Arthur was all alight because he had had enough bravery to go up to Gary Cooper and ask him the time, but alas, he was too timid to ask him to sign his autograph.*

So later, with a little urging, I took a piece of paper and boldly went up and had him sign it. Just as soon as I can get eyes on Arthur, I shall show him that I did not have cold feet, to put it vulgarly.

Well, I must rush off to my homework, so au revoir.

Before long, Mimi had her own day in front of the cameras as a French-speaking actress. Showing up on the studio lot with her finger-waved hair noticeably lighter and—after surgery for a deviated septum—her nose slightly smaller, Mimi mostly played bit parts. When she finished her first substantial role in a movie, she shared her elation with her brother, George Edward, who congratulated her in a return letter.

"So you have started in a new line of business and turned your first film. I am not really surprised, as I know you are somewhat of the pushing kind and the advent of talking films has revolutionized the whole industry. Your knowledge of French should be a great asset. If ever a film of yours comes to Havre we will book seats for the whole run, you bet."

But with France's protectionist quotas—one movie had to be produced domestically for every seven imported—French cinema began to revive. Mimi's work slowly dried up and her attraction to Tinseltown and its famous stars eventually ran its course.

Mimi was, at heart, always more interested in the refined denizens of Los Angeles. Soon after arriving, she had joined the local chapter of the *Alliance Française* and in due time, she returned to teaching. She became a French instructor at a private Beverly Hills school, where she taught the offspring of the city's most influential residents.

As her own children got older, Mimi continued to pay close attention to their artistic talents. She made sure they took music lessons, but Gwen played the piano with no more aptitude than she herself had as a child. Mimi steered her toward writing and poetry. Her younger daughter, however, displayed real musical ability and Mimi nurtured it.

Jane had composed three short pieces at the age of six, and three more at nine. Now, having become a teenager, she started to shine. She had outgrown most of her earlier disabilities, although she still struggled with dyslexia. It hampered her ability to read letters, numbers, and symbols—including music notation—but had no effect on her raw musical gifts. In the early thirties, Mimi was proud to show her off at parties.

"Mother would hold these soirées in which escaped White Russians and people of talent got together in our home," wrote Jane. "Sometimes the lesser stars would come, including Franklin Pangborn, who was a one-time concert pianist. One of our guests was Penelope Peterson, who had taught at the Sorbonne in Paris. I remember she was a sixty-year-old singer with hair on her face and a booming voice. Large and majestic, she recited poetry and sang *Oh, the Days of the Kerry Dancing* with much resounding. We even had a Middle Eastern man one night. His name was Sharbott Khan. He wore a gold silk turban, and I was fascinated by him.

"At the end of the evening, as a pièce de résistance, I always played my own compositions, which our Russian guests said were very Russian-sounding."

33

End of an Era

Mimi kept an attractive home in which to greet these musicians and international guests. She was adept at the American crafts of quilting and braiding rugs, but unlike most depression-era housewives who used leftover scraps, Mimi bought reams of new cotton for her quilts and chose fine wool for her rugs. She also engaged in European handiwork, fashioning needlepoint covers for footstools and narrow tapestries that mimicked the servant bell pulls of the Victorian era.

Her most prized possessions, however, were the family heirlooms—gilt-framed paintings, Queeny's silver tea caddies, and Limoges and Coalport broth bowls used by Jane Bennett—all of which Mimi displayed with pride.

Not all of her treasures were beautiful. Years earlier, her father, a kindred spirit when it came to family keepsakes, had sent her a two-hundred-year-old glazed ceramic jug to pass on to her oldest child, Gwen. It was one of three, given to him by his mother, that he had kept locked in a glass cupboard until passing on one to each of his children. In her thank-you letter, Mimi asked for more information about her newly acquired pitcher. He was quick to respond, and said, in no uncertain terms, that it was *not* a pitcher.

Although George James was fairly solicitous of Mimi's feelings on emotional matters, he rarely minced words when it came to facts. "What you are pleased to call a pitcher," he wrote, "is nothing of the kind. It is a hot-water jug . . ." He told Mimi how it had been passed down through the Gliddon line, belonging to his great-grandfather and then his grandfather, who had used it to make hot toddy in the winter. Henrietta had given the jug, which she "prized beyond expression," to George James on his twenty-first birthday.

Having clarified its origin, Mimi's father wrote at great length about the difference between a pitcher and a jug—the gist of it being that a pitcher holds only cold liquids—and ended with an academic discourse on the etymology of the two words. He was a tireless teacher.

Mimi regularly consulted him on family history because of his broad knowledge of all things Tate and Gliddon. He might have complained about it—"Some of your questions take me half an hour to find out as I have to rummage through so many papers and go tracing back a hundred and forty to fifty years," he once wrote—but he valued her queries and responded quickly.

He lamented that no one else expressed much interest in their shared ancestral history, referring to his research as a labor of love that "I could do only for you, as others don't enter into the spirit of the thing as you do, and as did my dear mother. I am very proud of it all, I can tell you."

Fortunately, Mimi's father not only kept notes on his ancestors but on Queeny's less documented side as well. Cut off from her family history by the early death of her mother, a remarried father, and the departure of her siblings, Queeny was left with little more than some china and silver, a few photos, and several oft-repeated stories. But George James recorded what he knew for Mimi and signed his letters "Your dear old Daddy, Pater."

He still missed Queeny terribly. With little else to occupy his time, he wrote to Mimi often. Although she herself was a faithful letter-writer, she could hardly keep up with him, as indicated in one of the letters she'd received from him during her first year in California. He hadn't heard from her in ten days.

September 16, 1930

My own Beloved Mona,

Confirming my letter to you of Tuesday last, I am without news of you since then, and it is ever a grief I may say, when on going to the letter-box Saturday and Sunday I find nil, as I count the days almost from Saturday to Saturday [American Mail Day], in the hope of getting a letter or card from you. It is the one joy and comfort of the week, and when nothing comes, well, my feelings of disappointment are beyond expression . . .

I am alas ever the same and do not know, nor have I known—save when you and yours were here—what a day's comfort, happiness and real light-hearted joy means. I think so much about you all and long to see you, as I know it would be such pure love and affection and welcome by all.

But there was even greater heartache ahead for him and his family in France. Queeny's death had been a blow to all of them, but the death of an older person, no matter how cherished, is not completely unexpected. Losing a child is different.

Three years after Queeny's death, just as everyone had gotten used to her absence, George Edward's seven-year-old son, George Rodolph, suddenly took sick.

"My eldest brother, George, was a lively boy, very healthy and dynamic," recalled his younger brother, Alain Tate, who had been five at the time. "I still remember a 'friendly' battle between the four boys on the top of our beds.

"He was taken urgently one morning to a clinic, with pain in the chest, and he died during an operation a few hours later. He was in reality suffering from an abscess in the lungs caused by an attack of 'streptococci,' which only antibiotics (still not available in 1932) could have healed. It was a shock for the whole family."

George James was once again bereft. Even if not a very huggable grandfather, he had deep affection for his grandchildren, not least among them his sweet namesake, the fourth George Tate.

In the 1930s, George Edward and Marthe had three more children. Denis was born a year before his brother died, and a few years later—after five boys—the family finally celebrated the birth of a girl, Monique. Two years later, they were back on track with another boy, Yves.

Accustomed to visiting his son's family one day a week and his daughter's another, George James didn't entertain at home. But one day when Alain was ten, he visited his grandfather.

"I remember very well, when my mother was expected to give birth to Yves in 1937 and I had been sent away to the Cantors [Rita's family] for a week. Aunty Rita took me to visit Grandpa in his house located somewhere in the suburbs of Le Havre ... He was warm and welcoming, trying to show me the house while speaking in English, which I did not fully understand, but I fully appreciated his affection."

Alain's older brother, Anthony, who went by Tony, also shared memories of their grandfather. "He was always so dignified and independent. Mind you, towards the end, he needed looking after because his hands had become a little unsteady.

"He came to our house every Friday to have lunch with us. Poor Dad used to come in for some stick from his father when they talked politics. Grandpa was a confirmed conservative and anything or anyone *not of his convictions* was a 'damned socialist' or even a communist, which of course was nonsense. Dad was always a staunch conservative, with a touch of 'liberalism' and 'humanity.' He could not accept the old attitude of the conservative class, whose treatment of domestics and retainers generally was feudal. But old Grandpa, though not unkind, had no time for 'damned peasants.'"

His mind still sharp, George James maintained his enthusiasm for chess, which he referred to as "the King of all games, as the apple is the Queen of all fruits." He was pleased when Gwen joined her school's chess club, and he sent her one of his books. "I have had this book in my possession upwards of fifty years," he wrote, "and it is, you may say, still quite new and clean. I beg you to study it well, as you cannot have a finer exercise for your mind."

Tony remembered his father and grandfather playing chess, "both puffing their pipes, a glass of whiskey nearby. I was occasionally allowed to watch *in complete silence* ... The silence was interrupted every four to five minutes with a terse ... 'Queen' ... 'Check' ... etc."

George James was none too pleased when his son—in a case of the student overtaking the master—began to beat him. But even if defeated in chess strategy, there was a security in the game's agreed-upon rules. There was no such assurance in the social and political arena.

"The only time I saw Grandpa really upset," wrote Tony, "was when the Duke of Windsor (Edward VIII) abdicated in 1936 to marry 'La Simpson.' He was really cut up about it. What was England coming to??? Constitutional crisis!!! My father could not do anything about it. All he could do was lend an ear and a shoulder for Grandpa to pour out his disappointment."

Life was getting harder for George James. Times were changing in inconceivable ways, with the younger generation discarding old values and Queeny not there to buffer the blows and calm his concerns. And old age, which often makes it hard to maintain one's decorum, did him no special favors.

"Grandpa used to have lunch with the Cantors once a week as well," wrote Tony. "It was in late summer and the Cantors were in their summer chalet outside Le Havre. So Grandpa had a way to go and the bus service was not very good. He had to walk quite a way. It had been raining and the country paths and roads were full of water holes and mud. Well, Grandpa slipped and fell headlong in a puddle.

"Although he was not actually hurt physically, he was a complete mess, covered in mud from head to foot and drenched. He eventually reached the Cantors' place, only to be met with a shocking display of hilarity by his grandchildren.

"Grandpa, who was always so neat and fussy about his appearance, was upset enough by his fall and the subsequent mess of mud and water, and I gather that he gave the kids a tongue-lashing for their lack of respect."

When Tony, twelve at the time, heard about the affront to his grandfather's dignity, he waylaid one of Rita's boys at school and hit him.

"Dad and Aunty Rita had an argument about that," wrote Tony. "I was not flavor of the month then. I'll tell you that for free...

"Still, old Grandpa had a bit of a temper himself. Aunty Rita used to look after him (cleaning and laundry) towards the end. Grandpa did not have much furniture then, but he had been hanging onto a beautifully carved Breton cradle. I understand it was used for my father.... However, Aunty Rita kept nagging him to let her have it, to match all her other Breton treasures (some were very old and quite beautiful).

"One day the old boy was so annoyed that he went into the courtyard, borrowed an axe from a neighbor, and before you could say 'Jack Robinson,' the old, valuable cradle was reduced into fire kindling. Boy! Oh, boy!

"Dad was called away from his office to mediate between the two because Aunty Rita was beside herself and Grandpa was equally determined to 'sort her out...'

"Oh, the rich pageantry of life!!!!"

Frequently miffed about one thing or another, George James sought solace from Mimi. Living so far from each other, neither had to endure the day-to-day irritations of family relations. Their correspondence—in which he freely expressed the warmth he often hid from others—was mutually supportive.

He moved a time or two in the thirties and by January 1938 had a single room, perhaps with his son or daughter, and was looking forward to getting a bigger place. Given the following letter, Mimi may have suggested he come to visit them.

> *My Darling Mo & Family,*
>
> *Thanks dear one for your loving lines. I was honored and full of emotion, and I appreciate it all. If I had the means, Los Angeles would quickly make my acquaintance.*
>
> *Well, dear, here I am till March 'ere I am installed in my own domicile. I wish I could write you free of all and any restraint or fear of comments ... you must read between the lines, but a one-room lodging is not conducive to happiness and comfort, as against a six-room house [of my own] ...*
>
> *Goodbye and God bless you. I fear we shall never see each other again so I miss you one and all. Goodbye dear Mo. My love and best wishes always to Fred and the girls, and thank Jane for her pretty card. Bless her kind little heart.*
>
> *Fondly, G. Pa Tate*

Six months later, on France's Bastille Day, the proud British patriarch passed away.

He was eighty-one when he departed this life, sitting in a chair with a book in his hands. He had his own place in Sanvic—perhaps the six-room house he wrote about—but had been spending a few summer weeks at a rest home at Montivilliers, about seven miles out of the city.

Mimi mourned his death but didn't grieve as she had for her mother. With her father's exacting nature—and severe parenting when she was a child—it had been hard to feel terribly close to him. George James was, perhaps, one better loved at a distance, and Mimi treasured his affectionate letters.

The late thirties were, for the rest of the Tates, a time of increasing financial security and the contentment that usually accompanies it. George Edward and Marthe enrolled their sons in a private school and bought a new automobile to take the family out to the country on weekends and to Brittany in the summer. They were also looking forward to another baby, expected at the start of the new decade.

In September 1939, however, France and Britain responded to Hitler's invasion of Poland by declaring war on Germany. The action would have dire consequences for those living in Le Havre and other towns on Normandy's north coast.

34

Ye Gods and Little Fishes

The early thirties had been relatively good for the Kramers, with the Great Depression having little effect on them. "A few less dresses in the closet," as Gwen described it. The family followed a routine of school, Saturday outings to Santa Monica Beach, and Camp Fire Girl vacations at Camp Yallani in the San Bernardino Mountains. Enjoyable as those activities were, Mimi was a formidable parent.

"Mother was delightfully, endearingly beautiful, kind, compassionate and creative," said Gwen. "People really adored her." Her daughters, however, saw her domineering side.

Devoted to their proper rearing, Mimi had developed into a mother who was as strict as her own grandmother, Henrietta, and as corrective as her father, George James. She may not have used a ruler on her daughters' piano fingers, but it was clear she wouldn't brook any disobedience.

Once Mimi sent a letter to the editor complaining about ill-behaved children who willfully destroyed property, created disturbances in stores, and barged into buses with no courtesy toward others. She assured other parents that consistent discipline and loving guidance would produce respectful and secure children. "No child admires a parent who cannot be trusted to determine the right course for him to take," she wrote, "and the spoiled child always lacks security."

Mimi had no problem determining the right course for her own children. An alert parent, she kept her daughters from trying the kinds of pranks she pulled as a girl, and oversaw every aspect of their lives. She kept them chaste and, despite the fact that they had both inherited the hefty Hayford bosoms, forbade them to wear brassieres until they were young adults. They were restricted to chest-flattening bust bodices.

Their outer garments, equally conservative, were in line with the styles favored by the royal family. "Mother dressed us exactly as you'd have seen Queen Elizabeth and Princess Margaret as they were growing up," said Gwen.

Although the fashions were a bit stiff for Southern California—and served to set the girls even further apart from their peers—Mimi was determined to provide her daughters with the restraint and refinement that would open doors to polite society.

Gwen attended Los Angeles High School and after graduation worked for thirty-five cents an hour at May Company, a classy department store on Eighth and Broadway. Then she expressed an interest in studying psychology.

Her dad, however, thought that was highly impractical. In a 1936 letter, when Gwen had newly turned twenty, Fred shared his view on the matter.

"Thru the years she has wanted to be everything down the alphabet until now she has reached 'psychologist.' Her idea of that profession is to loll back in an easy chair, listen to the troubles of others, and set them right. Just as easy as that! The years of hard work, the money to finance it all, the fact that only maturity and life's grinding experiences are genuine guides to success in a field notably dominated by men, she cannot or will not see."

He wrote that shortly before Gwen and Jane went to stay with their birth father, Herbert. And the letter was addressed to him.

After thirteen years of increasingly strife-filled marriage—and with her daughters nearing adulthood—Mimi began to focus on her own heartfelt needs. Although she and Fred had shared a strong attraction, their arguing had long since outweighed their making-up. Forty-two-year-old Mimi, still youthful in body and spirit, had found someone to fill her longing for both ardor and harmony. It was Fritz, Fred's boss and the company president.

Although Fritz lived in Connecticut, he had been spending more and more time in Los Angeles. Then, on one of his business trips, he suffered some kind of medical ailment, prompting Fred and Mimi to invite him to stay in their home while he recovered. Gwen and Jane remembered it well since it meant they had to give up their bedroom. Mimi fashioned an outdoor suite for the girls under umbrellas and tarps by the side of the house, which might not have been such a hardship in sunny California if it hadn't turned into a two-year living arrangement.

At some point, Mimi's and Fritz's nurse-patient bond developed into an amorous relationship. Fred, traveling for business during the workweek, knew nothing about it. But the girls did.

It was hard on Jane, who always championed her dad. It wasn't so bad when Fred was out on the road, but during his at-home times, Mimi used Jane to pass notes to Fritz. The teenager didn't relish the role but wouldn't think of refusing.

One day, Fred noticed Mimi slipping something into Jane's handbag and wanted to know what it was. Mimi said it had to do with his upcoming birthday. "You certainly wouldn't want to spoil the surprise, now, would you?" she asked. Jane kept quiet.

Gwen, who didn't feel the same loyalty to Fred, was more philosophical about the affair. "Uncle Fritz thought she was beautiful," said Gwen. "He loved her and he made her feel complete."

More important to Gwen was that the heady distraction of love had caused her mother to finally loosen her parental grip. When Fritz eventually moved back to his own home—and wife—across the country, Mimi made plans to follow him.

For Mimi, her relationship with Fritz was more than a distraction. She'd finally found true love. Not the girlish expectations of a somewhat reluctant new bride, or the "settling for" realities of a single mother with two small children, but rather the deep devotion between soul mates. Or so she thought.

It's not known—as it rarely is in matters of the heart—how things were all supposed to work out. But Mimi wanted Gwen and Jane kept occupied during the summer while she pursued her romance with Fritz, so she decided the girls should spend time with their birth father.

Considering how much she disliked Herbert, her choice is surprising. But she wrote to her ex-husband, with whom she'd had no contact in years, and asked if Gwen and Jane could visit him in New Haven. She suggested they go with him and Frances—whom everyone called Tish—on their annual visit to Sebec Lake. Mimi said it would be nice if the girls had a chance to get to know him and their Hayford grandparents, Wilder and Rose.

Fred was caught completely unaware. He didn't know Mimi was leaving; he didn't know she had been privately communicating with Herbert; and he didn't know his daughters were scheduled to visit their father. If there is any mercy in ignorance, it is that he also didn't know that Fritz, a man he'd always trusted, was at the heart of it all. It was enough that he had to deal with Herbert. Fred wrote him a tightly spaced, four-page letter, starting with the obligatory "Dear Herbert."

"As you receive this, the girls will be on their way. The Gods must sardonically grin at this situation. How amusing these humans! Fourteen years ago you were relegated to what has become popularly known as the 'doghouse.' The famous Tish was fearfully hated and reviled.

"The wheel of fortune spins round and round. By the caprice of the central figure, the situation is nearly reversed. Tish is now to mother the girls! The Hayfords, who once treated Mona rather shabbily because they felt 'she was not good enough for their son,' are to entertain them. Ye Gods and Little Fishes! Life is Funny!"

Fred's first priority, however, was for Gwen's and Jane's welfare. The main thrust of the letter was to tell Herbert about the girls, whom he hadn't seen since the divorce.

"You are about to meet two very attractive and charming little misses. I say this without the slightest reservation. We have never had any trouble or disobedience from them. In comparison with the average, they are angels. They should capture your heart to the Nth degree.

"Regardless of what you may hear, see, or imagine, no one can change the fact that I love them!"

He described Jane as having "an odd little personality. Less of the 'soft soap' that Gwen is so good at. Loves music and has artistic ability. Properly trained, she might develop it into something."

And Gwen . . . "is as gay as Jane is serious. Life rolls off her back. I envy her. She claims a belief in fairies, and no more apt description of her mind can be made . . . but by no means does she lack intelligence!"

As to her desire to become a psychologist, Fred, who admitted to being "serious minded," suggested she "take up a study which will help her out in a pinch: teaching, secretarial work, dietetics, anything that would allow her a few years in the adult world, getting experience, sizing up men, and life, before marrying. As it is, she knows nothing but schoolboys, who already know everything at nineteen, twenty, and twenty-one. Perhaps you can suggest a way to solve her problem.

"I understand you plan on letting them drive. Jane, of course, has never driven. Up to you, but I certainly would advise against it. Gwen has had all of two hundred miles actually behind the wheel. She managed to get stopped once, and even had a minor fender smack. I mention this because I would not want her hurt or in trouble, and you must take care until she gets considerable more experience."

But in spite of Fred's desire to smooth the way for his girls, his own confused and hurt feelings kept finding their way onto the pages. He thought the girls' trip to the Hayfords was a reprisal for something he had done to Mimi. "Being angry with me," he wrote, "this seemed like an excellent idea to hurt me."

Even if he had done something to precipitate her actions, it must have been galling to him—the man who had picked up the pieces when Mimi divorced Herbert—to have to now explain his inability to keep her happy.

"The close contact of daily living, the rubbing of personalities, Mona's strong mother instinct, the dominant personality she has developed, all were bound to excite some irritation," he wrote. He wasn't sure how much Herbert knew, though, since Mimi would only show Fred part of her ex's letter.

These clandestine arrangements were hard enough to accept, but most maddening for Fred—at least as regards him and his wife's first husband—was that Herbert expected him to pay the girls' expenses.

"Amazing viewpoint! Don't you understand this whole affair has been arranged without consulting me, entirely against my will? In secrecy? And that I think it can bring mostly unhappiness to everyone concerned? Under the circumstances you surely cannot be naïve enough to believe I would help finance it. You make a few cracks about earning power. Well, you are at your peak, too. You know more about money and finance than I do, being in the business. Here is your chance.

"Let me assure you, I have not grown horns. That I will reach Hell one of these days there will be no doubt, but I honestly don't think I will be the worst character there. So don't judge me too harshly. Remember, there are always two sides to any question. And speaking of Hell, no doubt I will be seeing you."

He signed it "Sincerely, Fred Kramer."

Although it's not known what Mimi told Fred about her own plans, it was apparent that their marriage was teetering, and his position as Dad to Gwen and Jane was in jeopardy.

As he drove his daughters to the bus station, he worried he might not see the two again. Before kissing them goodbye, he pressed a small piece of jewelry into each girl's hand.

"Please always remember me," he said.

35

Reconciliation

The girls' sweltering cross-country bus trip—before the days of air-conditioning and on-board restrooms—was not without its tests of fortitude and common sense.

"For my sister and me," Jane recalled, "the six-day ride from California to Connecticut was a memorable experience. Every two hours the bus would stop and we would be given the chance to go to the bathroom, often at an outhouse or equally dismal toilet. It was mid-summer in 1936. I was still fifteen and my sister had turned twenty.

"These buses weren't made like your now-a-day Greyhounds. They were just plain, ordinary buses with upright seats, and if you dozed, you did so sitting straight up. At night we'd try to sleep a bit, but then the lights would go on, and out we'd go again."

After passing through never-ending miles of farmland—and quickly-ending breaks at roadside eateries—they finally arrived in downtown New Haven. But, as had been Mimi's experience nineteen years earlier when she returned from France to that very same city, Herbert was not there to greet his daughters.

"Somehow he got the schedules mixed up and was still at home," said Jane. "I stood out on the road to wait for him, to see if I could see him coming, and this car stopped. I ran and got in, and he took off. I said, 'Wait for my sister!'

"I thought he was my father, having not seen him since I was a baby, but I'd been picked up by a masher, a skirt chaser. When I explained, the guy dropped me about a mile away, and I had to walk back carrying my suitcase.

"When Father picked us up, we had our first bath in six days and a change of clothes. I went fast asleep that afternoon on our shared bed."

Once recovered from their arduous ride, the girls became acquainted with the family. Despite Mimi's dire warnings, Tish turned out to be pleasant. She was a relaxed wife who didn't get upset about things—except perhaps her husband's attentions to a neighbor woman who always seemed to need help with home repairs. But overall, Herbert and Tish had an easy relationship and a peaceful home.

They had waited years before having children, and then had two. Four-year-old Joann inherited her mother's mild disposition and curly hair. Two-year-old Carol, with bright dark eyes and hair, looked a lot like Jane had at that age. But Carol had a severe skin condition that caused ulcerated blisters. Tish spent hours either wrapping her in gauze bandages—often head to foot—or slowly soaking them off. The toddler also suffered from asthma.

"The summer we were there," said Gwen, "Carol had terrible asthma attacks. One night I went into the kitchen and Father was carrying her. She was sitting up close on his chest, and he was walking her and walking her."

The toddler was a sweet girl but mentally slow, which Gwen attributed to too many asthma-induced bouts of oxygen deprivation. Mimi attributed it to inbreeding. And her curse.

> In the smile of a child you will find my tear
> From her heart you will hear my moan
> Tho you curse and you weep in your grief and fear
> My sorrow will be your own

It's not known if Herbert credited Mimi's words with having that kind of power. As a committed second-generation Christian Scientist, he likely followed the religious precept that Carol was the "eternal, spiritual manifestation of God." She was perfect. He and Tish relied on church practitioners and prayers to heal their daughter's recurring ailments.

Carol's frightening asthma attacks and skin eruptions did nothing to dampen Gwen's happiness at being with the Hayfords. She could now spend time with the father from whom she'd been so abruptly separated, and she cherished the chance to find out all about him—his version rather than Mimi's. He willingly obliged, starting with the marriage proposal itself. Although Mimi said it was Herbert who pressed her to marry him, he told his daughter a different story.

"As Father tells it," Gwen said, "they smooched and cuddled, silly words were murmured . . . and suddenly Mother flips out of the hammock, runs into the kitchen and announces to Grandfather and Grandmother that she and Herbert would be married next June, after his graduation. Presumably he didn't know those mumbling words were serious."

Since Herbert was a good storyteller in the best Maine tradition, the line between fact and fiction wasn't always clear to his out-of-state girls. Like the time he told Gwen they had Indian blood. Not realizing he was pulling her leg, she spoke for years of her father's descendancy from the Penobscot tribe. She liked being part Native American.

Gwen didn't share her mother's pride in their stuffy British heritage. She preferred the everyday folk she associated with her father. Herbert was a man with tools in his garage and root beer fermenting in his basement. Although he lived most of the year in New Haven, where he worked in real estate and stocks and bonds, he was a dyed-in-the-wool Mainer. He was happiest at the lake: swimming to their raft, waving greetings to neighboring camps from his sailboat, or batting the breeze with the local men in front of the store at Greeley's Landing.

Gwen loved everything about him and believed whatever he told her. Jane believed none of it.

Mimi's younger daughter wanted, more than anything else, to please her mother, and she knew the way to do that was to avoid getting close to the Hayfords. She maintained her distance for the sake of Fred, too, who was keeping house for himself back home. In letters, she sought to reassure him of her allegiance.

"Dear Dad, I just received your card describing your skill in cooking. How was it? Did you play Tarzan of the Wilderness? Well, coming down to brass tacks, I think H. is the [here she inserted a sketch of a spider with Herbert's head and a devil's horns], and I don't mean maybe. I know there is a true 'Dad' waiting in California. I think H. went a little too far when he started telling me lies about Mother."

Jane didn't elaborate on what lies "H" had told, but when it came to his first marriage, Herbert, of course, had his own view of events. The main parties in a failed marriage, or any collapsed relationship, inevitably tell different stories.

If they talk about it at all.

Mimi didn't leave any correspondence about Fritz, but it's clear her plans as an unencumbered woman did not go as she had hoped. In the end, Fritz didn't return her passion ... at least not enough to sever ties to his family and commit to her. Or maybe belated regrets about betraying Fred held him back. In any case, the affair was over.

Regardless of what Mimi had been willing to risk in her quest for love, she was no closer to finding it. She was hurt by Fritz's rejection, as well as embarrassed, but she focused on being practical and setting things in order. She returned to Los Angeles to reconcile with her husband.

Much as he may have wished otherwise, Fred needed her. Mimi radiated a life force that drew him into her orbit. He would have much preferred that she be in his orbit, but he took what he could get. In whatever way she explained the summer to him, he accepted it.

Jane told what happened next.

"So she made up with Dad, poor Dad, and relatives came to pick us up after the summer was over. The only problem was my sister felt such love for Father and our stepmother that she didn't want to leave. But because she was under twenty-one, Mother could have had the sheriff force her to leave. I was so mixed up and mental, I didn't care.

"In time, we were home again in California, as if nothing had ever happened."

36

Out On Their Own

The girls' summer stay with their birth father did not open the door for an improved relationship between Mimi and Herbert. Mimi was not thrilled that Gwen was so over-the-top enamored of all things Hayford. But even more important, Mimi needed to reestablish her loyalty to Fred, and so, as before, she directed that the Hayford name not be mentioned again.

Getting to know her father, though, had made an impression on Gwen. She found that she shared his love of recording numbers in ledgers and making them balance. It swayed her to the practical, and upon her return to California she studied accounting at Santa Monica Junior College, where she earned an associate degree.

Gwen and Herbert shared another trait, too. As she became a young adult, it was clear that she was less like her mother, who always wanted to sort out problems, and more like her father, who preferred to deflect them. If Gwen ran into opposition from her parents, she'd tune them out—quietly resisting more than openly defying—but in the end, she usually did what made them happy.

That is, until 1938 when twenty-five-year-old Sam Baer entered her life. Gwen was as outwardly agreeable as before—she'd say anything to avoid conflict—but her choice of a man made it apparent she would come to her own decisions.

Fresh out of college, Gwen met Sam, the owner of a small accounting business, when she answered his *Help Wanted* ad for a bookkeeper. He looked a bit like Herbert. Sam's face was broader and his hairline lower, but he had the same dark eyes, dark hair, and trimmed mustache. He hired Gwen, they fell in love, and within a few months planned a morning wedding in the historic Spanish mission in Santa Barbara.

On the day of the nuptials, Mimi gently placed a generations-old family tiara on Gwen's head, Fred escorted her down the aisle, and Jane stood beside her as the maid of honor. It was a felicitous ceremony, but both Mimi and Fred thought their daughter could have done better.

The groom was a Berkeley graduate and a hard worker, but he was also the son of poor French Catholics who had yet to rise above their humble beginnings. His mother was a washerwoman, brought over from France by her uncle to help in his San Francisco laundry. She eventually married and started a family, but her husband—Sam's father—developed schizophrenia. He was committed to an insane asylum and the young mother had to find a way to support her children on her own.

In the summer of 1914, with five kids and pregnant with her sixth, she drove a wagon down to the desolate Imperial Valley—fifteen miles north of the Mexican border—to claim free land. Beside a tenacious shade tree, she erected a ramshackle house that she added on to throughout the years. In the relentless desert heat, she brought in water from a ditch, and raised her brood by taking in washing and ironing. Gwen admired her and called her Mom.

By virtue of Sam's bloodline and background, Gwen probably couldn't have found a man Mimi and Fred would like less. Even so, the newlyweds had a standing date for dinner at her parents' home on Sundays. Before their first visit, Gwen made a point of teaching Sam which fork or spoon to use from the array of silverware she knew would be lined up on each side of his plate. Still, if he committed any social faux pas, Mimi, a gracious hostess, saved her concerns to share with Gwen later. In private.

Fred was less restrained. Despite his own fraught beginnings, he was now a sales executive with a self-assurance that occasionally verged on arrogance. During the weekly meal, he often ribbed Sam with thinly-veiled verbal jabs.

Not surprisingly, Sam was no more comfortable with Mimi and Fred than they were with him. The newlyweds stopped their customary visits.

In an attempt to establish a better rapport, Mimi started going to their apartment during the week, without Fred, but that didn't work out much better. Mimi could barely hide her dislike of their neighborhood in Huntington Park, a streetcar suburb of mostly industrial workers and, increasingly, dust bowl migrants. To make matters worse, the couple lived downwind of Vernon's hog rendering plant—which frequently emitted a putrid smell that lingered through the community for hours. And, worst of all, Gwen and Sam had decided to stay.

They bought a rundown place a few blocks away at 6504 State Street. The previous occupants, an old couple who had no energy for home maintenance or gardening, had left it a mess. But Gwen was attracted to the house from the start, and she and Sam went into debt to buy it. It was the man she chose and the house she chose, and she loved them both.

Emboldened by her success in heart and home, she asserted herself in other areas as well. She helped Sam enclose the front porch, which was to have its own entrance for their accounting office. The remodeling work, though, necessitated frequent stops at the hardware store where Gwen found she had to wait until all the male customers had been helped. It irritated her to no end.

Referring to the proprietor as a Bible-thumping chauvinist, she told how she dealt with him on her following visit. "I entered the store wearing only sneakers, shorts—hiked up to be shorter—and a flapping bandana on my chest. Every man turned to look. There was utter silence and the owner's face went purple. He waited on me quickly and I was out the door before the register stopped ringing. The next time, I wore my usual shirt and overalls and was served promptly."

Eventually, she and Sam finished the renovations. Mimi and Papa tried to share in Gwen's excitement but didn't have their hearts in it. It was bad enough she'd married down and lived in a blue-collar house without a proper lawn—prompting Fred to ask Sam if he raised goats—but perhaps toughest to accept was their daughter's name change. Gwen had started to use her high school nickname, Scottie, as her given name. "If movie stars and the Pope can change their names," she said to friends, "then I can change mine." Knowing her parents disliked the moniker, she refrained from making such a heady pronouncement to them. Still, they couldn't miss the sign on the office door, *Sam and Scottie Baer*.

She had declared her independence. She was Scottie.

Their second daughter was less of a problem. Unlike Scottie, Jane worked hard for her parents' approval. She was malleable and didn't resist them, actively or passively. It didn't hurt, either, that Jane had a sophisticated sense of fashion and a natural elegance that drew people to her. Where once she was described as odd, now she was unique. Moreover, her growing musical talent solidified Mimi's belief that her daughter was indeed the reincarnation of Jane's great-grandmother, Henrietta.

Before Jane's senior year in high school, Mimi arranged for her to go back east to study music. The budding musician earned two scholarships which, when supplemented by a little money Mimi had received from her parents' estate, allowed her to enter Massachusetts' respected Longy School of Music.

"I wanted to be a composer more than anything else in my life," said Jane. "Mimi took her inheritance money and sent me to Boston. I realized the sacrifice she'd made, and I was very grateful to her."

The stately three-story stone building, replete with gables and ivy-covered towers, sat adjacent to Harvard University. Jane lived at school and studied under Nadia Boulanger, a renowned French composer, conductor, and teacher. Although Jane was on her own for the first time, she wasn't far from Aunty Clara, who saw the music school as a stepping stone to "further study later on in Paris, if her work shows she has talent enough to earn her living through her music."

"I am helping with the lessons," Clara wrote to Fred in February 1939, "because everyone says she has talent and I care so much for Mona and the girls that I will do all I can afford to help them. I would have Jane here, but I am not well enough.... Jane is radiant since all is settled and she has to be held back as she is so eager to prove to us she will succeed."

She usually stayed on campus through the weekends to complete her homework and practice music, but sometimes she visited her aunty and when Clara's health permitted, they attended concerts together. Jane spent holidays with her or Mrs. Elliot, Mimi's one-time employer, who also lived nearby. Now and then Jane ventured out with friends, one day touring Mary Baker Eddy's old home. "Truly an inspiration," she wrote to not-very-religious Fred, whom she often tried to bring into the church.

Jane devoted considerable time to writing to her dad. Because his work had always taken him away from home, years earlier they had developed a close pen-and-ink relationship, and it flourished during her time in music school. One Christmas she sent a carol she composed for him, and every Father's Day she wrote a special poem. Her letters and cards were always adorned with cartoon drawings and clever verses.

In one no-special-occasion letter she described her day off. "Every Saturday, the rooms are used for giving lessons... If you think it was bad to hear a little practicing at home, you ought to be here where in every room, on every side, there is singing, violin playing, cello, trumpets and pianos from nine to two o'clock. I tell you, nothing could ever be worse."

Aside from her singing and instrumental abilities—especially on the classical guitar—Jane was also a talented whistler. Later in the same letter, she related a bit of mischief that surely made her dad smile.

"Under my window is a fire escape, and around the school is a high, ten-foot brick wall. The two help to conceal my window. Now much is my amusement when some old biddy goes walking by, I stand back, unseen, and whistle to the rhythm of her walk. Time and time again, the victim will look in all directions but never dream that it comes from my window. And try as she might, in a state of anger, to break that rhythm, I slow down as she does. Finally I stop when the woman is so enraged that she makes too funny a spectacle to allow me to keep a straight enough face to whistle anymore! Try it sometime. The tune of 'Pop Goes the Weasel' is very effective."

Along with her account is the sketch of an annoyed woman—one hand on hip and the other gripping a grocery bag—looking around for the source of her vexation.

But most of Jane's attention was on her music. She honed her skills and became an accomplished composer, singer, and musician. Every bit as important, however, was the personal confidence she gained during those years away from home. Mimi came to see her often, staying in Boston at length, but her maternal influence gradually lessened and Jane became more independent.

As Scottie and Jane were moving to new residences, so too were their parents. Fred, who had been successful in his work, was finally able to provide Mimi with the affluence she had been accustomed to as a child. Although he was always content to rent, in 1940 he bought her a home. The newly built house, with two bedrooms and two baths, was located in an upper-class neighborhood in the gently rolling Cheviot Hills, mere blocks from the more well-known Beverly Hills. White with blue shutters, a flower box under one window, and a picket fence bordered by wildflowers, it had the look of a city cottage. On the roof, Fred installed a rooster weathervane in a nod to those topping the Brittany churches of Mimi's childhood.

Their home was a fitting sanctum for Mimi's nineteenth-century reproductions of Raphael's and Botticelli's Madonnas, Leonardo di Vinci's Angels, and Perugino's Red Cardinal, all embraced by ornate gold frames. Sharing wall space with the famed works were portraits of her Tate and Gudgeon ancestors.

And for Fred, the two-car garage had enough space for a proper workshop, where a man could retreat when need be.

It was at this time, with everyone settled in their new places, that Pearl Harbor was suddenly attacked. Soon after, the United States entered World War II.

"It was noon," wrote Scottie. "Sam was painting rooms inside the house, and I had been to the store to get some things for lunch. Passing the gas station on the corner of State and Gage, the owner hollered at me, 'Hey, did you know that war was just declared?' I was too inexperienced to feel any emotion, fear or excitement. I went home and told Sam.

"We joined the neighborhood patrols and disaster crews, and took first aid classes. Here in California, though, we were mainly 'playing' at war. I was one of the air raid wardens, but most of what I did was get coffee and donuts. We were supposed to keep our windows dark, but I don't think I did a very good job because I went to bed every night. I really didn't care if people had their lights on or not.

"We used to meet in the police department basement. One day the whole country was going to be on alert and practice what we would do if attacked. First, they sent notice that Washington D.C. had been 'bombed,' then Chicago, then St. Louis, and then Denver. By the time Denver got 'bombed,' it was five or six o'clock and we were all tired, so we went home."

She had good reason to be tired. Their accounting business was booming. "As accountants we had to drive long distances to our clients, who were becoming prosperous. The companies that hired us were making ammunition and metal equipment for the war, so we got extra ration tickets for gas. Also, income tax started during the war, and accountants made money from that, too. Sam and I lived on the upper edge of life and had whatever we wanted or needed. Our monies bought property on Figueroa Street in Los Angeles, in Santa Barbara, Whittier Heights, and Torrance. And, of course, we paid off the $2,300 debt on our home."

Back in Boston, Jane finished music school. Only fifteen months after Aunty Clara wondered if Jane might one day polish her skills in Paris, the Nazis defeated the French army and overtook the capital. Now, a year into the occupation, any dream of studying in France had long been abandoned.

Jane returned to Southern California and by early September was engaged to Dick, a handsome, Mimi-approved man from a well-to-do Christian Science family in Westwood. The marriage was set for the evening of November 1, 1942.

But to the embarrassment of the groom's family and the humiliation of the bride's, Dick broke it off three weeks before the wedding. Scottie said it was just as well, telling Jane that Dick was emotionally unstable. He quickly proved her right. When Jane went to his place to talk things out, she discovered he'd eloped to Las Vegas with a flavor-of-the-week Hollywood actress.

The whole demoralizing fiasco took place less than a year after the bombing of Pearl Harbor, and the new Women's Army Auxiliary Corps was actively seeking recruits. WAAC posters of self-assured young women—faces forward, heads held high, chins up and shoulders back—declared, "This is my war, too!" "Going where we're needed most!" "Make your life exciting! Make it fun! Make it all worthwhile! See your Army recruiter today!"

And so, eight weeks after being dumped, Jane did just that.

Mimi, sympathetic about the jilting and convinced Jane was too delicate and thin to be accepted anyway—her wedding gown featured an eighteen-inch waist—thought it was a harmless enough diversion. She gave her consent. But before anyone knew it, Jane was inducted as a private in what was later renamed the Women's Army Corps (WAC).

37

A Close Call in The Pacific

After boot camp, Jane was assigned to the Motor Pool in Georgia, where she drove jeeps and troop trucks. It was a heady time of gaining confidence in her abilities. She made friends with WACs of all backgrounds, women who hadn't been hand-picked by her mother, and met exciting young men who hadn't passed muster with her dad.

In an atmosphere charged with the knowledge that life would be cut short for many soldiers, military couples didn't favor long engagements. In May 1943, Jane met Gene Smith, a soulful-eyed corporal on leave. They exchanged addresses and after a flurry of letters confirming her hopes that he was as good as he looked—a respectable Christian who had sung in both the chorus and glee club at his private Pennsylvania college—she looked forward to their next meeting.

That next meeting, on July 14th, turned into an elopement, with the couple—dressed for a day of fishing—saying their vows in front of the Justice of the Peace in Volusia, Florida.

Unfortunately, Gene's flowery letters never covered his rough ideas about consummating a marriage. He was a brute in bed. After the drunken groom passed out, she sneaked back to her barracks and one of the WACs took her to the infirmary. Jane quickly found a lawyer and filed for an annulment.

Gene begged on his knees—arms tightly around her legs—for another chance. She no longer wanted anything to do with him, but still active in her church, she was urged by Christian Science practitioners to take her vows seriously. She reluctantly tore up the annulment papers. Thankfully, Gene was soon deployed.

In summer 1944, she received her own orders to ship out. One night on a bus bench—wanting to leave something behind in case she didn't make it back—she composed *Softly, Softly Fell the Snow*, a gentle carol with a third verse befitting the times.

> Like the snow the Christ-child came,
> Holy is His very name,
> Bearing with Him precious light,
> To a world dark as the night.

Then it was off to San Francisco, where the WACs encountered a military mix-up. The women had been issued thick woolens and assigned to drive trucks somewhere cold enough to warrant such heavy clothes. But due to a clerical error, another group of women, highly trained in cryptography, were sent to drive the vehicles instead. Jane's unit, their woolens packed, were slated to board a ship to sweltering New Guinea.

Mimi vehemently protested Jane's assignment—all the way to the top brass—but to no avail. Jane may have been a wispy ninety-pound musician in civilian life, but that didn't disqualify her from serving overseas.

The family arranged to meet in San Francisco, where Fred had a branch office. Mimi and Scottie took the train up, and the four of them went out for dinner. Mimi, however, was suffering from a bad cold so everyone said goodnight by twelve o'clock.

The girls, though, who as adults hadn't had an opportunity to get to know each other, sat on their beds talking. By that time in their lives, Scottie was calling her sister "Jay," a nickname Jane had used since music school. The next day, Scottie made a note in her diary about their discussion-filled night.

Jay and I talked from midnite till seven a.m. She is so well and healthy. I like her very much. She had a hard childhood.

It was the beginning of a deep friendship. Separated in age by more than four years, and having occasionally been raised apart, they had vastly different experiences. But who else can understand one's early years like a sibling? Each a piece of the family puzzle, they worked together to make sense of the upbringing that had formed them. In the process, they forged a solid sisterly alliance.

The only downside to this newly minted relationship was the effect it would have on Mimi. Heretofore, Scottie was the rebel daughter and Jane the compliant one. But Scottie applauded her sister's decision to join the army and remove herself from their mother's sphere of influence. She also encouraged her to claim her right to be called Jay, a name Mimi deplored almost as much as Gwen's unseemly Scottie. But despite her courage in going off to war, Mimi's younger girl wasn't ready to openly rebel against her mother. Only her friends and Scottie called her Jay.

With a final wave, Jay boarded the ship to New Guinea. The *Going-where-you're-needed-most* part of her service had begun.

From his San Francisco sales office, Fred wrote her a letter of farewell addressed to "Jane dear."

"As I write this, your great ship rolls and pitches onward thru the dark night, carrying you with each vibration of its powerful engines always a little farther from those who love you . . .

"In the morning the sun rose over the Golden Gate. I stood on one of the city's hills gazing at the mist around the great bridge and, as sad as I felt, I could not help but envy your fine adventure, for many years have passed since my last crossing. Of all the experiences in a crowded and much traveled life, none were as satisfying as an ocean voyage. To stand at the bow, to watch it dip and rise and sway, all the while it plunges forward parting the waters into a foamy maelstrom . . . My! Perhaps I have been dreaming . . .

"I had hoped for a few more hours with you. The father is an individual in his own right, but under the spell of the maternal, he rarely shines in his own splendor. And to be the only male in the company of three of what is so gaily called the weaker or gentler sex, allows him a role about as important as a spear carrier in a Shakespearean stage production."

Before closing with the usual expressions of love, and six Xs for kisses, he included some fatherly kidding.

"I sent you the two sets of bras. Mother tells me you could use them. Also included the necktie. If the worst comes to pass, you can always trade them off to some jungle chief, who will no doubt prize the bras and give the tie to his favorite wife."

After three weeks on the ocean—during which time the women did their best to alter their woolens into tropical uniforms—Jay's ship arrived at the mountainous rainforests on the north coast of New Guinea. Stationed in Hollandia, home of General Douglas MacArthur's headquarters, she and her fellow drivers started the jobs the cryptographers were to have performed. With her talent in art, she became a draftsman in the radar countermeasures unit.

WACs were normally stationed in places already cleared of the Japanese Imperial Army, but that wasn't the case in New Guinea. Small groups of enemy combatants—who had retreated to jungle caves to await reinforcements—roamed the highlands. Because of that, Jay and the other women weren't allowed out of the compound without an armed soldier. Some of the WACs thought the restriction unnecessary, but others appreciated the protection—or at least the romantic possibilities—of escorted walks. Even with an able-bodied companion, though, there were risks.

Once, after a long shift at the drafting table, Jay wanted a brisk evening walk and her friend Tom was happy to accompany her. But treading the path, they suddenly saw a platoon of Japanese soldiers crest a hill and head towards them. Trusting they hadn't been spotted, they dropped and rolled for cover in the bushes.

The only bush near her was scrawny, but she flattened herself as best she could and relied on prayer and her camouflage uniform to conceal her. Holding her breath, she stayed still as the enemy soldiers approached and then passed by unaware. When Jay and Tom finally emerged from hiding, he noticed something on her sleeve. Jay looked down to find a muddy footprint from the cleft shoe of one of the Japanese. He'd nearly stepped on her arm.

One might wonder how a classically trained musician known for acute sensitivities as a child would fare in that environment, but she had developed into a steady soldier with a fighting spirit. One afternoon when she was out for a swim, a deranged GI tried to drown her but she stayed calm and fought him off.

She was not inordinately affected by the sights of war, either. Despite her keen sensibilities, she had a strong stomach. One day, she and friends were on their way to swim in Lake Sentani—a ten-mile hike through mountainous jungle—when she noticed in the bushes, lying on his back, the remains of a fallen Japanese. He appeared to have been dead for days.

Like any GI collecting souvenirs, she reached into his waistband to claim his country's flag, covered with the brown-stained autographs of his hometown well-wishers. From his shirt pocket, she fished out a photograph of seven sword-bearing officers. She put them in her pack and soldiered on.

Later, Jay was sent to Leyte in the Philippines, and then to the capital, which had suffered one of the most devastating battles in the Pacific. As American forces closed in on Manila, Japanese soldiers began destroying the city and massacring the men, women, and children who lived there. In the ensuing month-long conflict, over 1,000 U.S. troops and 100,000 Filipino civilians were killed. The carnage was staggering.

Jay was billeted in a classroom of the heavily damaged De La Salle College. Although the Japanese had been routed before the

WACs arrived, the fallen soldiers' remains were everywhere. GIs removed the dead as the women moved in. Jay remembered one corpse with his leg up and arm raised as if doing a jig. She watched the soldiers carry out his body. Then she laid a mat over his dried blood and set up her cot. But such attempts to hide the horror of their accommodations were futile. The shrapnel-torn walls and crumbling façade were constant reminders of what had happened. The view from the window was just as bad.

"It was the worst destruction we'd ever seen," said Jay. "My window looked down on a minefield where Japanese bodies were lying. We were so reckless in those days. A friend's boyfriend said he knew where the mines were. 'Just stay in my footsteps,' he said. So we followed him out to see the bloated bodies."

Jay's religious faith probably helped keep her on an even keel. During her enlistment she'd served as choir director, church organist, and chaplain's assistant. She tried again now to get Fred to take up Christian Science.

"Do it in secret for me," she pleaded in a letter. "It'll give you something you've never had before. Personal love from those held dear will never come as near to the heart as God."

Fred expressed appreciation for her sentiments and acknowledged that religion can help believers overcome problems, but he didn't plan to join the church.

"To my mind, a Methodist can be just as good as a Baptist or Christian Scientist or the reverse. In spite of my 'terrible character,' I honestly believe I am as good a Christian in the material sense of the word as any of them. I have no wish to do harm, nor would I willingly do anyone an unkind deed.

"Well, there is little use selling myself. I shall remember your good advice. In the meantime, if I could find a 'religion' of blarney and high-grade applesauce for everyday living, it would make it much easier for those about me."

Fred, remembering his war years, had wanted to enlist, too, but since he'd falsified his papers as a young man itching to join World War I, the records showed he was just past the cut-off age. Now the most he could wish for was his daughter's safe return. He and Mimi worried about her, yet both refused to give voice to it. With faith that she would return, they built a small cottage for her behind their home.

38

The War in France

In her living room window, Mimi displayed the Blue Star Banner, denoting a family member serving, and at her door she flew the Stars and Stripes. Just beneath it, she hung the British flag.

Mimi was anxious about the war in Europe and particularly worried about her sister Rita and brother George, who, with their families, had been caught in the midst of it for several years. The port city of Le Havre suffered terrible bombing, and Mimi had scant means of communicating with her siblings.

Their British roots were a liability, and George's French in-laws worried about the Tate children speaking English. It had generated neighborhood taunts in the past, but once the Germans occupied France, it became downright dangerous.

"Some of Mummy's relatives were paranoiac about us boys speaking English together," wrote second son Tony. "Their refrain was 'You are in France, speak French. After all, you are content to eat the bread of French people.'"

But it was a point of contention for the rebellious teenager who identified closely with his British heritage. "I'd reply that if we ate French bread, it was because we'd paid for it."

The decade had started out on a happy note, with the birth of the Tate's eighth—and final—child, Patrick. But that was the last joyful event for some time. In May 1940 the Nazis invaded and the Battle of France began.

Alain Tate later wrote about it. "Like hundreds of thousands of French citizens, George Edward Cecil and his wife fled with their family to Brittany in June 1940, hoping in vain that the advancing German army would be stopped along the Seine River."

Germany's victory, however, was swift. On June 3rd, the Nazis bombed Paris, and on June 14th, they captured the City of Light. Eight days later, an armistice, establishing the German occupation zone, was signed.

With France no longer fighting Germany, George's attention turned back to making a living, so he and Marthe brought their children back to Le Havre ... only to face a new problem. Now the British were bombing the occupying Nazis, and the Tates were in the middle of the fighting.

"In the early days of the German occupation," wrote Tony, "we were bombed regularly by the R.A.F. [Britain's Royal Air Force]. One night we had the most frightening experience. Bombs were dropping everywhere, though not particularly close to us. By the time we'd all been awakened and dressed after a fashion, it was too late to go to the nearby shelter.

"So we were all huddled up in the hall of our house, at the foot of the staircase, waiting for a lull in the bombing before dashing out to the shelter. We then heard a bomber diving (you cannot mistake the sound) and then the ominous 'whistling' of bombs. Sure enough, a stick [series] of six bombs came crashing down, one after the other, each one exploding nearer and nearer.

"My baby brother Patrick, about seven or eight months old, was in Mum's arms. Everyone was trembling. I was rigid with fear. Dad was calm but white as a sheet. The last bomb fell across the street from us, into a depot or laboratory where they stored chemicals and pharmaceuticals, mostly alcohol, in large demi-john glass bottles.

"Well, you should have heard the bang!!! We didn't know then where it had fallen. Our windows, and the windows of those all around us, just disintegrated and through the skylight in the roof, at the top of the stairwell, there came down a shower of earth, bricks, stones, dust and millions of bits of paper, invoices, tally books, etc. We thought that our roof had been hit and that we had had it!!!

"Then nothing happened. We were still in one 'shaky' piece. Complete silence for a minute—we were still a bit stunned. Suddenly, the younger kids started bawling their heads off. Mum was frantic. Dad, too, in a way. The bits of paper were still floating down. The smell of dust and burning was very acrid. It was eerie.

"We had a quick check to see that everyone was OK. Then we legged it like 'bats out of hell.' The German anti-aircraft batteries were hammering away. Planes were still droning overhead. In the street, as we came out of our gate at the end of the drive, Mum got caught up in telephone wires hanging from a broken pole.

"We could hear another wave of bombers coming closer. We pulled and tugged at the damned wires and eventually released Mum and Patrick just in time, because as we dived into an open doorway, two bombs dropped neatly in the middle of the street, wiping out everything in sight ... cars [and] people who, like us, were seeking shelter. Bits of metal were hitting the brick walls and the ricochets were whistling past.

"That night many of our neighbors were killed or maimed.

"Yet with the help of God, we survived those traumatic years. We went through dreadful times, and I grew up quickly. I was fifteen years old when we had that experience, but the following day, I can honestly say I was an 'old' fifteen.

"If one showed fear, the youngsters would be scared. Being the oldest in the family, since my brother George died, I was always expected to give a good example ... Not quite so easy, believe me."

Tony's younger brother, Alain, wrote that they were forced to spend many nights in the basement of a neighboring building, often distracting themselves by playing chess with their father. But seven times in the next two years the bombing was so fierce they were compelled to take refuge in other towns.

Life was especially dangerous for Rita and Dolphe's family. Their Jewish surname, Cantor, made them particularly vulnerable. Jay later recalled a story Mimi told her.

"One day, German soldiers were picking up boys and putting them in a truck to take them to God knows where. They grabbed one of Rita's boys, but a neighbor started yelling at them, 'You can't take *him*! He's *my* son!'

"So they let him go. She saved him."

Whether Rita's boy was specifically targeted—or merely one of many young men scooped up to provide labor for the Nazis—isn't known, but Jay said the Cantors used the Tate name for the duration of the war.

George and his family escaped the dangerous coast when he was offered a job promotion that included a move to the head office in Paris. They left Le Havre and moved into an apartment in the Passy district. But even in Paris, life was hard, according to Tony, especially with the food shortages.

"Mummy queued up for hours in the most appalling weather conditions to try and get extra food for the youngsters. We, the grown-up boys, never saw any milk, butter or meat officially for nearly four years. All our sugar, fat, eggs went to the nippers [the younger children]. Dad and Mum were horribly thin and yellow, due to undernourishment."

Some of the family heirlooms had to be sacrificed for food.

"Dad spent a fortune on what he could scrounge on the black market to feed us. He and Mummy sold a lot of their possessions, gold and silver, to meet the exorbitant prices demanded by black marketers. Mum and Dad never knew that 'we' knew what they had done for us. But we knew..."

George's British heritage and military service in World War I could have caused them serious repercussions, but the family was now legally French.

"Fortunately, they were never troubled by the German police," Alain wrote, "as George Edward Cecil had been provided in 1938 with French papers by the Rouen Prefecture. His lawyer had indeed discovered that, although he served in the British army during the First World War, he was considered a French citizen by the authorities because he had not officially chosen British citizenship at the age of twenty-one."

But considering that the French were not completely united against the enemy—which could refer to the Germans who were occupying their country, or the British and Americans who were bombing it—caution was always in order.

The youngest, Patrick, disclosed an incident that occurred one summer day in their fourth-floor flat in Paris. It was hot, so the windows had been left wide open while his dad listened to the British Broadcasting Corporation, which was a crime during the German occupation. Suddenly someone rang the doorbell. It was the son of a couple—an American lady and her French husband—who lived on the fifth floor of an apartment across the street. The young man at the door told them that "they already had their own radio set, and *they did not need to hear our radio, as the sound goes up, as you know.* Of course, they were warning us, and Dad took the necessary steps to avoid being heard when 'breaking the law.'"

Both Tony and Alain took up with the French Resistance, handing out leaflets and patriotic literature, but soon Tony joined the underground military forces.

"In 1943 (I was not quite eighteen), I joined a small group of students from our college," Tony wrote, "and ran away from home. We lived rough . . . and I mean rough. The Royal Air Force used to drop weapons, ammunition and food, which we collected at pre-arranged times at night from deserted fields and distributed to other Resistance groups.

"British liaison and intelligence officers, in charge of underground districts and groups, trained us in the use of Sten guns and weapon maintenance. We carried out raids on German depots and railway lines, which we blew up with plastic explosives.

"The French attitude then was 'France (Vichy) has signed an armistice with the Germans, therefore we are no longer at war with them... My attitude was 'Britain has not signed an armistice, therefore I must consider myself at war and do the best I can under the circumstances.'

"My greatest fear during the war was of being killed accidently in a British or American bombing raid (and that would have been ironical), but it was greater to me than the fear of being killed by a German bullet. Stupid, isn't it? Considering the ultimate result would have been the same. Still, when you are seventeen or eighteen, one's views on life are rather limited.

"Those dark years, in a way, had a 'plus side.' We grew up and matured spiritually more quickly, and it bound all of us Tates together very firmly and closely as a family."

39

We Are Free!

In August 1944, Paris was liberated, bringing great hope to all of France. Mimi received sporadic messages from her brother, letting her know that he and his family were okay. But it wasn't until the following spring, with the final defeat of Nazi Germany, that they could reestablish normal communications.

On May 11, 1945, George was finally able to send her a letter. It was three days after Victory in Europe Day.

"My dear old Mo and my dear old Fred,

"We are now free! We have been spending the last two days rejoicing over our good fortune and cheering the boys who risked their lives to free us. Will the world ever know the extent of the harm done to humanity by the Nazis? I doubt it.

"I hope letters will now travel quicker so we can get regular news of you all. We have just received your parcel for which many thanks. Dresses, socks, and vitamins! We shall gradually get out of this mess caused by the scarcity of everything, food and clothes specially, so please don't deplete your own wardrobe, we can carry on until the factories start work again over here. We are just a little worried about fuel for next winter. The powers that be don't seem inclined to do anything, pretending priority claims from industries. We nearly died from cold this winter.

"Our great preoccupation just now is to find out whether we shall be able to spend a month in Brittany. We have not seen the sea for five long years and we are all just dying to bathe and sprawl again on the sands. The difficulty is due to the mines, which have been sown in millions along the beaches, making them dangerous. Perhaps at La Grandville or Val André we may find something. Everybody has to fish for himself for a bathing suit. They will probably be made out of old black-out curtains!!

"We were delighted to learn you are all alive and well... I hope you got some of the messages I sent through different friends in Rouen. I wanted you to know we were well and very much alive.

"Rita and Adolphe have settled down in their new flat. I have only seen them once in about two years. They are well and have received [your] letters.... Adolphe's mother died in 1942 in the cellar where they had to live owing to bombardments.

"We shall send you some snaps as soon as we are allowed to do so through the post. You will be able to admire the Tate family... [The children] have all been jolly good during the war and never groused or complained about anything."

Recovery from the war slogged on, but communications improved quickly. Letters, which heretofore had taken as many as six weeks to arrive by sea, were now sent by air, bringing the following letter from George to Fred in a remarkably fast two weeks.

"Thanks so much for your news and for all you have sent us. Everything has reached us safely. I wrote you last week thanking you for the black shoes and brown women's shoes. Also the blue suit which saved Tony from walking about naked! The hot water bottles are also invaluable in view of the difficulty we have in keeping warm. Last winter we used ordinary glass bottles, but they kept breaking in the bed and drenching the bedclothes.

"This is a funny world in which you cannot buy anything, though you have the money! All those articles you sent cannot be obtained here, even in the black market. However, old man, you must not bleed yourselves for us. As I have already mentioned, things will improve one of these days, and as soon as the industries get going, the cost of living will come down. I have a very well-paid job and as soon as prices get normal, we will all be very comfortable . . .

"P.S. You mention the question of a suit. Frankly, I could do with one if it is possible. Tony got the first one you sent and I am now reduced to my last one, which was made in 1939. It is a bit worn round the sleeves, but then new suits are very rare. Don't be afraid of sending a really worn one, provided it has not already been turned, as the practice here is to turn old suits inside out and readjust them."

George's letters shared heartbreaking tales about old family friends, including the viscount who had arranged for his first job in the auto garage. "Alain de Lorgeril was shot by the Nazis for harbouring young men from the Resistance movement," he wrote. "They blew his brains out from behind, in front of his family!!!"

But most of his correspondence focused on the joys of postwar life, including a report a few months later about their Brittany vacation in La Cotentin, six miles from their old home in Hillion.

"If you do not remember where this lovely place is, I will tell you. Midway between Planguenoual and Le Val André . . . it is close to the beach and the food is plentiful. The fact that there is no electric lighting and that the cooking has to be done 'dans l'âtre,' [in the fireplace] made it picturesque. However, the kids all enjoyed themselves and lived on the beach eating cakes and God knows what all.

"We received another parcel of soups from Mrs. Paine [Clara] and I have just written to thank her for her kind thoughts. I hope the next time she will slip in a paquet of Camels, but no doubt she does not smoke. This is not a hint to you, old sweetheart, so keep your hair on. If you can spare a few Gillette blades, though, I would like to feel what it is like to have at least one decent shave. One gets tired of pulling the stubs out by the roots. I still have Fred's blade sharpener, but it is certainly the worst for wear.

"I hope to send you a bunch of snapshots. We are having them enlarged so that you can see how fine the family is! I must close down, so will say 'Goodbye, old Girl' for the present. Our united love to Fred and the girls. You must feel relieved about Jane now that the war is over!!!"

Jay, who was stationed in the Philippines when Japan surrendered, was celebrating the hard-fought victory with the rest of her army buddies. And she finally had real buddies. "The hard knocks of military life," she said, "got me out of my shell."

Removed from the milieu of students who amused themselves by poking fun at a classmate who was different—and removed, too, from the influence of her overbearing mother—Jay became confident and outgoing. She'd formed friendships with the other women, and some of the men as well. One in particular, a quiet Swedish-American from the Midwest, was Sgt. Robert Anderson.

During the Battle of Manila, Bob had taken part in a rapid march to rescue prisoners of war held at the Santo Tomas Internment Camp. Formerly a prestigious university, the prison held over four thousand civilians for three desperate years. Most were American or British, but the POWs included plantation owners, businessmen, missionaries, and hotel workers from over a dozen countries. More than a thousand detainees were housewives; four hundred were children. By the time Bob and the others liberated the captives, ten percent had died, most from malnutrition.

After the U.S. forces took back Manila and the most urgent needs were met, Bob and like-minded GIs used old lumber and salvaged nails to rebuild a bombed-out local church. He was a good man, and like Jay, he was a Christian Scientist.

And, like her, he was completely in love.

In September 1945, after a year overseas, Jay was discharged. Her first priority was a visit to Las Vegas to put a legal end to her fishing-date elopement, a regrettable union that for the previous two years had existed only on paper.

Back home, Fred wasn't inclined to think anyone—even Bob, a veteran decorated with a half-dozen medals—was good enough for his little girl. But Mimi was just glad to see her happy and marrying a man who shared their religious faith.

A few months later, on the day after Christmas, they said their vows. The next morning, Mimi wrote to Bob's mother to describe the wedding, held in the Kramers' living room.

> "Tonight Fred and I are seeing our children, your son and our daughter, on the train headed for your welcoming arms. We wish them Godspeed.
>
> I know you are anxious to hear about the wedding, perhaps in a bit more detail than two starry-eyed children could recall, so I am going to try, amid the unfinished duties which face any mother after a wedding, to bring the event to you.
>
> I should say here that the wedding march could not be had anywhere, so I took Bob to a recording place where we had one made. This recording was a bit different since a carol, *Joy to the World,* was played at the start, and about half way through, the wedding march began, which made it very nice at this season. On the other side Bob says a few words to Jane, followed by a pretty selection. This went off quite well, and the bride marched in on her father's arm in perfect time.
>
> The wedding was beautiful. Using the double ring ceremony, Bob got a bit bewildered and tried to put the ring on his own finger instead of on Jane's, until I heard Jane say, 'not yours, darling, on *my* finger.' I laughed inside and was grateful for the sense of ease and joy which

accompanied the gesture. Following the benediction, the officiant, Dr. Roberts, turned the couple to face us and said, 'I am happy to present Mr. and Mrs. Anderson,' and after that, as Jane said, 'the lip-rouge was passed around!!!'

The two went into the dining room, where a lovely cake was waiting to be cut. This they did well and with grace. After the cake and ice cream, the two started out towards a small guesthouse we built on the grounds for Jane long before we thought there would be a wedding, and the guests were waiting with rice and good wishes. They ran the gamut of flying rice, and Bob carried Jane over the threshold. "

Mimi and Fred took the newlyweds out to dinner and then dropped them off at their downtown hotel. Years later, Jay wrote about her wedding in a piece titled *My Most Beautiful Day*, ending on a sweet note.

"Of course, when I was married, it seemed almost surrealistic that the day had come when anyone would love me enough to marry me, but here it was. Afterwards, instead of rushing up to our hotel room, we went to church to see how it felt to be married and in church. The rest came later."

40

A Fruitless Marriage

Jay and Bob's wedding marked the close of a year of endings and beginnings—the cessation of fighting and the commencement of rebuilding—both globally and within Mimi's family. Scottie had also undergone a period of tumultuous change.

Eighteen months earlier, while Jay was preparing to deploy overseas, her older sister had been confronting an inner struggle at home. Although Mimi's and Fred's dislike of Sam caused considerable friction, it also masked a greater problem in the couple's marriage.

By early 1944, Sam was not doing well. He had been seeing a doctor for psychological problems. *He's tired and jittery,* was how Scottie described him in her diary. He took a few weeks off to visit family in Texas, but it didn't help.

Dr. Meyers at the Eighth Street Clinic diagnosed him.

They've found he's not only neurotic, but hysterical, she wrote that night. The doctor started treating him with hypnosis.

By May, Scottie had retired from bookkeeping to be a proper and supportive housewife. She bleached her hair, made curtains with the fancy new White Sewing Machine Sam gave her for her birthday, and volunteered in the war effort.

The following month, Sam was looking and feeling much better. Impressed by the results, Scottie—who had been depressed and gaining weight since she gave up work—made an appointment with Dr. Meyers for herself. Not one to want anyone to see into—or, worse yet, control—any part of her mind, she declined hypnosis. But they talked. She noted the gist of it. *He says I've been too "good" to Sam and am defeating my own desires.*

They had been married for almost six years and what Scottie desired was children. Sam didn't want them. "We talked about it before we were married," Scottie later said, "and it didn't make any difference to me then. I didn't care if we had kids. But by the time I got around to twenty-seven or twenty-eight, everybody was having children and having a good time and all that goes with it. And then I wanted children."

Scottie continued to see the doctor, who, in August, suggested a course of action. *I'm to leave Sam for trips and enter my own interests and stop living for, and around, him.*

Dr. Meyers provided the encouragement she needed to talk to Sam about what she really wanted. But Sam, concerned about passing on his father's legacy of mental illness, was clear about children. There would be none. Ever positive, Scottie tried to assure him that God would give them only healthy children. Sam, however, wouldn't relent.

Finally, Scottie asked him the most important question. "Do you still love me?"

He couldn't answer. She knew then there was no longer any reason to be 'living for, and around, him.'

It was at about that time that Scottie took the train up to San Francisco to see Jay off to New Guinea. Then she returned to her home in Huntington Park, where she had already started to throw her energies into the war effort. Despite her half-hearted work as an air raid warden, she had signed up to help at the Red Cross blood bank, taken the physical, and passed the driving test. The only thing left was to renew her first aid card, so she enrolled in the required night class at Huntington Park High School.

That's where she met Raymond Dole.

Ray was a man of contradictions, the result of a deeply conflicted childhood. He had come from Seventh-day Adventists, at least two generations back, and received the bulk of his education at an Adventist school. Although not unduly pious, he was a dedicated church elder and served as the Los Angeles Superintendent of Sabbath Schools.

Regrettably, his mother Inez—a Minnesota girl who wanted more than her small mill town had to offer—hadn't paid attention to her own church learning. She had grown up to be a smooth-talking con artist.

Ray had avoided getting involved in his mother's scams. She never told him what she was up to, and he didn't want to know. Especially after one of his well-insured stepfathers died of mushroom poisoning. It was a hard balancing act—following the Good Book while remaining a loyal son, but his healthy sense of self-preservation kept him walking that tightrope. After he took a wife, it became trickier.

At twenty-four he married Jeane, an anxious-to-get-out-of-the-house seventeen-year-old. When their son was born, Inez insisted they name him Ray Junior. Jeane was against it and saw her husband's easy capitulation as the sign of a momma's boy, but soon the Depression struck and everyone's attention turned to putting food on the table.

Determined to keep Jeane and Junior off welfare, Ray juggled several jobs. He parked cars, drove a delivery truck, and worked in gas stations. Still, they barely had enough to buy the baby's vitamins. The highlight of their week was Saturdays—the Sabbath for Seventh-day Adventists—when they put on their best clothes and rode the streetcar to church.

Finally, Ray got a job as a first aid instructor just as new government regulations required Red Cross certification for firemen, policemen, and lifeguards. First aid gained popularity with actresses and housewives, too, and soon his packed classes lifted him out of the ranks of the working poor.

No longer so fiercely focused on surviving month to month, Jeane—who'd matured into a no-nonsense, law-and-order wife—one day realized that her mother-in-law was supporting herself by swindling people. She wanted Ray to put a stop to it.

He knew better than to poke his nose in his mother's business and refused to discuss the matter. Although Ray wanted nothing more than to put his troublesome mother behind him, Jeane insisted on investigating Inez's cons and kept bringing her to the forefront of their lives. Things got bad between Inez and Jeane, and by extension, between Ray and Jeane.

They argued, separated a few times, and finally divorced.

When World War II broke out, Ray tried to enlist, but his poor eyesight prevented it. He continued teaching and picked up a second job driving an ambulance for the police department. He also volunteered for disaster relief. Manning the radio at a house fire or rowing out to rescue someone in a flood, Ray was quick-thinking, fast-acting, and calm in the face of danger.

And if he wasn't saving people, he was teaching others how to, like the evening in September 1944, when twenty-eight-year-old Scottie walked into his first-aid class.

41

A Delightful Chap

Ray, who depended on streetcars for transportation, had arrived at Huntington Park High that night well before the start of class. He was sitting at the teacher's desk with his newspaper spread out in front of him when Scottie strode into the room. Later, he recalled their meeting.

"She came into the classroom early, and I'm reading the paper, and she asked, 'What are you reading?'"

"And I said, 'I'm reading the ads.'"

"And she asked, 'Why?'"

"I think—this was what was strange for me—I'd never had anyone that was—I don't know if I should use the word 'bold' or not—but you know, she didn't mince around. And I said, 'I don't have a car.'"

"She said, 'You don't have a car!?'"

"I mean, like this was an unheard-of thing. 'No,' I said, I don't have a car.'"

Her forthright manner could have been annoying, but coupled with her blue eyes and blonde curls, it merely piqued his interest. After the class was discontinued for low enrollment—an unusual occurrence for the popular teacher—he suggested Scottie attend his twice-weekly Los Angeles night class at Metropolitan High. It was several miles away, so he said if she could make it there, he'd be happy to see her home safely on the streetcar.

She showed up at the new school and at the end of the night, Ray offered to buy her a sandwich on the way back to Huntington Park. He took her to Mike Lyman's Grill, not exactly on the route, but a trendy place to get a bite to eat. They shared a booth and their stories. Within two weeks, they were seeing each other outside of class. Scottie wrote about him in her diary.

October 3: Ray is much like Sam, same size, mustache, glasses. Forty-one years old and plenty of hair. A delightfully jolly chap.
October 12: Spent the day with Ray. A movie, then Bimimi [a popular bathing pavilion] for swimming, dinner, and home by midnite. I'm growing very fond of him.
October 22: Played tennis singles with Ray today. He is excellent and promises to make me into a good player.

Soon, hardly a day went by that she wasn't hearing from him or meeting him. He knew all the best diners in town and escorted her to the Ice Follies and *Dante's Inferno* at the Biltmore Theater. They spent Sundays bowling or playing tennis, after which they'd take in a movie. In spite of being thirteen years her senior, he was youthful in appearance and manner, a man of boundless energy... and growing ardor.

October 30: Ray phoned today that he had bought me the ring I admired in the jewelry window. He is such a kind man. I certainly like him.
October 31: Tonite after class Ray gave me my ring, a flat top with a chain for the ring part. It is even nicer than in the window.

After a full six weeks of this increasingly serious relationship, Scottie's husband, Sam, rallied and pleaded for a new start. But it was too little too late, and he couldn't compete with his wife's new admirer. Scottie wrote in her diary that Ray *took over the ship in great style.*

She also told her friends—after meeting Ray's sixteen-year-old son—that he'd make good babies.

Junior lived with his mom but attended church with his dad on Saturdays. Scottie, who was interested in all things religious, joined father and son for services a few times at their Seventh-day Adventist Church. She found the congregants nice, even if a bit provincial. Midwestern, is how she described them.

And they didn't seem to know what to make of her, an attractive young blonde in the company of one of the church elders. Her attendance was surely noted and whispered about. Although it's hard to believe he introduced her around as a married woman, people have a way of picking up on those things.

At some point, Ray, probably at the urging of the other elders, had to choose between Scottie and his religion. It did not prove to be a hard choice. The Adventists had provided Ray with a much-needed moral compass during a frightfully immoral upbringing. And through them he had secured respect. But Ray was in love, so he chose Scottie. He resigned his positions and left the church.

In early December, on a weekday when Fred was out of town, Scottie took Ray to meet Mimi. Knowing nothing about Ray's outlaw mother, she was just glad he wasn't Sam.

By then Mimi had realized her daughter wasn't going to be convinced to marry into high society and she looked at Ray for who he was. And there was a lot to recommend him. She approved of his Red Cross work, while his classes for Hollywood actresses reminded her of her own movie days. She liked that he drove an ambulance, the way Fred and her brother had in World War I. She appreciated his well-honed sense of humor, too. He was witty.

Despite her fine and proper heritage, Mimi was never dour. She loved jokes, especially Bob Hope's pithy one-liners, and was adept at reciting them—minus his deadpan delivery. She'd follow the punch line with a laugh and a womanly slap to her knee.

Ray liked Mimi, too, and didn't mind the extra effort occasionally required to keep her happy. Although he only knew his student-turned-girlfriend as Scottie, he quickly learned to call her Gwen in the presence of her mother. If he forgot and referred to her as Scottie, Mimi would stiffen her back and interject curtly, "Scottie? Who's Scottie? I have no idea who you're talking about." She didn't have to do that very often.

Scottie's beau soon passed muster with Fred, too. A confident man, Ray wasn't intimidated by him the way Sam had been. It may have helped, too, that Ray was only three years younger than Fred. And every bit as world-wise.

At Christmas, Ray proposed to Scottie, promising her all the children she wanted. She quickly accepted, went home, and told Sam she wanted a divorce.

Sam didn't fight her. *He doesn't seem upset*, she wrote. But she made that observation before her soon-to-be ex-husband—an accountant, after all—cleaned out the money from their joint bank account, re-deposited it in his own name, and rented a plush office in Los Angeles.

Even though Scottie had helped Sam build up the accounting office over the six years of their marriage, he saw the business as his. After all, he said, not only had he hired her, but she'd since resigned. Accordingly, he took all the upper-end clients—the munitions and war-equipment suppliers—and considered himself reasonably generous when he left her with a few little markets and Greek eateries.

In the end, he agreed to give her, in exchange for several other pieces of jointly owned property, their Huntington Park house. But that old place was all she really wanted. He said he'd vacate it that summer, after the upcoming tax season.

While Scottie was facing financial uncertainty, Ray was adding to his earnings. In January 1945, he hired on as an inspector for the Los Angeles Health Department. It was a good-paying civil service position. Finally able to afford a car, he bought a green

1936 Chevrolet coupe. It was nine years old but in decent enough shape to get them up to Lake Arrowhead for a weekend of hiking and boating.

In early March, Scottie rented a furnished apartment on busy Figueroa Street at Florence and moved out of the home she shared with Sam. Wanting to avoid the lengthy California dissolution process—*Might as well get it over with at once*—she went to Las Vegas to file for what was termed a "quickie" divorce. She arrived in the glitzy gambling town half a year before Jay would make the same trip for the same purpose.

Scottie took up the required six-week residence, worked the cigar stand at the El Rancho Vegas Hotel, and waitressed tables for two dollars a night plus tips. She wrote breezy love letters to Ray, who surprised her with an Easter visit halfway through her stay. They took a leisurely drive in the springtime desert. Scottie, who was partial to the stark landscape with its barely perceptible flowers, declared it wonderful.

But for all her bravado with her new flame, now—with lots of time alone to think about it—she was no longer so sure what she wanted. She was having second thoughts about both the divorce and the upcoming wedding.

On April 17, ten days before the planned nuptials, she wrote in her diary, *I'd have given anything to have had Sam phone and call off the divorce. If I have to go through with it, I hope it isn't legal and will be annulled or voided.*

The following day she recorded, *No dice, the phony divorce went thru without a hitch. Now to face home.*

42

Mrs. Dole

When Scottie returned to Los Angeles, Ray was there to meet her bus. He drove her to lunch at the Biltmore and then on to see Mimi, who was in the midst of planning the wedding reception.

Ray's presence and Mimi's excitement did nothing to ease her apprehension. And it only grew when Ray took her to the health department to meet his colleagues and get their required blood tests. It didn't help that she had a visceral fear of needles. It was a trying day for a woman who liked to be in control. In her diary that evening she wrote she was *leery about the coming wedding.*

Two days later, she was as uncommitted as ever. *Went down to State Street and cooked Sam a squab supper. Got him drunk and me, too. To the apartment and chinned with Ray a bit.*

The following evening, after another round or two of cocktails—this time with a girlfriend—she wrote that she had *decided against a marriage. I just can't face it, I hold Sam too dear still.*

But when she saw Ray the next day—three days before their planned wedding—she didn't mention her misgivings. Perhaps she didn't want to hurt him. Perhaps she changed her mind again. Perhaps she just didn't know what she wanted.

Ray knew what he wanted, though, and it hadn't changed since he'd bared his heart in a letter earlier in the year.

"Oh! Sweetheart, I love you. I feel so helpless when I go to tell you of my love—you say more in one page than I could say in a book.

"Speaking of books reminds me of the one I am reading. It's so fascinating that I first stole a glance at the last chapter. But now

I've started at the beginning. Each chapter becomes more exciting and in a few short months I will have reached the end. And, if it ends as all good books should, you will be in my arms.

"I am so happy when I am with you, and so lonely when I am not. Honey, you say and do so many nice things that I will never be able to catch up with you. I will love you always, darling. I just hope you will never get tired of me telling you about it."

But had she tired of it, now that her pursuit of love was quickly bringing her to the altar? Ray may have been love-struck, but he was always alert to pending disaster and probably felt her pulling away. When faced with the choice of waiting to see how things played out or taking action, he opted for the latter.

That morning he suggested they stop by the health department to see if the results of their blood tests were ready. Amused at her over-eager fiancé, Scottie laughed and said they wouldn't be in yet. After all, it had only been two business days and, being wartime, everything took longer.

Then Ray proposed a deal. If the test results were in, would she marry him that day? Go directly to the courthouse and get hitched? No fancy formalities, no parents, no ruckus.

The idea no doubt appealed to her rebellious nature, particularly the part about circumventing her mother's growing reception plans. But, bottom line, Scottie thought it was a safe bet.

Unfortunately, she hadn't taken into consideration that Ray was a well-liked employee who had more than one friend willing to falsify a form and sign it. Who wouldn't help a good man in a bit of a pinch? If Ray had any qualms about his victory, they were drowned out by the well wishes of his colleagues as they slapped him on the back and sent the couple off to marry.

Ray bought Scottie a yellow rose corsage for her dark wool suit. Then, saying nothing to Mimi, they drove to the courthouse.

That night, April 24, 1945, Scottie recorded in her diary: *To Santa Ana Courthouse and was married by Judge Cameron.*

That was the first sentence. The second was not celebratory. *I will still be single, as no one will know. Don't know why I did it, except for Ray.*

Setting aside her inner turmoil, she reported having a pleasant honeymoon on a ranch near Victorville. *Ray is a very dear person and adores me,* she wrote, as she chronicled two days of horseback riding, swimming, horseshoes, ping-pong and badminton. But when they returned to the city, Scottie asked him to drop her off at her own apartment.

A week later she wrote, *Shame Ray has to live alone, but I don't want to be married, don't consider myself so, and never have. Am Mrs. Dole to Ray's business associates to save him embarrassment.*

Although they were legally husband and wife, Scottie hadn't changed much from the girl who complied with her parents' desires while harboring her own contrary views. Ray may have won her hand in marriage, but marriage was what *she* said it was. What the law said was inconsequential.

Ray, having been raised by a strong-willed mother, knew when to follow cues, and he followed Scottie's. He gave her time to think it over and continued to court her. In early June, she found out she was pregnant.

A baby. Looks like we really are going to have one to love this winter. Ray is thrilled and glows. He's so dear and kind and loving.

A few weeks later, a woeful disappointment . . . she miscarried. Maybe, though, the pregnancy gave her a glimpse of the life she could have with Ray, the one she would never have with Sam.

Her parents wanted her to accept the marriage. When she had first told Mimi and Fred of her wedding, they were mad that they hadn't been included. But as soon as Scottie said she wasn't living with Ray, their anger was replaced with alarm. They liked their new son-in-law, if they could even call him that. They told her she was being unfair to Ray and putting him in an awkward position with his friends and family.

As much as Scottie had hated her parents criticizing her first husband, their championing of her second husband wasn't especially welcomed either. Determined to do things her own way, she ignored them.

In August—the month that marked the dropping of the atomic bomb and the surrender of Japan—Sam finally vacated the home he'd shared with Scottie. More than the filing of any legal papers, it was this departure that sealed the end of their marriage.

With Sam gone, Scottie returned to her Huntington Park house and slowly adjusted to the changes of the past year. At some point in the following weeks—no longer momentous enough to even be noted in her diary—she stopped resisting what Ray had to offer and let him move in.

During the time Scottie was fitfully ending one marriage and starting the other, Mimi was busy with legal concerns of her own. Like her mother, Queeny, and father, George James, Mimi had a special interest in the welfare of babies. In the early 1940s, she and Fred had taken in a series of foster children.

One bright five-month-old, Joné, became special to them. Unlike Gwen and Jane—Herbert's biological daughters—this girl belonged to them equally. A couple of years after her arrival, they applied to adopt her. But by then, Mimi was over fifty, and although she and Fred were granted guardianship, the courts said they were too old to be adoptive parents. It broke their hearts.

Wanting to ensure that Joné would have good parents, Mimi approached a childless couple who had been smitten with the girl from the first time they'd seen her attending church with Mimi. They had the love, financial resources, and Christian Science beliefs Mimi thought necessary to give her a good home. So before

Joné was five, Mimi used her position as guardian to place the girl with them.

The couple applied to adopt Joné and two years later faced off in court against her biological mother, who now wanted the girl back. Mimi didn't think the twice-divorced, former actress was responsible enough to take care of Joné, so she testified before the judge and made it her mission to attend every hearing. After a legal battle that was covered for days in the *Los Angeles Times,* Joné's mother lost her parental rights and the adoption was finalized.

It was a hard-fought victory for Mimi but did little to ease her and Fred's sorrow at not having been able to adopt Joné. Mimi stopped taking in foster children. But having learned something about child welfare laws and the court system, she now devoted herself to promoting needed reforms. She worked tirelessly for the establishment of a law to provide shelter for abandoned babies and was greatly relieved when it passed.

It was in the 1940s, during her years as a foster mother, that she became known as Mimi. Perhaps she chose that moniker as an appropriate name for a temporary mom—not as personal as Mona, as stiff as Mrs. Kramer, nor as presumptuous as Mama. Or maybe it started out as Mémé, the French word for grandma.

In any case, the name held special meaning for her. Mimi had been the nickname of her sister, Mary Kathleen, the one who died as a toddler and was always "looking down from heaven, disappointed" whenever mischievous Mona got in trouble. "Mimi" was unblemished, French, and youthful-sounding.

Mimi never wanted her own daughters to call her Mother in public—early on she asked them to call her Pan, and then it was Peg—so when the time came, she surely wasn't going to let herself be called Grandmother or any variation of it. She would be known to her grandchildren as Mimi, and Fred as Papá.

Despite a precarious start, Scottie's marriage to Ray gave her the babies she wanted. In 1946, their first, Michael Frederic Raymond Dole, was born. Although Mike was given one more name than the average American male, it was the usual amount for a Tate heir and reflected their custom of paying homage to relatives.

Mike's birth occasioned another connection to the past. Years earlier, Mimi had promised to give Queeny's garnets—a Victorian necklace, bracelet, and earrings—to the first of her daughters to have a child. She presented them to Scottie, who was delighted.

But now for the hard work of parenting. From the beginning, Scottie was a hesitant mother. She fed, burped, and changed Mike, but if he persisted in crying after his bodily needs were met, she had no idea why... much less what to do about it.

Mimi, however, was a hands-on grandmother who knew best. A few days after Scottie left the Christian Science maternity home with her newborn, she went up to stay with her mother. *Out at Mother's for the week,* she wrote in her diary. *Am still tired a bit. Her handling Mike will give him a break and teach me a lot.*

He was three weeks old when Scottie took him back home, but a month later she dropped him off at Mimi's and embarked on a postpartum vacation with Ray. In keeping with the British Tate upbringing—in which nannies and grandmothers could do every bit as well as, or better than, their mothers—Scottie didn't show much concern about leaving him. Aside from a note in her diary the first day—*Took Mike to Mother's while we are gone up to Seattle*—and another on the seventh day—*Called home. Mike OK*—the two weeks' worth of entries focused on sightseeing.

43

The Matriarch

I was born a year later and, like my brother, given several names. The first, Raymona-Jane, was to honor family—Ray for my father, Mona for my grandmother, and Jane for my aunt—but no one ever used it. My middle name, Bridget, was chosen for its diminutive, Biddy. That's what they called me, after Mother's best friend from high school, a tall, big-boned woman who from then on was known as Aunt Big Biddy.

My arrival didn't have much effect on my parents' routine. When I was two months old, Mother and Father took another postpartum vacation, this time up to Utah. Throughout the eight-day trip, my brother and I warranted a diary entry only on the first day. *Left Biddy with Mother, and Mike farmed out to Jay.*

For all her desire to have kids, Mother, raised by those from the emotionally distant Victorian era, wasn't nurturing. She delighted in watching us toddle around—and didn't much mind the extra cooking and laundry—but she didn't want to be pulled on, or cried at, or have her work interrupted.

She'd had us close together so we could entertain each other. As soon as I was old enough to walk, each day after breakfast Mother put Mike and me in the backyard and latched the screen door. At noon, she set sandwiches on the back stoop, but apart from potty breaks, she rarely let us in until naptime, a quiet hour during which she'd lie down with a science fiction novel. When it rained, she kept us in our rear-of-the-house bedroom behind a Dutch door she'd installed so she could look in on us without having to risk our escape into the house at large.

Most comfortable at her desk, coffee mug within reach, Mother spent her mornings in front of thick ledger books and an adding machine, her fingers rapidly pressing the keys by touch, her hand instinctively pulling the crank between each entry. *Chik, chik, chik, ka-chunk. Chik, chik, chik, ka-chunk.* At regular intervals she totaled the numbers, producing a swift and satisfying, *ka-chunk ka-chunk*. It was the rhythmic backdrop of our home, the reassuring pulse that reached Mike and me as we played.

Father, who inspected hospitals and jails for the county health department, was home for our five-thirty dinner and then left again to teach first aid.

In spite of their full schedules—or perhaps because of them—several times a year my parents got away for the weekend, and also made vacations out of Father's health department conferences. During these trips, we usually stayed at Mimi's. Mike didn't get "farmed out to Jay" anymore. She no longer lived in California.

Jay and Bob had begun their wedded life in Hawthorne, half an hour from Mimi's, and soon started their own family. Their firstborn, Susan Neville Anderson, arrived three months after Mike. Then, one year behind me came Mona. Her full name was Mona Louise Anderson, but Mona was the important part and a much stronger homage to Mimi than my watered down and never used Raymona.

In terms of grandmotherly affection, Cousin Mona may have had an edge over the rest of us, but any competition for Mimi's attention was short-lived. Mimi was scrupulously fair in her treatment of us—what she bought for one, she bought for all. Besides, it was only a year later that Aunt Jay's family went to Minneapolis and settled near Uncle Bob's folks.

After Aunt Jay left, Mimi's influence over her was restricted to letters, holiday phone calls, and vacation visits. But whenever

Mimi took the train to see Aunt Jay—whom she called Jane—she stayed for weeks at a time and did what she could to infuse the Tate heritage into the Andersons' Midwestern lives.

By then, my mother was known as Scottie to all but Mimi. Although she hadn't changed it legally, she used it for everything. Mother also bucked convention by holding on to her first husband's name. When she married Father, she kept Sam's surname as her middle name—so as not to confuse her bookkeeping clients, she said—and posted a hanging sign in the front yard advertising the accounting office of *Scottie Baer Dole*.

Father didn't seem to mind the *Baer* part, but the conspicuous proclamation that someone named *Scottie* lived in the house behind the sign galled Mimi every time she came to visit ... which wasn't often.

Our home was orderly as long as Mike and I—not yet old enough for school—were corralled out back or in our bedroom. The living room, with its floor-to-ceiling library, was off limits, made clear by a small gate at the hallway entrance. We were fairly well-behaved, but any change in our routine—like being allowed through the gate to greet Mimi—often generated more excitement than we could contain.

On one visit, when Mother and Mimi disappeared into the kitchen, Mike and I climbed the back of the sofa to reach the silver tea caddies displayed on one of the shelves. There were two, and at some point since discovering them, Mike had claimed the short squared-off one and I'd called dibs on the delicate one with a cupid-like figure on top. We'd long since figured out how to open them, and with pennies filched from the top of our parents' dresser, made them into loud metallic rattles.

When Mimi heard the clatter, she came in and saw us jumping on the sofa, whooping and hollering and shaking the tea caddies.

Queeny's tea caddies.

"What in heaven's name are you doing?" Mimi exclaimed as she rushed over and reached for the ornate canisters.

The look on her face silenced us. We handed them to her.

"These are precious," she said. "They're not toys." She turned to Mother. "Gwen, dear, how could you let them play with these?"

"Oh, they weren't hurting them." But Mother's airy response only fueled Mimi's anger.

"How can you have so little regard for family heirlooms? How will Michael and Biddy ever learn to care for fine things?"

Mother didn't answer.

"I didn't give you my mother's tea caddies for them to become children's noisemakers." Mimi put them in her bag and left.

Mother went into her office and closed the door. Mike and I slunk back outside.

My brother and I were better behaved during our Sunday visits to Mimi and Papá's house—a safe haven for all things precious. The brocade-upholstered sofa and chairs, Chinese table lamps, and gold-framed paintings of Renaissance angels quelled any inclination to fool around in the living room. Even her backyard, with its manicured lawn and flowers, was too formal for roughhousing. We weren't dressed for play anyway. Family dinners of Continental cuisine served in the dining room meant a scratchy dress for me and wool shorts for Mike.

Mimi presided over the meal, usually a roast, fresh vegetables, and in keeping with French tradition, an after-dinner salad. As matriarchal as her mother and as exacting as her father, she made use of these weekly gatherings to teach Mike and me manners. Mother was happy to let Mimi deal with decorum and, under our grandmother's tutelage, we demonstrated we could be perfectly well-behaved eating off bone china, holding fine silver, and handling the tiny ivory spoons nestled in antique salt cellars.

On Christmas—a day when Mimi turned her culinary talents to ham or goose—Mother and Father brought us mid-morning, before it was too late for the annual nine-dollar-a-minute transatlantic phone call to her brother in Paris.

"Quick," Mimi always said, "Say hello to your little cousins."

Suddenly shy—and confused by the people on the other end who spoke with accents and sounded more like adults than "little cousins"—I couldn't wait to pass the phone to the next person.

Among the Christmas presents was usually a ball for Mike and a doll for me, but most important to Mimi was the thin turquoise box tied in a white ribbon that she presented to each of us grandchildren. Tucked under tissue paper was an engraved piece of sterling silver: a knife, fork, or spoon. With another one on every birthday—making two utensils a year—Mimi was assured we'd have a complete set of decent tableware by the time we married.

Shortly before dinner was ready, Papá and Father would leave to pick up a couple of Mimi's "dear friends," elderly ladies who had no one with whom to celebrate the holiday. They joined us at Thanksgiving and Easter, too.

Our two-week vacations at Mimi's were less formal, but still included lessons in the social arts. It was, after all, about the time of Queen Elizabeth's coronation. Aside from teaching me how to curtsey and Mike how to kneel for knighthood, she instructed us in the proper use of *Shall* and *Will*, and relentlessly corrected each misused *Can I?* to *May I?* She patiently explained the difference between first and second cousins, and once- and twice-removed. Then she quizzed us on the *first* and *second* and *once* and *twice* of our "little cousins" in France . . . and we had to start all over again.

Most days, though, were less Euro-centered and more typical of Los Angeles in the early 1950s. A youthful grandmother, Mimi was always up well before us and never left her bedroom until her short blond curls were coiffed and she was properly dressed, normally in a crisp white blouse with a flowery skirt and low espadrille wedges. By the time we awoke, she had already picked juicing oranges from the yard and was in the kitchen whistling along with the radio's classical station.

She served breakfast in the kitchen nook. Papá read the newspaper and had shredded wheat cereal and grapefruit, while Mimi made us *Eggs and Soldiers*—soft-boiled eggs propped up in little cups accompanied by buttered strips of toast to dip into the yolks.

If the day was warm, before going to work Papá would set up our canvas wading pool. But Mimi generally took exception to wherever he placed it. She'd complain and he'd have to move it—sometimes more than once—before he'd mutter something, get into his Buick, and drive to his office.

On weekends, Mimi and Papá took us to the ocean at Santa Monica where they went through the same routine with the beach umbrella.

They were more fun when they weren't together. Once Papá took me to the Los Angeles airport and parked at the end of a runway on a street deserted except for aviation buffs waiting to see a Pan Am Clipper take off. We got out and stood by the chain link fence under the flight path. When the plane thundered toward us, I crouched down, terrified it wouldn't clear the fence. But Papá was unafraid. He stood on his toes and stretched out his arms as if trying to touch its underbelly.

Mimi's jaunts were less exhilarating. She regularly took us to Farmers' Market, on Third and Fairfax, where she bought bread, creamery butter, and fresh rhubarb for her pies. Sometimes she treated Mike and me to lunch at one of the little stalls, but she kept an eye on her wristwatch to make sure we were home in time for her fifteen-minute television serial, *Guiding Light*.

Mimi didn't talk much about watching daytime TV—she considered herself above such middle-class pastimes—but she loved the heart-wrenching *Queen for a Day* show and the heart-stopping soap operas. Captivated by the romantic dramas, she composed a story of her own. She told me she was "writing a book in her head," adding a chapter a night, about a man named David. Although Mimi didn't describe him, he was surely handsome and so in tune with the heroine that he'd instinctively know where she wanted him to set up the pool or place the umbrella.

My brother and I, of course, knew little of her longings. She was just our grandmother who seemed to want nothing more in life than to correct our English, bandage our scraped knees, and make our nightly cup of hot milk and honey.

44

Return to Brittany

When she wasn't fulfilling the duties of a housewife or grandmother, Mimi's days revolved around friends and neighbors. Most in her circle were devoted to her, and for good reason. She listened attentively to others and let them know how important they were. Generous with her time and possessions, she passed on jewelry to her women friends just as Aunty Clara—who had died a few years before—had given gold necklaces and bracelets to her.

She also passed on her heartfelt advice. In the same way that she had never been shy about asking for help when she needed it, Mimi didn't hesitate to assist others with their problems. Although never a busybody—she usually waited to be asked her opinion—she gave them her best counsel. She had a clear, decisive manner, characterized by such expressions as "Well, my dear, you simply must . . ." delivered with a certitude that was reassuring to those who sought her guidance.

Many of her friends were people Mimi met through Christian Science. On Sundays, attired in a conservative hat, white gloves, and a stole of Russian sables with their tails clamped in each other's jaws, Mimi attended the fashionable Beverly Hills church. Despite Aunt Jay's earlier attempts to convert Papá, he refused to go except on Easter. But Mimi sat with her friends and after services often took homemade soup to ailing congregants who hadn't been able to join them.

Mimi was particularly solicitous of the elderly and lonely. Her cleaning lady was an older woman with a slight limp who needed Mimi's help more than she needed hers. Sitting together polishing the silver, Mimi always asked after her family. And when Mimi paid her, she'd also give her a bag of groceries or some small thing to brighten her day.

In like manner, Mimi and Papá opened their quaint backyard cottage—the one originally built for Aunt Jay—to Emil, a wizened little man from Switzerland. He lived his last years with them, helping in the garden and around the house.

Perhaps these people reminded Mimi of her Aunty Harrie, Nanny Adele, and the inhabitants of her village in Brittany.

In 1951, when war-torn Europe was up to receiving visitors again, Mimi planned a voyage to France. It had been twenty-two years since her last trip and she was anxious to meet her brother's youngest children—Denis, Monique, Yves, and Patrick—and reacquaint herself with the older ones.

Tied up with work, Papá couldn't go with her. Sailing cabin class—a step below first class but superior to tourist—she crossed alone on the *SS America* the summer she turned fifty-eight.

She disembarked in Le Havre, where she spent time with Rita and her sons, now with wives and children of their own, except for Maurice, who had become a priest. Then Mimi went to Paris, where George and his family had remained after the war.

Mimi and her brother and his twenty-year-old son, Denis, took the train to Brittany. In a letter dated July 2, she wrote to Papá about the trip, reminding him of their own visit to Hillion.

> "George is so well known and loved that his presence is like magic; as soon as he entered anywhere, there was a welcome. He and I are so much alike, and love the same things, that even before I express a wish, somehow he mentions it.
>
> We departed here Friday night on the ten-thirty train for Saint-Brieuc. No sleepers on that train, but we didn't

give a damn. The three of us had seats in a compartment, which we shared with a couple (who had slung a hammock across for their fourteen-month-old baby) and two old maids.

George and Denis dozed, but I was wide awake, afraid of missing a thing. At Rennes we got off, as there was quite a stop, and bought sandwiches and beer and laughed our heads off!

We arrived at Saint-Brieuc at five in the morning in a drizzling rain and, as everything was closed until at least eight, we took a room with a double bed and a single bed at the hotel near the station. George and Denis shared the bigger one, and I threw myself on the small bed and fell asleep immediately.

At seven-thirty I awoke. George and Denis were sound asleep in the other bed, but soon awakened and we packed up (we had scout-bags slung on our backs and later tied to our bikes). We went downstairs for a good breakfast, after which we walked into town.

The rain had stopped and the sun was shining as we went through the familiar streets, and into the little *bazar de quatre sous* where Mummy used to buy us a toy for four *sous* every time she came in town. We entered the market near the cathedral, just as you and I did in 1927.

The *sabots* [wooden shoes], meat, and rolls of cotton are sold at the same spot. Nothing has changed, except for the prices. I bought Jane's *sabots* there for six *francs* then, the same today are 375 *francs!* We bought *des crepes suzette* and a Brittany cake, and walked through the fish market where the women were yelling about their good fish.

Then we pedaled to Yffiniac, down that long hill. On the left we saw the sands where the horse races are run (and were being run as we passed!). In the distance we saw Villa St. George standing as always, dominating the other houses under the shadow of the old Castle de la Noue.

At Yffiniac we called on our friend, Maurice Chalois, who was preparing to leave in his car for Le Val-André (a lovely seaside place where George often goes, somewhat like Dinard and Saint-Malo) to join his wife, daughter and grandchildren. He sees George almost every year. He was delighted to see us and kidded us about a song we all used to sing. They are quite wealthy and hid Rita and Dolphe for a while during the war. We promised him we'd stop at Le Val-André the next day as it is on our way.

We lunched at Yffiniac and cut across the little footpaths towards Villa St. George. It is just as it was, but for the electric lights and radio and butane, and also a spring discovered in the garden. It was wonderful to be there.

We ran upstairs and found where George had carved his name in the stone when he was a kid. The old ladder, which reaches up to the loft, still leans against the house! George and I once prided ourselves on the ability to walk up and down that ladder without holding on, much to our mother's fear.

We rode our bikes to the familiar fountain and up the hill from whence we could see Villa St. George and the bay, where the yellow gorse looks like pieces of gold from a distance. And we even saw a skylark, one and only one, just as we did when children!

At Hillion we went straight to St. Nicolas, which is now a modern inn. Bombs destroyed the thirteenth century building and an ugly hotel is in its place. But of course it has every comfort—bathrooms, toilets (remember when you were there?), electricity, radios, dining rooms, and modern beds. George and Denis had a double, and I a single. We reached there about two. After registering, and being waylaid by the village folks who recognized us, we went to our dear little cabin—you remember on the rocky point where we took the movies? Everything is much the same, except that the barbed wire the Germans strung all around the cliffs still remains. We took off our shoes and waded, threw stones, and picked up shells just as we did years ago.

We came home by the lovely old house by the sea… and stopped to see my little sister's grave. Then we had supper, after which we called on my school friend, Marie Campion, who was so nice. Her brother paints beautifully, and I'd give anything to have one of his paintings of the Hillion church.

The next morning we all three went to the seven o'clock service and sat in our old family pew, still with its door. I tell you, many memories went through me. I saw women I had known when a child, now gray-haired and old, and I wondered if I might suddenly open my eyes and find myself back again with my mother and father beside me! When George walked down the aisle alone to the altar for communion, I cried, remembering we had walked down that very aisle together for our first communion."

Mimi returned that summer with eight pieces of luggage full of treasures from Brittany and France. She brought back several children's outfits, complete with woolen berets, for Mike and me. With his hair slicked down and mine curled, we self-consciously posed while Mimi took photos to send back to our "little cousins."

45

Sebec Lake, Maine

A couple of years later, there was another grandchild to include in Mimi's photos. Father, almost fifty, and Mother, thirty-six, had thought our family was complete—a boy and a girl, both of us finally in school. Then Mother, finding herself queasy all the time, discovered she was pregnant again. In early March 1953, my baby brother was born.

Father wanted to name him Jonathan Christian, but Mother favored Timothy Xavier. So they settled on Jonathan Christian Xavier. When they brought him home, though, Mother said he looked like a Timothy, so—birth certificate be damned—that's who he was.

My parents, Scottie and Ray, with Mike, Tim and me in 1953.

Despite his unexpected arrival—at the beginning of Mother's hectic tax season, no less—Timothy was the child she enjoyed the most. In her diary, she wrote: *Mike and Biddy wrassle all day and nite until I'm almost witless. Timothy sleeps well and is pleasant.*

She kept his playpen in her office, where she was as busy as ever with her ledger books. But by then she'd expanded her scope beyond accounting. Like Father, she taught first aid at night, and the previous year had been named co-chair of the regional branch of the Red Cross.

Shortly after Tim's first birthday, Mother ventured into local politics. Committed to improving Huntington Park, she ran for City Council. Her values had changed little from the time when, at seven, she got a policeman to stop the junkman from whipping his horse. It's not known what 1954 "city junkmen" she thought needed reining in, but with age, her belief in her ability to make a difference had only increased.

Although I envied my friends with moms who devoted their days to baking and sewing, when I saw Mother's name and photo in the paper, I was proud. I didn't see the next article that announced she came in last. If it bothered her, she didn't show it. She said it was the city's loss, not hers, and never mentioned it again.

At about that time, my parents hired a live-in helper, Virginia. Soon Mother turned her office into a bedroom for herself and Father, and rented workspace in an accounting firm several blocks down the street.

In 1955, with our family now truly complete, Mother decided to take us to Maine to meet her birth father, Herbert Hayford. They had written letters back and forth, but she hadn't seen him in two decades. Mike and I, nine and eight years old, had never heard of him. As for the trip, all we'd been told was that we were driving to Boston. But after pulling out of the driveway in our Ford station wagon, Mother said we'd spend a few weeks at Sebec Lake with our Grandpa and Grandma Hayford.

Grandpa was thin and fit and had lively brown eyes, while Grandma was plump and had fluffy hair. Aunt Joann, a student at

Principia, a Christian Science college, worked as a summer lifeguard at the nearby beach. Aunt Carol was pretty but quiet.

The lake was so clear I could see schools of fish swimming under the dock, and the pine trees, although no good for climbing, smelled like Christmas. The night was filled with stars, as well as the occasional ghostly wail that Grandma assured me was only a harmless loon—even while Grandpa raised a brow and said it was the Lady of the Lake.

But they both agreed the woods were full of bears. One day Grandma gave Mike and me metal pails and took us to pick blueberries. But when we got to her favorite berry bushes, we saw a black bear already there and helping himself. Grandma stood still, put a finger to her lips, and hustled us back down the trail.

We met our great-grandmother, Rose, when Grandpa brought her to the camp for a visit. A little woman leaning on a cane, she wore a polka-dot dress, a small church-going hat, and a white necklace. At ninety-one, she couldn't see well enough to tell me from Mike, but she was nice.

Grandpa invited her to stay with them the following month, but she said she wouldn't until they moved the privy closer to the house. Later my cousin Joe told me Rose was fearless and once even set her own broken arm. But she was smart, too, certainly smart enough to avoid the rocky path to the outhouse.

Sebec Lake was heaven for a city kid. Rocks to climb, a raft to swim out to, a boat to row. Grandpa took us in his motorboat to a shoreline strewn with huge boulders, and then to a lakeside store where he bought us real moccasins. At dusk each evening, he had Mike lower the flag from the camp's pole and fold it into a triangle, and he taught us both how to choose a good skimming stone and skip it across the water.

But the most important thing we learned while staying on the shore of a deep lake—over a hundred feet down in the middle—

was how to swim. Aunt Joann taught Mike and me to dog paddle and tread water. Tim, a toddler with a mop of blond hair, was too young for lessons, so Mother played with him in the pebbled cove that she herself had splashed in as a child.

One day when Grandma and Mother were in town shopping, Grandpa took Father and us three kids out on his sailboat.

Mike, who was more cautious than I, looked nervous as we pulled away from the dock. "What if it tips over?" he asked.

"Don't worry," said Grandpa. "I've been on this lake all my life and haven't tipped over yet."

At nine, Mike already knew there was a first time for everything, and he clung tightly to the edge of the boat.

Half a mile out, Grandpa asked Father to take the tiller while he fiddled with the sail. Suddenly the heavy boom swung around. "Coming about!" Grandpa yelled. "Watch out!"

We ducked so we wouldn't get hit in the head, but the boat started to roll. Grandpa tried to correct course, but it was too late. We were all thrown into the water.

Mike and I swam up to the surface and grabbed onto the overturned hull. Tim, though, went straight down. Father dove after him, got a hold of him by his hair, and brought him up. Tim, coughing and sputtering, looked surprised.

Father grasped the side of the boat with one arm and held Tim in the other. He bounced him a bit, repeating, "You're okay, kid . . . you're okay."

Mike, his fear now vindicated, was screaming bloody murder, which got the attention of a man on the other side of the lake.

The far-shore dweller pulled up in his motorboat, hauled us on board and took us back to our dock, all the while saying he couldn't believe that Grandpa, of all people, had turned turtle.

As soon as we got to camp, Grandpa changed and went out to get someone to help him tow the boat in and right it.

We dried off in the house. By then Father was laughing about how he'd lost a shoe, but despite diving down for Tim, his glasses and hat had stayed on his head. We put our wet shoes and socks on the back porch and laid our dripping shirts and pants on the railing. Father, who changed Tim's clothes, hung them by the potbelly stove in the living room.

When Mother and Grandma returned and approached the porch, they saw the clothes drying and knew something had happened. Mother quickly noted the men's things, and Mike's and mine, but she didn't see Tim's. She rushed inside.

While Mother hugged Tim, Mike and I—both vying to tell the story first—shouted over each other about the boat flipping bottom-side up and Timmy almost drowning and Father saving him. I'd never seen Mother cry, but her eyes got red and watery that day.

Grandpa, who was proud of his sailing skills, wanted it on the record that the capsizing wasn't his fault. That night he wrote in the camp journal: *Went sailing and, with Ray at the tiller, we all got wet. Bill Levensalor came out and got our boat. Nothing lost but moccasins.*

Grandma added a note of her own: *The girls had gone to town for the morning... proving that you can't leave these men alone. None seemed perturbed at the dunking. Timmy's description of it was in one word—Wet—much repeated. Biddy said she nearly lost her bubble gum.*

One morning before we left for home, Grandpa said he wanted to show me something in the boathouse. He pulled an old canoe paddle down from the wall.

"This was your Mimi's," he said. He rubbed the smooth wood with his sun-browned hands. "She and I went boating on the lake together all the time." He smiled at me and winked. "You tell your grandmother I'm keeping this for her. She can come back here for it any time she wants."

I was thrilled to be chosen the bearer of this message. Unaware of Mimi's bitter divorce, I was sure she'd want to know he was saving her paddle for her.

It wasn't until we started back that Mother said our vacation in Maine was a secret. We could talk about our on-the-way stops at Washington D.C. and Coney Island, or our on-the-way-back visit to Boston and Niagara Falls, but nothing about Sebec Lake. She didn't worry about Tim saying anything—he wasn't yet making sentences—but she told Mike and me that Mimi and Papá were never to know.

"Why not?" I asked.

"Mimi doesn't like Grandpa and Grandma," Mother said.

"Why not?"

"Oh, that's just the way she is, dear."

Sensing that I'd keep up the questions, Father jumped in. "Don't worry about it, kid. Just do as you're told."

Mimi had thought she'd put the whole Herbert Hayford thing behind her in 1936 when she reconciled with Papá and brought her girls back from the East Coast. But Mimi had underestimated Mother's determination to keep her father in her life.

And, clearly, Mother underestimated Mimi's ability to ferret out secrets. Mimi had a way of detecting things, and in this case it wasn't hard since Mother and Father had stopped to visit George Paine on Maine's Sutton Island, just south of Bar Harbor. Mimi knew Mother wouldn't have gone all that way and not driven the extra three hours to get to Herbert's place. All Mimi needed was confirmation.

A few days after we got back to California, Mimi dropped by. Mother was still at work, but Mimi said that was okay, since I was the one she wanted to talk to. She came into my room, sat on the bed, and took my hand.

"Now Biddy, dear," she said. "A little bird told me you went to Lake Sebec and met the Hayfords and had a marvelous time. Tell me all about it."

I wouldn't have said anything if she hadn't made it clear she already knew. But relieved it was no longer a secret, I delivered Grandpa's message about Mimi's canoe paddle and blabbed everything else she wanted to know.

Mimi said she was glad I had a nice time at the lake. Then we heard Mother arrive home. Mimi said that the next time I came to stay with her, she'd tell me things I should know about Herbert and Tish, but for now she had things to discuss with Mother.

What had been guaranteed to cause resentment soon developed into something worse. When fifty-five-year-old Papá found out about our visit with the Hayfords, he had a heart attack.

It may have had nothing to do with our visit to Maine, but Mimi, who was shaken by Papá's brush with death, said it did. She blamed Mother, who refused to be made responsible. After all, Mother complained privately, Mimi herself had sent her and her sister to see their father twenty years earlier.

But maybe Papá had become a bit inured to Mimi's doings and didn't feel them as keenly as he did his daughters'. Although he seemed to know he hadn't become the husband Mimi wanted, Papá was proud of being the dad Herbert hadn't been.

Papá stayed in the hospital a while, and then Mimi took care of him at home. She was as supportive and protective of him as she had been during his breakdown after their wedding. It was a quiet time of remembering how deeply they cared for each other. Setting aside their differences, they focused on the future. At her urging, he began to take life easier and vowed to retire early. He said he'd quit work in five years.

In spite of Jay's fears for Papá's health, she also wanted to visit her birth father. As she had gotten older, she wished she'd given him more of a chance to be a dad the summer she was fifteen. Hearing from Mother about our trip only increased her desire to meet him and see what she thought of him now.

But no matter how curious she might be, she didn't want to risk hurting Papá, the man she still called her *real dad*. So the next summer, she told her parents she'd be vacationing in Colorado and gave a friend a series of prewritten letters to mail to Mimi from the Rocky Mountain state. The ruse worked. Jay and Bob—with Susan, nine, and Mona, eight—flew to Maine and enjoyed an undetected vacation at Sebec Lake.

Jay recognized things she and her father shared in common—faith in Christian Science, a bit of restless energy, and love of their stringed instruments—she for her guitar and he for his mandolin. Bob joined in the fun on the living room's old pump organ.

The next year, Jay and Bob had a third daughter. They named her Wendy, a shortened form of Gwendolyn. Having established a life two thousand miles from Mimi, Jay was more relaxed in her mothering this time around and delighted in her last baby the same way Mother delighted in Tim.

In 1959, Jay's family returned to Maine, taking two-year-old Wendy to meet her grandpa. They had a good time boating and swimming. Herbert made his acclaimed root beer, too, and whenever the phone rang, he had eleven-year-old Mona answer it with a sassy, "Duffy's Tavern and Duffy ain't here."

Jay was glad she'd gone to see him, but it didn't alter her first allegiance to Papá. She was careful to keep both trips a secret, and Mimi and Papá never found out.

46

The Grand Tour

After forty years of dedicated service to Seamless Rubber, Papá retired. He was sixty. Traveling was one of the things he and Mimi both enjoyed, so they planned a year-long trip through Europe.

But first, in July 1961, they sold their Cheviot Hills home. This was easy for Papá, who saw the sale as a practical matter, but hard for Mimi. She loved her home and once wrote of "dressing it as I would a child, with every lovely charming thought. I cannot visualize my treasures in another place." It was with a heavy heart that she put their things in storage.

When they arrived in Paris, Mimi and Papá bought a brand-new Peugeot. The beginning of their trip, however, was less about driving to famous sites and more about reconnecting with family. And saying goodbye to one of its members.

Their first stop was Le Havre, to see Mimi's sister, Rita, who was seventy-one and dying of liver failure. Even though they had not been close growing up, the ensuing years had smoothed over the spats of childhood and Mimi was eager to see her.

> "We talked about all our good times, and as she didn't know she was passing, we made plans together for later on because I wanted her happy to the end."

Mimi was grateful to have a couple of weeks with Rita but upset by the rituals of her sister's Roman Catholic funeral, which she described in a letter to Mother and Jay.

> "Yesterday was Aunty Rita's funeral, a miserably sad day, and one I shall not soon forget. The entire affair was a farce and mockery to a loving God. Priests chanted in Latin—no one understood a word—and said prayers, very few, in French, in which they implored Jesus and the virgin, *not God*, to keep my sister from eternal damnation in hell. Then they threw so-called holy water on the coffin, which the men almost dropped on their way down the steps. It was very bad, and I am still under a sense of shock from it all."

Perhaps more upsetting than the religious rites and the coffin-fumbling was the depressing realization that her generation was passing away. A sibling's death is a stark reminder of one's own mortality. Mimi still had her brother, but it was a sad time for the two of them.

> "George and I stood together knowing it represented the closing chapter to our family because he and I alone remain of our generation."

Mimi and Papá visited Hillion, but with her sister's suffering fresh before her—and without her brother there to bring back the happy times of earlier years—she was more mindful of the outer changes. She wrote unhappily of the modern inn with its bland cuisine—"food cooked to tickle the palate of the peasant"—and of the dull contemporary houses that replaced the traditional ones bombed by the Nazis.

Although the farmers were happy to enjoy the conveniences of the twentieth century, Mimi missed the old days when life in Brittany was more picturesque.

“The peasantry no longer wear quaint starched caps, gay colored aprons and wooden shoes, nor ride to church on Sunday in a two-wheel cart or on horseback. Today they wear our clothes and shoes, have bobbed hair, ride expensive bicycles or cars, listen to plays and news on the radio, and see things on television.”

The least appealing facts of country life, however, had not changed in the decade since her last visit to Hillion.

“There are, of course, signs of the good old days. Men and boys still relieve themselves against the church wall or by the side of a road. When the wind is 'right' (as it was last night) one's nostrils are filled with the smell of cows, pigs and horses, because farms still abound around here. As cows pass along the village streets, they drop great pancakes where one can step in them. This is somewhat disconcerting for us gentle folk who are not used to nature in the raw. The flies are fierce, huge, and persistent. And although much is said about them, nothing is *done* about them, so our meals are a constant battle.”

Mimi took great pleasure, however, in their Moncontour stop at the chateau of the Countess de Bélizal. Queeny's dearest friend had long since passed away, but her daughter-in-law and granddaughter, who was close to Mimi's age, still lived there.

“We drove up to the beautiful old place, and as soon as I said who I was, the granddaughter, Genevieve, ran out and recognized me at once. We were invited in for drinks, and Dad had a chance to see the splendid interior. There is even a garage which holds ten to twelve cars!”

From France they were off to other lands. Mimi wrote long letters chronicling their daily activities, while Papá imparted his observations on postcards, the backs of receipts, and once on a piece of sturdy toilet paper. But he also wrote serious letters in which he shared his views on political affairs. He kept up with the newspapers—particularly articles concerning the Cold War—and wanted to see the Berlin Wall.

Construction on it had started only three months earlier, just after midnight on August 13, 1961. When the people of Berlin woke up that morning, they were caught on whichever side they had fallen asleep the night before, with their connecting phone wires cut. People from East Berlin couldn't go to their jobs in West Berlin. Families, friends, and lovers were separated for what would turn into decades.

Papá and Mimi made the drive to West Berlin—surrounded by communist-controlled East Germany—and entered the Soviet Zone. They slogged through an hour of red tape and passed between two checkpoints manned by scowling police with Tommy guns before being admitted.

They found a hotel for the week and the next day went to the Berlin Wall. Although it hadn't grown into its final twelve-foot-tall height—and did not yet include its inner barrier and broad no-man's-land—it was still brutally effective. Eight people, including an eighty-year-old woman, had already been killed trying to cross over it.

"Everything you've read about it is true," Papá wrote. "Barbed wire, bricked up buildings, the six-foot solid wall topped by wire and behind it the East German police. We cruised through several streets and made numerous stops. We were allowed within about twenty-five feet. I climbed several clumps of ruins to look over. In contrast with the lively scene *behind* us, it was dead looking. We saw an older woman with a young couple and a baby standing on ladders, waving and waving, holding the baby high for someone on our side to see."

By Christmas, Papá and Mimi were at her brother's in cheerier Paris. In the same way that Mimi was comfortable having long-term visitors in her own home in America, she was a relaxed guest with her family in France.

My mother, who greatly valued her alone-time, wrote to Mimi and asked how it was working out, spending weeks on end with one relative or another.

> Being with the family, or kinfolk as you say, never troubles me. I feel absolutely at ease with them because I can do as I please. It is funny that after all these years the feeling of 'home' with my family is the same. It is a relief to be able to say anything, knowing you are accepted and understood. No 'airs' are put on, your good and bad are recognized and you are still loved. It is much the same as a mother and her children, they know each other's frailties, but they love each other regardless.

Revitalized by loved ones but chilled by the Parisian winter, Mimi and Papá headed to the warmer climate of Spain. Mimi, however, didn't find the country to her liking. The lack of sanitation and the repressive politics grated against her sensibilities. She blamed General Franco's dictatorial regime and the Roman Catholic Church for keeping the farmers in poverty.

> Taxes to the government and the church keep these poor ignorant peasants with little hope of gain. What money they derive from marketing, taking their produce to town on the backs of overburdened donkeys, is hardly adequate for more than mere existence. Consequently,

they have no way to better themselves. The rich pocket their money and are content to keep the peasants ignorant and poor."

Mimi didn't think that the farmers' goats, which were herded through the villages, were much better off.

"The male, who wanders among thirty-odd females, has a contraption hanging under his belly shaped like a plate, and every time he jumps on a female, the damn plate forms a wall between the 'active part' of his lovemaking and the mark he is shooting at. Of course, this is very frustrating for the poor old buck, and I imagine there are moments when, for him, life is pretty futile."

Mimi and Papá planned a side trip to Morocco and headed down to Gibraltar to board the ship. But while driving along the stunning seaside cliffs of Spain, their steering suddenly went out. The car careened toward a precipitous drop.

A rock barrier by the road was the only thing that prevented them from going over the edge. Although neither of them was badly hurt—Mimi's knee was gashed and her arm bruised—the accident forced them into a lengthy stay in a country that Mimi was already anxious to leave.

"I cannot go into the details of our outrageous treatment by the police and a bastard of a judge. The complete helplessness of not knowing the language, the hours and days of being told *mañana,* the confiscating of papers, the car in a filthy garage where anything not nailed down is stolen. The rock was moved two inches, but *we had to pay for it,* one hundred and fifty pesetas!

> We got in touch with our Consul, who is indignant at the third-degree tactics of the police. When, as strangers and citizens of a friendly nation, we were in need of help and completely innocent of any wrongdoing... we were treated as criminals and our papers taken (they still have them). I am certain there is going to be action. I shall personally write Franco (I mean it!) and tell him I think that judge should be castrated. I never want to set foot in this country again!"

Much as she hated the place, they were stuck there. Finally they arranged to have the car towed to Gibraltar. "Thank God we got permission to take it on British soil," she wrote, "away from these fools and barbarians!" But even the mechanics at the repair shop in Gibraltar said the work could take three or four months.

Mimi and Papá decided to wait it out in a little fishing village about eight miles outside Malaga, on the southern coast of Spain. Several times a day, a train went into town, giving them a way to get mail and necessities, but for the most part, Mimi stayed put at their hotel not far from the shore. Papá, who loved the ocean, had made sure they had rooms with a good view of the sea. For hours at a time he gazed out at the water, which Mimi, even in the face of her slump, had to admit was lovely.

> "From our door we see the blue Mediterranean, and on a clear day, Morocco. The small fishing boats start out in the morning and, at sunset, it is a sight to see them return with their catch of fish and, the breeze permitting, their small sails unfurled. Or, on a calm evening, their chugging engines pushing them thru the water. We sometimes walk up along the cliffs where an ancient watchtower stands. From there we can look out to sea towards the town of

Malaga. At night it is especially interesting. The lights gleam across the water like so many silver ribbons."

Still wanting to see Morocco, they decided to take a plane, but unusually strong winds on their return flight made for a landing so harrowing Mimi didn't think they'd survive.

All in all, their stay in Spain was stressful. Mimi was sick much of the time, and then increasingly anxious about small festering sores that appeared on her face. Nevertheless, she refused to see a Spanish physician, preferring to hold off until they returned to France, where she trusted the doctors.

Two months later, they drove back to Paris. Mimi found a dermatologist and her skin cleared up. Papá sold the patched-up Peugeot and bought a Volkswagen Beetle. It was springtime, and the two of them took a much-needed rest in "le gai Paris."

"I am better, and have put on some weight. I was very thin when I returned from Spain, and was extremely depressed, but the delayed spring is finally here and it is quite impossible to contemplate shooting oneself when the boulevards are streaming with lighthearted people. Small tables shaded by gay umbrellas line the sidewalks, and people sit at them and drink delicious wines and give you the glad eye as you pass!

The Bois de Boulogne, where we love to go and sit on the grass under the trees, is beautiful. The tulips are in full bloom and the wild fruit trees breathtaking in their brilliance. Bright hats are appearing, although most women now go without hats. This fashion, I believe, was brought over by the American tourists, as gloves and hats go with a well-dressed French woman. I personally love to wear a hat, and usually do!"

47

Fate, Who Picked Me

While Mimi was relaxing at her brother's home, Mother was busy with her annual income tax work. It was always a fend-for-yourself time at our house, but this year Mother seemed more distant than usual. She had received word from Grandma Tish that Grandpa, seventy-one, was seriously ill.

Herbert had diabetes but, in keeping with Christian Scientist doctrine, declined medical care. Instead, he relied on church practitioners and prayer. He was getting worse, though, and Grandma thought Mother should know.

By then a freshman in high school, I lived most days in a world of my own. But early one morning I heard the phone ring, and when I walked into the kitchen a few minutes later, Mother was doubled over and crying so hard she couldn't talk. Father helped her to their bedroom. Then he came out and told us Grandpa had died and we should get our own breakfast and go to school.

The next day I asked Mother if she'd written to Mimi about Grandpa's passing. She said she didn't want anything to do with it, but I could write to her if I wanted.

In the months following our visit to Maine, Mimi had told me how Grandpa had cheated on her with Grandma Tish and how it tore the family apart. But despite her long-held bitterness, I didn't think Mimi would like to be kept in the dark about his death.

I tried to keep my letter short and straightforward. I don't remember exactly how I worded it, but I guess it was something to the affect that Grandma Hayford had let us know that Grandpa had died, along with the date and cause. I asked if she'd heard.

> "Yes, I received news of Mr. Hayford's death, both by newspaper clipping and a letter from New Haven. I think the paper should have specified that *two* of the daughters were from a previous marriage. I heartily hope this will end the nonsense of *Grandma from New Haven*. She is *not* your grandmother and I deeply resent her usurping this privilege, which can only be applied to your father's or mother's parents, or as an honor to a dear aged friend. Mrs. Hayford is neither of these."

By the end of June, Mimi and Papá had recuperated from their travails in Spain and were en route to the Edinburgh Festival in Scotland when they happened upon the town where George and Henrietta had lived as newlyweds. Mimi wrote a friend about it.

> "As we were nearing York, we came by a town marked Bawtry. I said to Fred, 'Why that must be where Bawtry Hall is located!' So we inquired and sure enough, it was well known and we were directed to it. I am sure you have seen that lovely etching of Bawtry Hall in my front room. It hung over the 'Victrola.'
>
> Anyway, we drove up to the gates and a guard said it had been taken over by the British High Command, and before I could go *near* Bawtry Hall, I would have to see its commanding officer, who proved to be a charming gentleman. I told him I was here from the States, and wanted to visit my ancestral home and perhaps take a photo of it.
>
> He said this wasn't allowed due to the type of secret military work going on there. He saw my disappointment, though, and said he would make an exception and have a guard take us to the front of Bawtry Hall, where he would even allow two photos!"

The manor now served as the Strike Command Headquarters for the Royal Air Force, but the exterior and surroundings looked much as they had a century earlier.

> The spacious grounds are shaded by large old trees, with beautiful gardens heading down to a lake. I imagine that my grandparents walked by the water with their baby, as my father's sister, the first born, made her debut here in 1848. I left that beautiful place quite emotionally stirred, I assure you. I almost wondered if voices, long since mute, could be heard above the excited beating of my heart!

Although that was the emotional highlight of Mimi's visit to Bawtry Hall, she was also interested in what the officer had to say about the town's history.

> He told me it was at Bawtry that the Pilgrim Fathers assembled to make their plans before sailing for Plymouth, and it was from Bawtry that they received aid! All this, he said, is in the Hall of Records in the town of Bawtry, as well as the birth records of my family!

It was already too late in the day to visit the archive, but Mimi marveled at "Fate, who had picked me" to look up and notice the Bawtry sign that day.

As excited as she was, Mimi may not have remembered that Herbert Hayford was descended from quite a few of the Pilgrim families. Hopefully it didn't come to mind. She would have taken no pleasure in thinking that Herbert's ancestors may have strode through the town of Bawtry more than a century before hers did.

48

Facing the Ocean

Mimi and Papá returned from Europe by freighter since they were bringing their Volkswagen with them. He was more of a big car man—he favored Buicks and planned to buy a new one when they got home—but she wanted the Beetle for herself.

Arriving in New York on October 1, 1962, they drove up and down the coast to visit friends, and then went to Minnesota for Thanksgiving and Christmas with Jay and Bob and their girls: Susan, sixteen; Mona, fourteen; and Wendy, five.

Jay, Susan, Wendy, Bob and Mona in 1961.

Just as Jay had blossomed in music school and the military—out from under her mother's watchful eye—she flourished in Minneapolis, where she'd established herself as Jay Anderson, a local musician.

Softly strumming the guitar, she sang poignant ballads about shepherds, maidens, and gentle woodland creatures. She entreated her listeners to *Come away with me* to a world of green valleys, meadowlarks, and love. But her sweetest song was one that told of her affection for her daughters long before they were even born. It ended with the refrain: *Now I must tell you, My dreams have come true, Children, my darlings, Those dreams were you.*

In a rich voice that resonated with confidence, she performed on local radio and TV stations. Always stylish, she'd made a few changes. She still sported a carefully penciled-in beauty mark, but her dark, tied-back hair had given way to soft, platinum-blonde curls. She was slender and stunning. The cameras loved her.

Bob had also done well for himself. After working an engineering job at Honeywell, he and a few colleagues set out on their own and formed a profitable electronics firm. He and Jay moved into a large house near the university and started hosting international students, mostly older doctoral candidates. Their home became a hub of intellectual and cultural exchange with people from around the world.

Jay developed a special affinity for the Japanese scholars who lived with them. They were clean and quiet. Although she had heretofore known the Japanese as ruthless warriors, she began to see them as members of an ancient and refined civilization. One guest was, indeed, the son of an Imperial Court artist. His social graces, cultural sensibilities, and artistic view of life echoed her own delicate esthetics. Jay was soon taken with all things Japanese and set about learning the language.

When she finally published her pre-war carol, *Softly, Softly, Fell the Snow*, she no longer saw an embattled *world dark as the night*. Rather, she answered the call of her last stanza—*Loosen all the hearts that are bound*—and arranged for the song's royalties to benefit the atomic bomb survivors of Hiroshima.

The contribution was a noble gesture but didn't raise much money. The world of music was not very profitable for those only moderately successful. So Jay, who wanted to visit Japan, took a job as a nurse's aide and started to bank her paychecks.

It was into this busy household that Mimi and Papá came to stay. They were happy to be with Jay and her family, but their visits were never without tension. Through the years, Mimi and Papá had competed for Jay's sympathy, each wanting her to see their side of any given argument. Now the two of them unpacked their disagreements as easily as they unpacked their clothes.

Having suffered their quarrels as a child, Jay had made sure her own home was free of noisy parental squabbles. If she and Bob disagreed, they handled it quietly. So the girls, especially Wendy who hadn't spent much time with Mimi and Papá, didn't know why they would be dancing one minute—smiling as they quick-stepped to *The Lion Sleeps Tonight*—and shouting and slamming doors the next.

But it was probably hardest on Jay, who was already juggling the needs of her family, lodgers, and hospital patients. She was the dutiful daughter who tried to keep both parents happy.

After Christmas, Mimi and Papá headed to Southern California and their thoughts turned to the task of finding a new home. En route, Mimi wrote to a friend.

> " We are anxious to be back, the question of whether to buy or rent has been discussed, and to date renting seems ahead. Fred just can't see buying a house, and though *I do*, I am afraid, for the sake of peace, I shall have to accept things as *he* sees them. But I will have the 'say' as to what and where! "

Once in Los Angeles, she decided on a pleasant downstairs apartment in Westwood. Because it was only a couple of miles from their old house, they returned to the same friends and church, but this time they resided in less space. They still had their own bedrooms to retire to, but it wasn't like it had been before, when Papá could retreat into his well-equipped garage workshop, or Mimi into the cozy den. Their year abroad, however, had accustomed them to closer living quarters.

The hiatus had also provided a good transition from employment to retirement for Papá, who'd spent much of his career on the road. Now home all the time, he was at a bit of a loss. He had his interests—with Cold War books newly added to his library of war pictorials—but after decades in corporate sales, a work-free lifestyle was an adjustment. Mimi kept him busy socializing with old friends, new neighbors, and people they had met abroad.

Then, in July of 1963, Papá had another heart attack. He was hospitalized for a week at St. John's in Santa Monica. After his discharge, Mimi put all her effort into nursing him back to robust health. She watched his diet, oversaw his medications, and with the *Key to the Scriptures* as close as her nightstand, prayed for him. Again, he recovered.

A year later, in the summer of 1964, they once more ventured out to Minnesota. Of all the people he loved, Papá was happiest in the presence of his youngest girl, who doted on him. Like many dads and daughters, they had a close relationship.

Mimi and Papá were back in Los Angeles when, just before Thanksgiving, he had a third coronary. He pulled through but was noticeably slower and more tentative in his movements. He looked older than his sixty-four years. And now if the two of them left the house at all, Mimi had to do the driving.

On Christmas Day, she made her traditional dinner and we joined them, but it was a quiet occasion with none of their special guests. Papá was dressed in his usual tie and festive red shirt, but he was thin and pale and didn't say much over the holiday table.

At the beginning of January, he wrote to Jay, starting out with, "This, my first letter of the New Year, goes to you..."

"This summer's visit with you was wonderful. And your treatment of me was so much of *what I rarely get*. I love you for it. Even then, I was under wraps for I know Mother well enough, and since have heard veiled remarks about favoritism.

"Mother has been dominant in her way so many years she has never known the real 'me.' She is often surprised to hear I have 'opened up' to others, not realizing I cannot and probably never will to her, for she finds it difficult to separate mere discussion, or even conversation, from the personal. Her life is so based on her inner feelings, the Victorian creed of her father, and memories of her childhood... She has no other standard.

"However, we know she is an unusual woman, a fine character, and generous. Certainly so toward her friends, and feelings toward her family (although not always toward her husband, who feels she takes some of her resentments out on him).

"I never thought, or knew how, to confide in her during my working years. I was anxious to avoid arguments. Perhaps that is the fate of marriage. How can you take a male and female, with diverse interests and ways of thinking, and expect them to agree?"

Papá then went on to chide his daughter for buying them an expensive writing pen and a meat cutter for Christmas. "One simple, nice present, not over seven or ten dollars would be just as gratefully received," he wrote. He compared her desire to buy them nice things with my mother's indifferent gift-giving.

"Your sister has no such compunction. She presents us with some 'doodad,' usually of minor value, and *she* could afford more. She laughs and makes a big story out of it, and gets just as much thanks, I assure you.

"She also wastes little affection (outwardly) on us, though I must confess she has come five or six times to see me since I have been ill. I believe she 'loves' me, even if rarely with great outward enthusiasm. Of course, she explains that by saying she rarely shows it with her own family (and observation confirms this). She is a warm-hearted girl, but outside of a few romanticisms and queer ideas (space ships, and some odd religion or other) is very much possessed of herself. . . .

"I would like nothing better this moment than being allowed to sit around your little sunroom and look out on the snow. But you are far away and choose your own way of life, and it's a bit late to quibble about it, tho I still wish you lived nearer . . . .

"I am getting along these days, staying still most of the time. This physical situation might be one prolonged a couple of years. Or days. Everyone eagerly tells you of the fellow who recovered from a heart attack and lived umpteen years. No one ever tells you how many died. So while I am not moping around about it, I don't expect to hit ninety or even eighty, and am dubious about seventy. Years, that is, not speedometer readings."

He signed off, "Remember, I love you, darling daughter."

In mid-January, Papá was feeling better so he and Mimi started going out to dinner again. Soon he was back behind the wheel, and on the last day of the month, the two of them drove out to Sherman Oaks for a Sunday afternoon visit with friends. They enjoyed a pleasant meal together and retired to the living room where Papá made himself comfortable in an easy chair.

At some point in the after-dinner conversation, Papá sneezed, put his head back, and closed his eyes. Mimi, accustomed to his recent habit of dozing off, let him be.

Later, when it was time to go home, she tried to rouse him. It was only then that she realized he was dead.

Mimi called his doctor and then Mother, who was up in Mt. Baldy. By the time Mother arrived, Papá's body had been taken away. Mother drove Mimi home and spent the night with her.

Jay, in Minneapolis, flew in the next morning. She said she knew the minute he was gone. She was at home standing on the stairs when her attention was drawn to the cuckoo clock Papá had brought her from Switzerland. The pendulum quit swinging. At that moment, she knew her dad was dead.

"His heart just stopped," Jay said. "I'll always remember 1965 for that, the sudden stopping of his heart."

The elderly George Paine came from the East Coast to attend the service, held on a rainy Saturday morning. Friends and former colleagues paid their respects at his flag-draped coffin.

Papá was remembered as a man who had worked hard and, from harsh beginnings, made something of himself. He didn't have family other than the one he'd married into, but he had done right by his wife and daughters. He had been a steadfast husband, loving father, and caring grandfather.

A month later, Father drove Mimi and Mother down to Fort Rosecrans National Cemetery in San Diego to attend a military observance at the plot where Papá's ashes had been interred. Afterward, Mimi wrote about it, describing it for friends and Jay, who had been unable to return to California for the ceremony.

> The National Cemetery is on Point Loma, a promontory jutting out to the sea. On a gentle slope facing the ocean, away from the wind, is the place where Fred lies.
>
> Fred always had a great love for the sea and ships, and whenever we found ourselves near a large body of water, he would spend all the time he could watching boats, and their coming and going around the piers.
>
> The ceremony was an emotional experience for me, and Gwen. It was most reverently done. I had never seen a military funeral before, and I felt the deep significance of the honor bestowed upon a simple soldier.

I am sure, were Fred able, he would approve, for he lies in an honored spot, between two men who, like himself, had given themselves at some time completely to their country. I am proud my husband lies there, in hallowed ground, as indeed it must be, and I feel I have done all I could to honor him.

This closes the book, the last chapter, of the life of the man I loved most deeply, and with whom I spent the largest portion of my life."

49

That Name Means You to Me

Mimi was seventy-one when Papá died, but he had left her financially secure. According to Mother, she had around $75,000 in investments—equivalent to over $730,000 today—as well as a generous monthly pension. Paying the bills and tending to legal papers, however, was difficult for Mimi, who was unaccustomed to dealing with finances. Mother, whom she came to rely on for practical matters, helped with banking and taxes.

For her emotional needs, Mimi had the support of her church and loyal friends, but life without Papá was a painful adjustment. Despite the imperfections of their relationship—spanning forty-one tempestuous years—she had loved him.

Grief, though, did not long dampen Mimi's enthusiasm for life. She and her friends went to luncheons and bridge games, and attended performances at the new Los Angeles Music Center. She was still partial to movies, too. One evening she noted in her diary, with a well-deserved exclamation point, that she had just seen *The Sound of Music* for the twelfth time. She loved the story of the courageous, upbeat governess—a heroine she resembled in both looks and spirit—who endured hardships but triumphed. And, not incidentally, found true love.

The summer after Papá's death, Mimi boarded the train to Minnesota to visit Jay, and the following year she sailed to France to see her brother. While in Europe, she traveled to Germany to buy a new Volkswagen and drove it to Hillion. Booking a room at the same hotel she'd stayed in with Papá five years earlier, she walked barefoot on the beach at La Grandville, visited old friends, and on Sunday morning, once again attended the ancient stone church of her childhood.

In 1967, she went to Sutton Island for six weeks to see George Paine. Although Mimi noted one day that he was feeling dizzy, he seemed in good health for a man in his early nineties. But three days after waving goodbye to him at the pier, she received a phone call that he'd died. That night she wrote in her diary: *Uncle George died this morning. Alone. Heart attack. Fell from upper piazza on Sutton, Maine. My best oldest friend is gone.*

Mimi attended his service at Christ Church in Cambridge. She sat in the front pew with his son Lyman, just as she had sat beside him when the Reverend Paine preached sermons half a century earlier. They both missed the other Paine boy, Alfred, a World War II casualty whose funeral had been held there in 1944.

Mimi routinely stopped in Minneapolis on her treks across the country, but she didn't this time because Jay wasn't home. She had finally saved enough money to take a trip to Japan.

A few former lodgers-turned-friends had offered to host Jay— now proficient in conversational Japanese—and arranged for her to serve as a summer resource teacher. But along with providing cross-cultural education, there was something else Jay wanted to do while there.

One of her friends helped her contact a major Tokyo newspaper, *The Mainichi Shimbun,* in an effort to return the photo Jay had found in the pocket of the dead soldier in New Guinea. Now, two decades after the war, a reporter published the photograph, located one of the seven men in the picture, and arranged for Jay to meet him.

The Mainichi was there to record the meeting of the former enemies, the WAC and the Japanese Imperial Army officer. A journalist wrote an article about their encounter, but there wasn't much new to report. The veteran said none of his friends in the photo had survived, so he couldn't know which one she'd seen in the jungle. But he bowed and expressed his gratitude for Jay's gesture of reconciliation.

At the time, Jay wasn't thinking about the Japanese flag she'd taken from the dead man's waistband, but four decades later she arranged for it, too, to be returned. Its owner still unknown, she was pleased that it was at least back where it could rest with other combat souvenirs returned by ex-GIs who no longer saw them as trophies but rather as sad reminders of a horrific war.

On Jay's way home, she stopped to see Mimi in Los Angeles. During their five-day visit, Jay said how much she'd like to live in Hawaii, the lush paradise she'd fallen in love with on her layovers to and from Japan. Oahu's tropical greenery, set against its red-brown earth and blue skies, reminded her of New Guinea.

Jay's two older girls, Susan and Mona, were already out on their own, but she thought the move would be especially good for her husband. Not yet fifty, Bob had recently suffered a heart attack and Jay didn't want to lose him. He needed a change in his sedentary lifestyle and Midwestern diet, as well as a break from shoveling snow every winter.

Bob embraced the idea. He had an in-law who sold real estate on Oahu and decided to try his hand at that. Jay was ready to start their new life in the islands.

Mimi, however, had reached the age when endings overshadow beginnings, as she was reminded with each old friend's obituary and each grandchild's departure from home. She wanted her daughter closer, not another thousand miles away. But Jay promised that she and ten-year-old Wendy would stop for a visit on their move from Minnesota to Hawaii.

Much to Mimi's displeasure, though, Jay wrote the following month that she was anxious to get Wendy enrolled in school so they would only be able to manage a four-day stay. Mimi, who measured a proper get-together in terms of weeks instead of days, wanted more time with them.

In her hurt and anger, Mimi wrote Jay a withering response. Although she included a gentle expression of heartfelt disappointment—*the guitar under the bed has until now been a reminder that soon you'd be here and we could finally have the pleasure of hearing you sing*—she was harsh about recent changes Jay had made, including surgery to sculpt the nose she had always thought too big for her face. But never one to pass up an opportunity to denounce Jay's chosen name, Mimi began with that.

> Dearest Jane (not Jay, or any other bird!),
> I won't go into detail about your idea of names, it remains to be said that we believe (in our family) in proudly keeping our given names. I gave it to you, as my grandmother [Jane Bennett] loved hers, whose it was. So I gave you that name. You are discarding it. I gave you a beautiful nose. You discarded that. I also gave you beautiful brown hair. You discarded it. Let us hope the heart I gave you, which came to life and truly beat against mine, will ever remain the same!!
> I cannot, and will not, hesitate in expressing my complete dismay at your sudden plan to make your visit merely a passing one. Gwen and I are both deeply disappointed . . . We cannot see why you even bother to stop over. It will be a matter of meeting you, and taking you back to the airport, hardly worthwhile.

If this was meant to guilt Jay into extending her itinerary, it did not work. Jay's heart may have been the same, but her backbone had strengthened. It was stressful enough to pack up her life in Minnesota and start a new one in Hawaii without having to accommodate her mother's desire for a mid-move holiday. Jay took Mimi at her word that the stopover was hardly worthwhile and changed the tickets to fly directly to Honolulu.

Mimi later expressed regret for her words and also addressed her daughter's desire to be known as Jay.

> "I cannot see you by any other name. To me and to Daddy you were always, and will be always, our lovely little black-eyed Jane. And thus you will stay to me. You must forgive me. I am only a mother and no doubt have queer ideas, but that name means you to me, and I must therefore pray for your patience."

A truce was called, but the issue of names remained contentious. The patience that Mimi requested in her letter was not meant to imply she planned to change her position. If anyone—and I was often the worst offender—unthinkingly referred to my aunt as Jay, Mimi was quick with her correction. "It's Jannnne, dear," she would say, stretching out the N as far as possible.

Although Mimi had inherited her own mother's grace and charm, she also had her father's proclivity for directness, probably best illustrated by the attitude that "if it's wrong, it's wrong, and someone needs to tell you." But whereas her father's matter-of-fact criticism was tempered with an emotionally soft core, Mimi's was steeled with determination. As the head of the family in the States, she felt it was left to her to uphold the motto emblazoned on their Tate coat of arms—*Virtue for King and Country*. And virtue was manifested even in dress and hairstyles.

A few years after Jay's cancelled visit to Los Angeles, Mimi and Mother went to see her in Hawaii. By then, Bob was a fit-looking advocate for health foods, and Jay was as lovely in her flowing muumuus as she'd been in her chic concert dresses. She had, however, long since tired of her limp Hayford hair and taken up gently puffed wigs. She was wearing henna-colored curls when her mother arrived.

Mimi held her tongue during the visit, but after getting home and sharing vacation photos with friends, she took pen in hand to express her opinion of Jay's new locks.

> Everyone, and I mean everyone, hates your damned red hair. Everyone—and I'm one of that clan—says for gaud sakes, go back to your other blonde, mixed gray, or what-have-you wig, and throw that fuzzy-red bale of hay in the rag-bag... As usual, no one had the guts to tell you, I had to be the goat.... When we saw you in Hawaii, loving you as we do, we looked for that beautiful gal we all adore, and found Madame Zizi!

When it came to letters, Mimi was a master of the acerbic. But Jay found no humor in the clever barbs and didn't respond, which quickly brought another missive. Mimi wrote that she liked Jay's blonde wig—"I love it and you look ravishing with it"—but she made sure Jay knew, just in case she thought her mother was backtracking, how she felt about the others. "The white one you can give to Grandma Moses, and the red one you can put in the toilet and pull the chain!"

Mimi's assistance in grooming was, needless to say, unappreciated by Jay, who never felt she quite measured up to her mother's standards. Since they lived so far apart, she could, of course, safely wear what she pleased. But Mimi's words, despite the splash of humor, had ruined the henna wig for her.

It was the hypocrisy, however, that galled her most. Mimi had changed her own name from Maud, had surgery to shape her nose during her Hollywood years, and had been bleaching her hair since then, too. But Jay wasn't foolish enough to point that out to Mimi. Instead, she poured out her frustration in letters to my mother.

It was different for Mother. She also received her share of unwanted assessments, regarding everything from fashion to family duties, but it didn't seem to faze her. She said she'd learned how to keep herself from being hurt by Mimi's disapproval—she ignored it. "When she was critical," Mother stated, "I didn't believe a word she said."

Mimi, however, didn't see herself as critical. She was helpful. After all, what are mothers for if not to correct and guide their children?

Mother and Jay were in frequent contact, writing each other letters of support and commiseration while Mimi navigated her lonely widowed years.

50

The Third Act

Despite her active social life and occasional dates, this was a difficult period for Mimi. Her daughters and grandchildren were busy with their own lives, and she no longer held sway over them the way she once had.

And if the younger generations' growing independence had precipitated her diminishing influence, losing Papá had furthered it. Not only had his death left her emotionally fragile, but his faithful veneration had served to legitimize her rule as the head of the family.

Perhaps the greatest setback to her status, however, occurred years earlier with the sale of her home in Cheviot Hills. For what is a matriarch without a manor? Lacking a spacious dining room to preside over at holiday dinners—as well as a man to carry the turkey and carve it—she resigned herself to being a guest, even if an honored one, at our unadorned kitchen table.

Life moves on, though, always beyond the control of even those once most confident in their ability to dictate its outcome. Maybe, however, it is precisely during those futile times when individuals wield the least power that they are most open to new experiences.

In September 1967, when Mimi was seventy-four, she made plans to attend the International Expo in Montreal. With an aristocratic bearing that still turned heads, she walked into the Union Pacific Railroad's Beverly Hills office to make reservations. Her attention was drawn to the distinguished-looking gentleman running the agency.

A young man hurried to the counter to wait on her, but Mimi brushed him off. Indicating the manager with silver hair and a matching mustache, she declared, "That man will help me."

"That man" was the one . . . the one she'd been looking for all her life. She knew it the moment their eyes met.

His name was Harold Friedman. He was as charming as he was handsome, and soon Mimi was like a schoolgirl waiting for the phone to ring. And it did. He took her to lunch, and in two weeks she was lamenting how hard it would be to leave him for her ten-day trip to Canada. The feeling was mutual.

Two days before boarding the train, she wrote in her diary, *Harold came for lunch. Wonderful time. Hate to leave him, and he doesn't like it too well, either.* The following day she recorded, *Lunch with Harold. Hated to leave him. He is upset. Two weeks without me.*

Harold was taken with Mimi, who was as playful in spirit as she was sophisticated in manner. During her absence, he called her on the phone several times, wrote her five letters, and was waiting at the train platform to greet her when she arrived back at Los Angeles' Union Station.

From the time Mimi returned home, she referred to Harold in her diary as M.A. for Mon Amour.

Younger people often make the mistake of looking at older people and thinking that the core of their being is as aged as their bodies. But it isn't. Unlike the sagging of flesh and weakening of organs, the spirit at one's center doesn't change. That was especially true for a forever-young woman like Mimi. In spite of her age, she felt at times as insecure as a teenager, once writing to Jay:

> "I have, as you know, grieved for Daddy for almost three years, longing for love and attention from a man. I have that now, but I am anxious and constantly wonder

when this newfound happiness will be wrenched from me. I cannot seem to grasp the fact that it might last. I am ever conscious that one day, like Madame Butterfly, 'I will neither sigh nor cry, I just must die.'"

Unlike Madame Butterfly's faithless Lieutenant Pinkerton, Harold seemed true and steadfast. He and Mimi saw each other almost every day. Still, she worried what he would think if he knew how old she was. Attractive and stylish, she radiated vitality, but Harold was only fifty-one, making Mimi twenty-three years his senior.

She fretted about the faint facial lines she had acquired over the years, and in another letter to Jay she briefly toyed with the idea of a facelift.

"In a way, I am all for it, but there is also the fact that hands, body, and legs tell tales. One can't wear gloves all the time, and after all, one must undress!"

Harold, however, was too much in love to notice creases in her skin, and she quickly dismissed the thought of cosmetic surgery. She really didn't need it; her youthful appearance and passionate nature easily disguised her age.

But even if she could pass for younger, she didn't want Harold to know the truth. She had never been one to discuss her age—not ever owning up to more than thirty-nine—and that wasn't about to change. She was careful not to leave her mail out, just in case he dropped by on the day her monthly Social Security check arrived. And when they got to the point of sharing family photos, she blacked out the dates on the back before she brought them out to show him. Harold may have suspected she was older, but he was a gentleman and never asked.

Of course, her subterfuge required some cooperation from Mother and Jay when they finally met him, since Mimi had to shave a considerable number of years off their ages, too. Although Jay and Harold had both served in the Philippines, Jay had to stay mum about her war experiences when he talked about his.

If the girls did slip up, Mimi was adept at changing the subject, or interjecting that one or the other of her daughters was too young at that time—during whatever era was being discussed—and couldn't possibly know what she was talking about. This was particularly annoying to my mother, who had to let four-months-younger Harold think he was two decades older than her, but she decided it well worth it if Mimi was happy.

And she was.

For the first time, Mimi truly gave herself to another person. She may have deferred to her first husband for a while, but if she submitted to him, or to her second husband, it wasn't for long. Never completely trusting their abilities—whether it be to forsake other women or to set up a wading pool—she had always needed to be in charge. Now, however, she had someone in whom she was completely confident, and she handed him the reins. Harold was in command and her life began to revolve around him.

Unfortunately, though, Harold wasn't exactly free to pursue a relationship with Mimi.

He was married.

51

God Show Me the Way!

When Mimi met Harold, he wasn't living with his wife, as Mimi explained in a letter to Jay.

> Harold was, at the time, and had been for a long time, separated from Helen, living with a brother and sister-in-law. He was completely free, as she was, to find a companion. He never cheated on her, and indeed still does not. It is a wonder he waited so long to find someone to love, and who could give him the comfort and love he had missed so long. He is a clean and moral man, and though Helen does not know me, I am sure she realizes he is free to find his own pleasures.

But soon after Mimi and Harold began dating, circumstances changed. Helen was diagnosed with stomach cancer.

> When this was discovered, two or more months ago, she went into the hospital. He returned to their house to take care of his fourteen-year-old daughter, Judy, whom he adores, and who could not be alone.
> After some time in the hospital, and an operation, the doctors told Harold nothing could be done, and said to take Helen home and do what he could to ease her life. That is, the short life she has left. So he has remained, but *not in the capacity* of a husband, because as he told me, he has 'neither the desire nor inclination' to resume spousal

relations, and neither has she. However, someone must care for her part of the time, and he does.

He is a kind man and wants to do all he can to ease her remaining months, and I desire that he do this because it proves he would treat me well, too. "

Even faced with this heavy-hearted turn of events, Mimi's letter ended on the sweet here-and-now she shared with Harold.

"We are counting only each day, being as happy as we can, helping others, hurting no one, and thanking God for our love. "

Harold stayed with his wife, tending to her and ferrying her back and forth to the oncologists at the City of Hope.

Although earlier Mimi had considered her relationship with Harold—then estranged from Helen—as semi-acceptable to society, he was now living with his wife. Thus, what for Mimi had started out as a budding romance with a for-the-most-part eligible man, had turned into a hidden affair with a married man.

Mimi shared with Jay, often her confidant, the difficulties of arranging meetings, as well as her fears for the future.

"Yesterday makes five months we have been together, and they have been marvelous and, at the same time, miserable. I can't explain how that is, but weekends I am tortured alone without him, not being able to call him, as he is home, though he calls me whenever he can get away. I hate to leave the house, fearing he will try to call. The other day he was going to drive to the valley to see a client and wanted me to go along. He called, but I was out at the grocers so he had to go alone. Another time I came home and found his card in the door. He had rushed over just to see me a minute, all for nothing.

Also, I wonder what the future holds, as he has no idea how old I am. He speaks of others as 'our age,' but I know years do take their toll and I can't hide those wrinkles that are bound to appear. Our life together is ideal. I could not imagine such a lover and he is constantly telling me he never knew anyone like me. We have everything; we get on beautifully, never an angry thought even. He loves to come here and he relaxes and we talk in each other's arms. What will happen if the day ever comes that we must separate? I dare not think of it. I never knew anyone quite like him, tender, gentle, handsome, six-foot tall, loving me, worrying about me so much that he neglects his work.

So I repeat, it is wonderful, and also a torture when I allow myself to doubt the future.

I shall go to Maine this summer for Uncle George's memorial service on the island. I don't want to be away more than three weeks or a month as I know I shall die of loneliness for Harold, and he for me, but as he says, it will be all the sweeter when I return. "

Having made Harold the focus of her life, Mimi was distressed sometime later when his wife, who had outlived the few months the doctors had predicted, turned her attention to their marriage. Helen suddenly confronted Harold with her suspicion that he was having an affair.

Mimi's joy, tortured as it was, turned to alarm. She wrote in her diary, *Disturbing news regarding Helen, who accuses M.A. of having another woman! Puzzling. Very upset.*

Had Helen misunderstood Harold's intentions when he had returned? Or was Mimi the one confused about how things were?

Harold called Mimi and assured her he'd never loved anyone more, but his commitment to his ailing wife and worried daughter had to come first.

They didn't see each other for several agonizing days. *Difficult decision,* she wrote. *I must separate from Harold. How can I? God must decide.*

Still nervous and confused and lonely, she wrote the next day. *God show me the way!*

In the end, Harold and Mimi simply couldn't stay apart. They wanted to do the right thing and "hurt no one," as Mimi had said, but it was a grievous time for him and an anxious time for her. They needed each other. For several months they curtailed their visits until eventually he was back to dropping in at her place for lunch, or tea, or on his way to the bowling alley in the evening.

Despite Helen's initial reprieve, the cancer relentlessly spread, and close to two years after her diagnosis, she passed away.

Harold's mourning and Mimi's propriety ensured that their relationship would be kept under wraps for the foreseeable future. Harold was especially concerned about his daughter, a teenager grieving for her mother. It was a sensitive enough time without adding complications.

In the late sixties, even before Mimi met Harold, she had kept a fairly busy social calendar. She engaged in volunteer work, too. The Vietnam War was uppermost in the American consciousness and she wanted to show her support for the brave young men in combat. She signed up at the Veteran's Administration to help wounded soldiers.

But she didn't care for her assignment—in what she referred to as *the old men's ward*—so she gave that up and devoted her free time to charitable work through her church. Her active life had her driving all over Los Angeles.

Mimi had been a fairly good driver when young, but in recent years she'd become nervous as she clutched, shifted, and steered her way through the increasingly congested streets. After a minor accident a few years earlier, she had traded in her small Volkswagen for a larger car: a sturdy Volvo.

In September 1969, a month after Helen died, Mimi was on her way to church when she swerved to avoid an accident. She lost control of the car, jumped the curb, and hit a tree. Worse yet, she had left her seatbelt unfastened—so as not to crush her satin dress—and was thrown forward with such force she smashed her face and broke her nose. An ambulance rushed her to the hospital, where she was also treated for a lacerated leg and bruised ribs. The Volvo was demolished.

Harold hurried to her side, and—as Mimi had predicted to Jay—he was as attentive to her in her hour of need as he had been to his wife.

The surgeons did what they could with Mimi's nose, but the operation she'd had back in the 1930s left the doctors without a lot of bone and septum with which to rebuild it. Her nose ended up looking a bit too small and pert for such a stylish woman. She was unhappy with the results, but there wasn't much that could be done about it.

Harold was just happy she was alive.

In spite of a few false starts through the years, Mimi never gave up hope of finding true love, and she'd finally found it in Harold. They were in some ways an unlikely couple. Their ages aside, his family, immigrant Jews from Poland, had arrived in the lowly steerage class that had broken Mimi's young heart when she had sailed to America first class. But regardless of their individual histories, their temperaments and personalities were well matched.

He was devoted to her while still being his own man. He treated her like a queen without giving in to her, as Fred had. And he never ignored her, as Herbert had. With a self-assurance as strong as her own, he was her dashing prince.

Eight months after the auto accident—and nine months after his wife's passing—he introduced Mimi to his daughter. From then on, Mimi and Harold enjoyed a public relationship.

Harold was traditional enough in his religious beliefs to insist on affixing the mezuzah to the right-side post of his front door, but unconventional enough to consider marrying out of his faith. In 1973, six years after they met, they set the date.

Mimi was overjoyed. But my mother, who still handled her finances, didn't think it fiscally wise to marry, which would mean giving up Papá's pension and Social Security. Harold and Mimi wanted to be husband and wife, though, so Mother suggested a wedding ceremony sans the legalities.

The night before the nuptials, Mimi wrote in her diary, *This is my last day as Mona Kramer. Tomorrow I become Mrs. Friedman.*

The bride-to-be was eighty, but her age was easily concealed by her radiance. The couple had a wedding day with everything one would expect: bustling guests, a formal ceremony, and a happy reception. Everything except for the lawful paperwork. Their union wasn't registered with the State, allowing Mimi to keep her benefits. But the part that mattered most—the sacred commitment voiced between two people in love—was blessed by those present and made official by the pronouncement of the clergy.

Performing the marriage rites was my mother, who had in recent years given up her accounting work to become a minister in the Church of Religious Science.

52

Power of the Mind

Although Mother had not realized her youthful goal of becoming a psychologist, she was finally able to fulfill her religious leanings, along with her desire to "loll back in an easy chair, listen to the troubles of others, and set them right," as Papá had off-handedly described her career ambitions forty years earlier. It had taken a while to get there, but the clergy was a good fit for her.

Mother, having been raised as both a Christian Scientist and an Episcopalian—with a strong dose of Catholicism during her year in France—gave considerable thought to the religious education of us three kids. When we were school-aged, she took us to the Episcopal Church.

"I didn't want to raise you as Catholics," said Mother. "And Christian Science, especially in those days, was so frigid. It was totally knowledge, knowledge in an ice cube. I wanted you kids to have ritual and beauty. I wanted you to know, when you grew up, what certain words and symbols meant. I liked the formality of the Episcopal Church and wanted you to have that."

On Sundays, she drove us to St. Clement's, arriving early so Mike and Tim could prepare for their duties as altar boys while I donned my choir robe. Father went with us on special occasions, but he didn't usually attend. He said he held church at home.

I wasn't sure exactly what he meant, but I knew that religion for Mother, too, wasn't limited to the confines of a house of worship. Every weekday morning before we left for school, she gathered us by the front door and led a recitation of the *Apostles' Creed*. After our choral "Amen," Mother—taking the role of the minister and standing every bit as straight as one—would pronounce, "The Lord be with you." Then we'd respond, "And with thy spirit," before grabbing our lunch boxes and dashing out.

Mother, however, was too broad in her beliefs and too inquisitive about religion to find any deep or lasting satisfaction in the Episcopalians' Book of Common Prayer. She considered other religions and met for a while with door-to-door Mormon missionaries, but no faiths accommodated her other spiritual convictions. Mother's childhood belief in fairies had now, in her late forties, been supplanted by an interest in unidentified flying objects. The latter caused problems between her and Father.

Mother began attending flying saucer conventions at Giant Rock, out in the Mojave Desert. They were organized by a man who claimed he'd met aliens from Venus, toured their spaceship, and learned from them the principles of human cell rejuvenation.

Father went with Mother a time or two, hoping if he humored her, she'd "get it out of her system." It didn't work. She was fascinated by extraterrestrials, telepathic communication, and psychic phenomena, which began to show up in her diary in 1964.

February 23: Enjoyed hearing Gina C. on "Precognition." The psychic club is made up of nice and sensible people.

They may have been nice and sensible people, but Father wasn't buying anything they had to offer. Having been raised by a con artist, he wanted nothing to do with what some trusting souls called *the unexplained*. He was sure the flying saucers were scams, and the séances and bending spoons were simple conjuring tricks. He didn't know if Mother was being set up, or if the whole lot of them were delusional.

Dismissing his concerns, Mother continued to go to metaphysical meetings, and through them met Frank, a kindred spirit in the New Age world. The more evening gatherings she spent with Frank, the less Father liked him.

September 29: Because I was interested in metaphysics through Frank, Ray consulted a lawyer and doctor and I came out with egg on my face and looking like Hester with a capital A.

Getting the icy treatment from Mother, Father backed off and gave her time and space to "come to her senses," but contrary to his hopes, she moved even closer to her new freethinking friends. Although he never raised a hand to her, he raised his voice a lot, and the house was full of his arguing and her silence.

The next summer, she began to write about another man, the proprietor of a clock repair shop in downtown Huntington Park.

June 8: Evan is a large, ugly man, with a vague lisp and a very beautiful and gentle soul. He gave me a clock! The clock.

July 15: Evan is the entity I knew in Utah 115 years ago and even before the world began.

Her interest in reincarnation was not surprising given that she'd been raised on Mimi's belief that Jay was the incarnation of Great-Grandmama Henrietta. And as for precognition, Mother had heard firsthand the tale told by George James, her grandfather, about foreseeing the sinking of the SS Hilda and how he'd saved the family by making them change their tickets.

Like Mimi, Mother had ghost stories, too. She talked of finding spirits in our house when she first moved in—a woman in an old-fashioned dress examining the contents of Mother's jewelry box, and an unseen man who thumped through the house on a wooden leg until she firmly told him it was her house and he'd have to leave.

She grew up on one form of spiritual consciousness or another, and so did we. When I was nine, Mother made a concerted effort to teach us kids extrasensory perception. She decided three-year-old Tim, not as far-removed from "the other side," was the only one good at it. She said he had an old soul.

Back then, Mother's beliefs hadn't caused strife in the family. Father occasionally teased her about them, but their exchanges had been good-natured. Now, a decade later, her spiritual seeking was taking her out more frequently, and with people Father did not trust. Suspecting Mother had something going on with Frank, Father didn't pay heed to Evan, the clock man who wasn't a part of the New Age crowd. But Evan was all Mother could talk about to Jay, who came out to the West Coast the summer of 1965.

August 14: Jay's visit was wonderful. She opened doors to past lives. My last Mormon life is becoming clear. The nicest verification is that Tim chose me for his mother in Utah. I had one husband [Evan] and one son [Tim], who looked all his life for his gentle father and has unknowingly found him this time.

Mother may have seen Evan as Tim's past-life father, but in this life, Evan was married with boys of his own. And Tim, newly a teenager, showed no particular interest in the man, who had become a weekly guest at our supper table. Mother had encouraged Evan to teach a clock repair class and then presented him to us as a night school colleague. But by the end of the year she was recording in her diary that she and Evan were finding places to rendezvous for a day or two at a time.

Father and Mother still had their Friday night dinner dates, and occasional weekends away, but tensions between them grew. He knew her heart was elsewhere; he just wasn't sure where. Finally, Father took a stand.

September 23: Ray has asked that I divorce him, or he will divorce me in November. He's still picking on poor Frank. He is his own enemy.

It was a short-lived stand. She denied any impropriety and he backed down again.

In much the same way that Mother's upbringing influenced her perceptions, Father's childhood had influenced his. Having been raised by a deceptive and not-to-be-argued with mother, he was particularly vulnerable to falsehoods. "The truth" was what his mother had said it was, and now it was what his wife said it was. And his wife told him he was suffering from an overactive imagination.

As astute and confident as he was in the work world, with women he could easily be made to doubt his own observations.

Eventually Mother found her way to Religious Science, an all-inclusive haven for spiritual seekers interested in exploring the power of the mind to better their lives. The church's founder, Ernest Holmes, was from a poor family in Maine, and espoused healing ideas similar to those of Christian Science, although with greater warmth. Mother felt right at home.

The religion itself wasn't entirely new to her. Mimi, who'd always been interested in the power of the mind, took her daughter to hear Holmes speak shortly after they moved to Los Angeles. Mother, then a junior high student, was unhappy that day because she'd been invited by a boy to the beach and would much rather have been splashing in the waves with him than sitting in the Wiltern Theater next to Mimi. She slouched in her seat, sulking, throughout the talk.

Despite her displeasure on that occasion, she hadn't forgotten Holmes' words on the interrelatedness of mind, body, and spirit, and by the 1970s, she embraced his precepts and was studying for the ministry.

Mother and Father's relationship improved a bit once she embarked on her religious coursework. She spent less time with the more frivolous fringes of the New Age set and asked Father to escort her to church. His insular Adventist upbringing made it hard for him to accept her new religion, but he was proud of her groundbreaking accomplishments—from establishing her own business to running for city council and now becoming a woman minister—and he often accompanied her on Sundays.

The Church of Religious Science, however, did little to help their marriage. Mother's adoption of loving affirmations and positive thinking should have, in theory, radiated out to benefit all those around her. But she had also become an adherent of a popular book, David Seabury's *The Art of Selfishness*, that advanced the theory that if you are happy, everyone else will be. Others' needs got short shrift. It wasn't long before she said Father's continuing skepticism weighed her down and kept her from moving forward in her spiritual growth.

Mother's trickle-down theory of family fulfillment didn't sit well with Mimi either. At the same time that Mimi was complaining to Jay about discarding her name and her nose, she was protesting Mother's decision to send thirteen-year-old Tim to board with friends of hers in Mt. Baldy. Mimi didn't begrudge Mother her affair with Evan or her new career, but thought she was shirking her responsibilities to those at home.

I wasn't around for Mimi's wedding or the final rending apart of Mother and Father's marriage. By early 1969—when Mimi was still hush-hush about Harold, and Mother was several years into her affair with Evan—I'd left California. Having romantic dramas of my own, at twenty-one I'd decided to make a fresh start and went to stay with Aunt Jay, Uncle Bob, and Wendy at their home in Kaneohe, on the windward side of Oahu. Although I'd never spent much time with Jay, I'd always looked up to her: a fearless soldier, an explorer of exotic lands, a folk singer with a strong, vibrant voice.

We took brisk morning walks along the beach and miles-long hikes at the foot of the mountains. Jay had a purposeful stride that didn't allow for leisurely conversation, but we had lengthy after-dinner talks in her lanai.

Knowing how much Jay loved her big sister, I hesitated to complain about Mother, with whom I was usually at odds, but it often slipped out.

"Well, I can't say I'd like to have her for a mother," Jay said one evening as she settled into her wicker chair. "She isn't very maternal. But she's a wonderful sister. And she's kind to the flops and failures of the world."

"How so?"

"For example, on her thirteenth birthday our mother threw a small party for her. It was very fancy, with proper china and even little finger bowls to clean your fingertips. Well, one of the girls mistook her bowl for a water cup and drank from it. Scottie didn't miss a beat. Before anyone could point out the error, she picked up her own bowl and took a gulp." Jay laughed. "Soon we were all drinking from the finger bowls as if that was what they were there for. Your mom is thoughtful like that."

My evenings with Jay gave me a broader perspective of my mother and I began to see her for who she was rather than who I wanted her to be. Her hopes and dreams didn't revolve around home and family. She would never be wifely or motherly.

Before leaving the mainland, I'd gone to hear her speak at a Religious Science church a couple of times. I saw how her eyes sparkled when she took the pulpit, saw her confidence and how she made people smile or nod or laugh with her. Drawn to people who sought spiritual advice, she delivered it to them with warm-hearted assurance. She was born to be a minister.

I had to let her live her life and get on with my own.

Through one of Jay's local connections, I landed a job as an office cashier at the Hilton Hawaiian Village, rented an apartment in Honolulu, and went back to college. Throughout my four years on the island, Jay and I were close. She took a position at the Hilton too, and we worked together, although on different shifts and in different capacities. In the morning she checked one set of guests in, and in the afternoon, I checked another set out.

Jay's love of Japan rubbed off on me and after graduating, I took classes in Japanese and accepted a job at a newspaper company in Tokyo. For the next five years, our communication was mostly confined to the mail, but she wrote long weekly letters that kept me up to date on her life in Hawaii, as well as what was going on with my mother and Mimi on the mainland.

By then, Mother had been ordained and answered the call to the pulpit of a small, struggling church in the California desert town of Barstow. In pursuit of her new career, she left behind her old life. And Father. After three decades together, she was finally clear on what she wanted, and it didn't include him.

Apparently, he wasn't so sure about wanting her, either. Following his retirement, he moved out once but then returned. Now they agreed that he'd live in their Huntington Park home, while she spent half the week with him and the other half in Barstow. That worked out until Father realized that her friend Evan was keeping her company in the desert. It may have been the swinging seventies, but Father was too conservative to accept a flaunting of marriage vows. He confronted her, but she refused to end the relationship with Evan. He filed for divorce.

Mother, who stood to lose his retirement benefits—which she felt she had earned through twenty-nine years of marriage—was furious. In the end, she said what he wanted to hear, that she wouldn't see Evan again. But as soon as Father withdrew the legal papers, she went back to doing as she pleased.

At seventy-one and starting to experience a cognitive decline, Father didn't have what it took to refile divorce papers. He gave up and agreed to Mother's offer of a legal separation. They sold their home and he found an apartment in Huntington Park. She made the final walk-through of their old house, the one she had purchased with Sam a lifetime earlier.

"I sat on the front steps for half an hour," Mother wrote of her final goodbye to our family home, "just as I had the day I moved in and waited for the furniture (a bed, bureau, oak icebox, stove, two desks, rocking chair, and two throw rugs).

"I cried and touched the iron railing and steps . . . they had felt so many feet. 'The Lord be with you,' I would holler as you kids left for school, and you'd holler back, 'and with thy spirit.' I cried through each room. I literally touched every wall, every window, the doorknob, the light switch, the icebox (electric this time!), the sink and stove. I touched everything. And in the back bedrooms I heard the squeals and thumps and tiny fast feet of small children, growing children . . .

"When I closed the door, there was no going back. I never knew it would take so much courage to walk over the threshold. To say goodbye to everything of my adult life, the only life I recognized. I caressed the door frame and the black safety-chain, closed the door with a gentle click, and drove to Barstow."

Mother returned to the tract house she called "the parsonage," and settled into her late-in-life career. In this newest incarnation, she tinkered with her name once again, dropping the final 'e' from Scottie, to become Reverend Scotti.

As a minister, she served her congregation with thought-provoking sermons, well-prepared classes, and reassuring "you-are-loved" counseling. She embraced the town and, in turn, was well liked by those who poured her coffee in the diner or waited on her at the bank. She joined the local chapter of the Soroptimist Club, attended luncheons, and gave invocations.

Later, she bought a barren piece of property on the outskirts of town and designed a home with huge windows and a view of the distant mountain range. The house was exactly the way she wanted it—white walls, glass tables, and a long, mirrored closet for her collection of colorful vestments. In the front and back yard, she planted mulberry trees and nurtured a growing array of plants with a system of hoses and positive, encouraging words.

Free from the everyday demands of her out-on-their-own-children, and her left-on-his-own-husband, Mother truly thrived. If there is such a thing as one's place in the world, it was clear she had found hers.

Mother continued to visit Father to take care of their bills and financial affairs. She attended his retiree parties, too, always by his side and solicitous of his needs. She was as polite as she had been when they'd first married and she'd agreed to be known to his business associates as Mrs. Dole. But if, for a while, she had considered herself married to him, she didn't anymore.

No one can force what isn't meant to be, nor put a halt to what is. Back in the same year that Mother and Father had gone their separate ways, Mother acted as wedding officiant for Mimi and Harold. On November 3, 1973, Mimi summarized it in her diary.

This is our wedding night! Married at 7:30 by Gwen.
We're happy. Ceremony lovely.

53

At Long Last

Even after the newlywed period had long since passed, Mimi and Harold remained honeymooners. He hung on her every word, unless she was complaining about his occasional cigarette. And he willingly repaired things around the house, living up to his nickname, Honeydo. She decorated their home with her ancestors' portraits and European finery, and cooked him gourmet meals. She found everything he said amusing when he was being funny, and astute when he was serious. Playful together and supportive of each other, they were well matched.

Harold was as energetic as Mimi, and a bit restless, too. He had a hard time staying in one place for long. In their first decade of marriage they moved at least five times. Each new house had Mimi at his side painting, papering, hanging drapes, and decorating. She never complained—after all, she wasn't supposed to be anywhere near her eighties—and enjoyed the constant activity as much as he did.

They embarked on their biggest move in the year after their wedding. Harold—still a couple of years shy of sixty—took early retirement and they went two hundred miles up the coast to the seaside community of Cambria. In the woods just out of town, they found a two-story house and hung a sign above the entrance declaring it *Halcyon*. Shortly after they settled in, Mother gave them a little dog, the first of two they'd call Missy.

Even with Missy, and a cat that made his way to their door, Mimi was lonely. A month after arriving, she confided in her diary she was depressed and homesick. She had made new friends, but there were far fewer of them, and Mimi's church didn't offer very many social opportunities, either. When she'd entered the town's small Christian Science Church, she was disappointed to discover only twelve congregants—and all of them dressed rather casually.

Harold acclimated more easily. Having been an avid bowler in Los Angeles, he found a team in San Luis Obispo, half an hour away. He got involved with service organizations too, attending breakfasts with the Kiwanis and volunteering at the Lions Club. He took Mimi to the Lions' dinners at the local Veteran's Hall, which she found a bit dull. Nonetheless, she was a good sport and even became a Lady Lion.

Although Mimi and Harold had traveled together before marrying—they visited Jay in Hawaii and went to Sutton Island in Maine—she hadn't yet taken him abroad to meet her brother, George. Perhaps she worried someone in the Tate family might inadvertently reveal her age, or that Harold would see her passport. On medical forms, she'd taken to using her daughter's—my mother's—birth year, which was the same as Harold's. But government documents were another matter. In any case, if Mimi did have concerns, they were overruled by her desire to see her brother again. So a year after their move to Cambria, they planned a one-month vacation. Favoring Europe in the autumn, Mimi booked a September flight.

George and his family thought Harold was a splendid chap. And Harold, a gregarious man, liked them as well. Aside from attending family gatherings, Mimi took her new husband to see the sights in Paris, Normandy, and London. They had a good trip and made it back to California without any embarrassing revelations about age.

As soon as Mimi and Harold returned, they put their woodland house on the market and bought a sunnier, single-story place with—if you stood at just the right spot in the yard—a view of the ocean. The redecorating chores started again. But fixing up the house and volunteer activities didn't pay bills, so Harold obtained his real estate license and went back to work.

In spite of the pleasure they took in their new home—out from under the dark pines—the weather was still overcast much of the time, which exacerbated Mimi's gloominess. She needed sunshine as much as she needed people.

Family members visited as frequently as they could, but Mimi wanted to be an active part of their lives. Before moving north, she'd become especially close to her granddaughter and namesake, Mona, who'd moved to Los Angeles after following her mother's path with a stint in the army. But it was farther to get together now. Everyone was moving on with their lives. Harold's daughter, Judy, was married, as were most of us grandchildren. Our kids, the great-grandchildren, were starting to arrive, but Mimi was missing out on their first steps and first words.

Mimi and Harold still made it to family occasions, but they were becoming weary of the four-hour drive south. In the end, Cambria's charms couldn't offset its cloudy skies and remoteness. Three years after moving there, they returned to Los Angeles.

They rented a place in a housing complex in Century City. Six months later, Harold was hired to manage the apartments, and he and Mimi moved into a spacious unit with a large dining room. Mimi was able to host proper family dinners again.

About a year after that, I moved from Japan back to Southern California and rejoined the holiday gatherings. Mimi, with help from Mona, set the table with her china and sterling silver, stuffed the turkey with her chestnut dressing, and filled the serving dishes with potatoes and gravy, fresh cranberry sauce, and rutabagas.

Mimi resumed her position as presiding matriarch, complete with an adoring husband at her side and a few great-grandbabies at her feet. In 1981, with six great-grandkids, she arranged for a professional family photograph. Susan and Tim couldn't come, but the rest of us showed up in our best clothes. With too many to fit in the living room, we posed outside. Mimi and Harold sat on folding chairs in the middle, holding hands.

Harold enjoyed his work at the apartments. A gallant and responsive man—with tools as well as manners—he was well-liked. But the never-ending needs of the tenants were exhausting. At sixty-five, Harold was happy to retire for good.

Mimi, close to ninety, and Harold, now a bona fide senior citizen, headed out to the desert to savor their golden years. They bought a ranch-style home bordering a golf course in Sun City, a retirement community in Riverside County. The town, which featured green gravel yards in place of grass, provided neither the natural beauty of rustic places she'd loved, nor the level of city refinement to which she had once been accustomed. There were no sophisticated restaurants or high-end department stores. But during her years of marriage to Harold, who saw no reason to pay more than necessary for anything, Mimi had given up the need to have the finest goods. She had what was most important... and that was Harold.

Their move to Sun City worked out better than their relocation to Cambria. As the name promised, it had plenty of sun. And, although Mimi missed her Los Angeles friends, there were, sad to say, fewer to miss. Her diary contained more and more entries recounting their strokes, hospitalizations, and funerals. Most of her dearest friends had already passed away, with few of her new acquaintances in Sun City healthy enough and witty enough to take their place.

Her social life dwindling, Mimi turned her energy back to poetry, a talent perhaps passed down from her Gliddon grandmother, Henrietta. Mimi won a local award for one poem, and Harold arranged to have two others published in anthologies. He was proud of her talent.

In 1984, she wrote a poem in tribute to her brother, who had died the previous year. In it, Mimi referred to a skylark, perhaps remembering the lone bird they had seen on their last visit to Brittany, when they rented bikes and peddled to Villa St. George.

> You left us broken hearted
> Ere the sun had risen high,
> You closed your eyes in silence
> With a quiet peaceful sigh.
> What were you thinking, darling
> As o'er your grave the lark
> Sang notes of joy and gladness
> To guide you through the dark?
> Could you feel our hearts were anguished,
> Could you see the falling tears,
> As we stood beside you mourning
> For the happy, vanished years?
> Will you recall the loved ones
> Who led you through the way
> From early daytime shadows
> To the end of another day?
> Will you be there, my darling
> When I step within the door,
> And see the vision of beauty
> And those who've gone before?
> May our love and true devotion
> Raise you above the sod,
> And may we meet again in wonder
> As the loving sons of God.

Mimi never made it back to Europe after the death of George, but she kept in contact with his children, particularly Monique, her only niece, and Alain, who had chronicled the Tate heritage in a book he'd written a couple of years earlier. Delighted that he had a passion for keeping the narratives alive, Mimi shared with him photos and stories about the family's roots and their life in Brittany. As her father had before her, Mimi now served as the Tate-Gudgeon authority.

And, like her father in his last years, she was the only one left of her generation.

54

Like Mother, Like Daughter

In her light-filled home in Sun City, Mimi finished recording the account of her life in Brittany. She hoped to preserve not only her childhood but part of a way of life unrecognizable today. In like manner, she wanted to protect her family's long British history and the trappings that went with it.

At ninety, after giving careful consideration to her legacy, she sat at her polished breakfront desk and wrote in longhand a detailed will, noting which heirloom from amongst her silver, china, and jewelry was to go to which daughter or grandchild.

On the back of each forebear's portrait, she attached a small envelope addressed to "Gwen & Jane" and inserted a handwritten note identifying the ancestor and what was notable about them. There was lovely Jane Bennett, painted "by the court artist," an etching of mutton-chopped Edward Barnaby Gudgeon, "Consul General of Liberia," and an oil painting of the first George Tate "in his college robes." Mimi had no plans to leave this life anytime soon, but with these few acts, she was assured that her most important affairs were in order.

Even if Mimi occasionally sighed and said one relative or another didn't visit often enough, she and Harold weren't lacking in company. In 1982, a year after they'd moved to Sun City, Aunt Jay and Uncle Bob followed them there.

It was hard for Jay to leave her lush island for the sunbaked desert. And she didn't want to live so close to Mimi, who despite having mellowed with marriage could still be demanding. But

Bob had started to display signs of Alzheimer's, and my mother convinced Jay they would be better off living near family.

They purchased a single-wide mobile home two miles from Mimi's house, and Jay bought a used golf cart, the only mode of transportation needed in the retirement community. Jay adapted to the dry climate but bent it to her will where she could, creating a leafy green sanctuary on her porch, which she called the lanai. Still favoring her muumuus, sandals, and kukui nut lei—unless she substituted the lei with her jade medallion and gold chains—she stood out from the other residents with their cotton shirts and khaki shorts. But she had long since given up her youthful desire to fit in. She had a bold and confident style of her own.

When Jay wasn't taking care of Bob or doing chores for Mimi, she was writing. She penned a number of articles for the local newspaper—interviewing senior citizens for the Sun City Profile column—and wrote poetry or recounted funny incidents for the *Show and Tell* newsletter she created for family and friends. A writers' group invited her to join and she wrote *The Gypsy Wind,* a manuscript about her life in the army, which she fictionalized just enough that she could complain about her imperious mother without catching hell for it.

Mimi liked having Jay close by for practical as well as emotional reasons. Although Mimi was still independent in spirit, she was limited by failing vision. A decade earlier, she had been prevented from renewing her driver's license. *Eyes found weak,* she'd explained in her diary. She went on to endure several operations with minimal improvement. So while Harold was off bowling, Mimi relied on Jay for assistance with household tasks and her correspondence, which was still considerable.

Aside from letters to her family here and abroad, through the years Mimi had also written to various heads of state. She sent condolences to the royal family when King George VI died in

1952, and regularly sent birthday greetings to the Queen Mother. She mailed a letter of sympathy to President Reagan after the Challenger Disaster, and later, when he left the White House, she congratulated him on a job well done. Mimi never felt unimportant to anyone.

Decreasing eyesight, however, lessened her sense of influence in the world as well as her control at home. She worried that the Tate-bound letters she dictated to Jay might end up with traces of her daughter's dyslexic spelling as well as extraneous greetings that Mimi hadn't authorized. Or, heaven forbid, be signed "Jay."

Nonetheless, Mimi's reliance on Jay to be her secretary only grew. She had her last eye surgery—as unsuccessful as the others—when she was almost ninety-two. Her diary entry on June 21, 1985 noted, *Eye badly infected. Using antibiotics. Painful.* The next day Harold took over writing in her diary. No day could be properly put to rest without recording its events, and Mimi trusted him to do it.

While Mimi was suffering visual problems, Mother was facing setbacks of her own. The year before, Evan had died of cancer. She'd been with him for almost twenty years, up until he was confined to bed and his wife refused Mother's request to see him. With no sense of closure and only casual sympathy from family members—most of whom believed they were merely friends—Mother was left to grieve alone.

Then in 1986, a long-time Huntington Park friend contacted Mother to report that eighty-three-year-old Father wasn't doing well. He had fallen at the curb of a busy street on his way to the grocery store, she said, and only by the grace of God been spared serious injury. He was suffering from increasing memory loss—more apparent every day, she added—and really shouldn't be left to live on his own.

At one time, Mike had suggested Father live with him and his family in Covina, and now I offered to get him into a small bungalow in the backyard of the place I rented in Long Beach. But Mother decided to move him into a renovated guesthouse on the edge of her two-and-a-half acres. She tasked him with watering the trees and coming in to feed her cat when she was out of town, which was often.

Mother, however, didn't plan on being a caregiver and wasn't cut out to be one. Her positive thinking, which had enabled her to accomplish notable goals, clouded her perception when it came to the ability of other people to reach theirs. Especially if those other people were dependent upon her.

More than a decade earlier, when Father had surgery for detached retinas and was declared legally blind, Mother insisted he could see just fine if he really wanted to. And now that he was experiencing dementia, she was convinced that his leaving the hose running on already soaked bushes or putting her sneakers in the freezer were acts done intentionally to aggravate her.

In 1987, a year into Father's stay with Mother, her church organist introduced her to a motorcyclist in a black leather jacket and riding chaps. David was blond with a sensitive expression that was as appealing as his biker attire. But his endearing demeanor didn't rest on an appropriately aged face. He was only thirty-two to her seventy. Mother, though, didn't see their age difference as a problem. That Christmas Day, she wrote in her diary, *Last year I was so surrounded by old people. God granted my wish this year—David.*

Given her own mother's May-December romance—as well as Mother's fondness for shocking people of a more conservative bent—it is perhaps not too hard to understand how Mother and David became a couple. And while she occasionally joked about wanting to be surrounded by a troupe of dancing boys, he was no mere amusement. She wrote in her diary that *God will delight, love and cherish me thru him.*

Father, who in better days would have warned her about being taken for a ride, was now having a hard time putting his thoughts together and making sense of his surroundings. He watched passively as David and others entered and left his field of vision, making small talk with him. And big decisions for him.

Mother arranged to board Father with a church couple in town, and by year's end she'd given the guesthouse keys to David.

Mimi didn't approve and said so. While concerned about the pitfalls of navigating an age gap even wider than her own—and with such a young man—she was dismayed that her daughter had shuttled her eighty-four-year-old husband off to live with people she'd described as "loving, but a little slow."

Mother sent a letter to Jay, reporting that Mimi was "hurt and mystified and angry that I don't respond more to the concept of 'family,' and I just could not care less...." By then, Mother was inured to Mimi's disapproval, and Mimi, ninety-four, wasn't as powerful in delivering it.

But with Mother's busy schedule—gone as much as she was home—Father had been mostly isolated on her property. According to a diary entry made after he'd left, Mother seems to have at some point recognized his needs. *Ray is doing very well. He needed the stimulation of people and activity.* A couple of months later, she wrote that *it was really abusive to have left him alone so much.*

Fortunately, Father's caretakers doted on him and gave him a lot of attention—notwithstanding their losing him once when he wandered off to the local Del Taco.

Despite their care, he had heart issues—atherosclerosis and a pacemaker implanted five years earlier—and soon suffered mobility problems that required him to replace his cane with a walker.

A year after Father had moved in with his caretakers, Mother picked him up for a visit. He wasn't feeling well.

August 20, 1988: Ray is very weak and cannot stand, nor hold his bladder. I have him this week and we shall receive Medicare aid.

The next day, she and David bundled him into an old camper and drove him the two-plus hours to Mimi's birthday party.

August 21: Camper broke down, and David and Harold fixed it. Mimi looks well. Ray very fragile.

They made it back home, but two days later, he was worse.

August 23: The paramedics picked up Ray and took him to the Barstow Community Hospital. Doctor suspects a prostate cancer.

August 24: Ray died 8:15 this morning. I visited him at 6-7. I returned at 8:15 and he had just slipped away.

Although the doctor listed Father's cause of death as cardiac arrest after years of heart disease and dementia, by the following day, Mother referred to his passing as a self-willed act.

August 25: Ray was healthy. X-rays showed perfect body. Blood pressure also perfect. He stopped his heart. I closed his eyes.

His funeral service was well-attended and very New Age, complete with an analogy of Father having emerged from his cocoon to become a butterfly. His old Seventh-day Adventist self might not have welcomed the airy comparison, but he'd come to enjoy Mother's church with its upbeat, smiling parishioners. In his final year, Father had largely retreated into himself, but when he did engage with others, his overriding outlook was one of gratitude. He would have appreciated all the fuss and flowers.

Mother's romance with David was liberating for her and unsettling for the rest of us. The winter after Father died, she brought David, garbed in his leather chaps, to our family Christmas party. Everyone was polite and nobody made reference to their relationship, except for Tim, who asked the one-year-younger David if he should start calling him "Dad."

Mimi privately cautioned Mother about David, probably in the same way Henrietta's relatives had warned her a century earlier about William Whitehead, the young rake who had caused her financial ruin. But Mother was no more interested in naysayers than Henrietta had been. By then, Mother had already bought an apartment building and a rental house, and added David's name on the papers of both.

Two years later, she noted in her diary, *In order to protect our mutual funds, David and I will marry (secretly) in the future.*

It didn't happen. In December 1990, on the third anniversary of their first date, she wrote she was *lonesome for nice love*. And, although she had two years left to fill in her five-year diary, she stopped there, found some ink-dissolving agent, and thoroughly scrubbed out most of the entries that mentioned him. Then she closed the book, bought a new one, and started over.

The David years cost her a piece of investment property, but she brushed it off and refocused on her church work. Known by then as Dr. Scotti—in 1983 she had received an honorary doctorate from Religious Science—she attended Science of Mind retreats at Asilomar and redoubled her efforts in the Barstow community. Aside from her regular ministerial duties, she had added an AIDS support group and increasingly conducted commitment ceremonies for gay couples.

Like Mimi, who years earlier wrote letters to the Los Angeles Times decrying social and racial injustice, Mother was outspoken in championing those with less political clout. In a letter to a local paper, she took objection to an article that referred to a couple of parks as those that served primarily as recreation sites for "minorities." Mother disapproved of the term and used the dictionary to make her point. "Minority means the lesser part," she wrote. "What part of Barstow is lesser than the whole? And what man is lesser than I?"

She served as president of Desert Manna, a non-profit which supported the hungry and homeless. Answering her phone with a comforting, "I'm here," she brought hope and acceptance to those on the fringes of society.

But the next few years were hard on her. She developed debilitating fatigue and baffling aches and pains that often kept her in bed. And there was no one to fill her loneliness. She wrote increasingly of missing Evan. And even of missing Father.

While Mother was helping those in Barstow, Jay directed her energy closer to home. Bob was declining. It had been eight years since they had moved to Sun City and his Alzheimer's had finally robbed him of not only his thought processes but his physical functioning as well.

Jay had inherited her mother's caregiving side. Like Mimi, who'd once tended to the old grandmother in the Elliot family, Jay had worked as a hospital aide in Minnesota and encouraged her oldest daughter, Susan, to pursue what had turned into a rewarding career in nursing. Bob, too, had once been a fount of information about vitamins and supplements, and Jay followed his lead. Mimi and Mother looked to her regularly for nutritional advice.

But there were no longer any health foods that could help Bob. Jay devoted herself to his daily needs—even warming his clothes in the morning before dressing him—until she lacked the physical strength to do so. In the end, Mother encouraged Jay to put him in a convalescent hospital. At the age of seventy-two, he passed away.

Mimi had outlived both of her sons-in-law.

55

Goodbye, Mon Amour Chéri

Although essentially blind, Mimi remained vibrant and enjoyed the company of family. Harold's daughter, now with children of her own, lived near Palm Springs, and Mimi's great-grandchildren all lived within an hour or two.

It was a bit far for frequent visits, but I brought my son and daughter whenever I could. By then, Harold did most of the entertaining, making us lunch and treating us to his homemade lemon cake. He took the kids to feed the ducks in the nearby pond and when we said our goodbyes in the driveway, he gave each child a roll of quarters.

It was on one such visit, when Mimi was in her mid-nineties, that she revealed how vibrant she still was. My kids and I had just arrived and Harold had taken them into the kitchen. Mimi patted the space on the sofa next to her and asked me to sit down. She wanted to tell me about *the awful thing that happened to them*.

"Last week, suddenly, out of the blue, Harold and I weren't able to enjoy each other's company in bed. He couldn't do it. Of course, as you can imagine, this was quite a shock to us."

Uncomfortable discussing such things even with my women friends, I made sympathetic sounds and hoped her story would be a short one. And hoped, equally, that it wouldn't veer into questions about my own sex life. Once when I was eighteen, she asked me some fairly innocuous questions about my boyfriend, and I gave some fairly innocuous answers. But then she said, "That's all well and good, dear, but does he satisfy you?" With that exchange etched in my mind, I braced myself, but her story stayed on track.

"Absolutely nothing like that had ever happened before and we couldn't figure it out," she said, furrowing her brow. "Then we realized it must be his new medicine. So he stopped taking the darned pills right away and called the doctor to ask him to give him something else." She laughed. "Thankfully we got it all sorted out, but we had a few anxious days."

"What a relief," I said, glad both that their crisis was averted and that I'd been spared the details. "Let's join Harold for lunch."

Not an hour later, as Harold and I walked behind the children while they raced to the duck pond, he leaned over and said, "You won't believe what happened to us last week . . ."

Although they were discreet in their disclosures, it was clear they continued to share a strong passion for each other. Once Mimi had stitched a sofa pillow for Harold with the playful message, *You're Gonna Get It!* The saying became his favorite, and he still regularly turned to Mimi with a twinkle in his eye, and a tease in his voice, to repeat the phrase. It always made her smile.

This late-in-life marriage brought Mimi the love she'd sought throughout her life. She found an ardor to equal that of her grandparents, George and Henrietta, who had met on the train and wed the next day. And she enjoyed a husband's dedication to rival that of her father's for his beloved Queeny.

But even the most loved and vital must eventually say farewell. A couple of years after the pill incident, we arrived one day to find Mimi napping on her bed. She woke up sunny and happy to join us. But by the next year, she was often under the covers, a wheelchair nearby, and too deeply asleep to notice us. Even on those occasions when she was in the living room waiting to greet us, she seemed increasingly frail.

Harold had to help her more, but as she had predicted, he was a willing caregiver. He cooked for her, tended to her wardrobe—she was never one to lounge around in a sweatsuit—and took her to weekly hair appointments. Still, her age began to show. After seeing Mimi on her ninety-eighth birthday, Mother wrote, *She is very fragile, like old tissue paper around an ancient baptismal dress.*

A year later, Mimi suffered a couple of small strokes that impaired her speech and hindered her movements. Harold kept her active and helped her eat, and when we visited, he sat by her side to assist her in finding the words she struggled to recall. She sometimes fell silent from frustration, but she never lost her gracious smile and regal posture.

Then one winter evening she had a third stroke and fell into a coma. Over the following days, she was aware of Harold and those of us who came to see her in the hospital, but her responses were barely perceptible. And she wasn't getting any better. Only when Harold insisted the nurses continue every effort to keep her alive did Mother step in. She told Harold he had to let her go. When he disagreed, she told him Mimi's true age. She was ninety-nine.

Through all the years of juggling driver's licenses, insurance records, and a few unwitting comments from family or friends, she had managed to keep her age a secret. Harold remarked on it in her diary. *Visited Mimi six times. No improvement. Doctor said it's very bad. Discovered Mimi would be one hundred years old August this year.*

He didn't say how he felt about this revelation. He may have been a bit chagrined at his gullibility, or impressed by her spirit, but those things mattered little. Particulars of her age paled in comparison to his anguish over the inevitability of losing her.

The next day he wrote, *Nothing new. Mimi opened her eyes for me a little today.*

Harold started looking at convalescent homes, but the hospital wouldn't wait for him to find the perfect one. On Valentine's Day, a week after she had been admitted, a hospital administrator authorized her to be transferred to a drab facility eighteen miles away. *Mimi was taken to Meadowbrook in Hemet today without my consent! I could shoot the guy. She's very bad.*

She was barely alive, but having been born with a powerful life force, it was not in her nature—conscious or unconscious—to let go. The same innate will to live that had allowed her to survive when she entered the world as a premature infant now prevented her from leaving it.

After three long weeks of visiting her in the nursing home, Harold noted, *Mimi is worse. God, it's so hard for her and for me.*

Four days later, March 11, 1993, Harold recorded her death. *Today, Mimi passed away at 3 PM. I loved her very dearly!*

In her will, signed nine years earlier, Mimi had requested a modest burial, typical of Christian Science funerals. In accordance with her wishes, Harold planned a no-frills service at the National Cemetery in Riverside. A few dozen of us, mostly family, stood waiting under the outside committal shelter.

Jay, who'd provided much of Mimi's care, was unsettled. The week before, she'd walked into the nursing home and discovered her mother's body. "She was all alone," she said to Mother, not for the first time. "How could the staff have been so oblivious?"

Mother, who had tried to comfort Mimi by speaking French during her own last visit, clutched a tissue and nodded.

"She looked stricken," Jay said. "She fought death to the end."

That haunting image aside, Jay was hurting for another reason, too. She had written a song for Mimi, but Harold didn't want her to sing it for fear it would "turn the funeral into a circus."

Finally, the cemetery workers wheeled in Mimi's pale pink casket. Someone placed a lone bouquet of cellophane-wrapped flowers on top, and then my brother Mike delivered the eulogy. Following Mimi's wishes, a poem of hers, *Weep Not For Me*, was read. She had also requested Psalms 121 and 139. The words were humble—*O Lord, Thou hast searched me, and known me*—and the service simple.

After we shared hugs and lingered a few minutes, Harold hurried us back to our cars, leaving Mimi's casket sitting alone under the shelter. It didn't feel right to me, especially given that her death had been unattended. I thought we should have been standing by her grave, marking her final resting place in our memories, seeing her off properly. But the cemetery didn't offer graveside services, and the shelter had to be readied for the next bereaved family.

Even if the funeral seemed too rushed and perfunctory for a matriarch like Mimi, it was probably as much as Harold could endure. They'd been hand-in-hand for twenty-five adoring years, but their last month together had been agonizing. He wanted everyone back at his place to eat and share memories of happier days.

Later, going through her desk, he found a letter Mimi had left for him. Although written years earlier—when she still had her sight and distinctive script—it was eternal in its message.

> Dearest Mon Amour Chéri;
>
> Should I leave you (and if you are reading this, it is because I am no longer by your side), you must not grieve for me. Remember rather our every tender moment, and let it lift you when your spirits sag and the hill seems hard to climb alone. I shall be at your side, loving you as I do now, and knowing we shall meet again, and recall—in a measure—some past encounter.
>
> Thank you, my darling, for every precious moment with you, for loving me and making me feel a woman much loved!
>
> Goodbye, mon amour chéri, my love—until we meet again, adieu.
>
> Your own, Mimi

56

Mimi's Will

Following Mimi's funeral, Harold's diary entries focused on mundane things—visits from family, bowling scores, and each hopeful purchase of lottery tickets. He was ready, however, to move on with life. He may have been seventy-six, but he was still healthy. And lonely.

A couple of months later—after entries mentioning a lunch and dinner with a bowling friend named Sue—Harold scrawled out, *I'm not writing in Mimi's diary anymore! H.*

Nine months after Mimi's passing, Harold married Sue, a perky widow in her sixties. It was a bit quick, but Aunt Jay said that Sue, being a good Catholic, wasn't about to spend the night with him without the blessings of the Church. And Harold was simply not a man accustomed to living alone.

By then we had all gotten to know Sue at family gatherings. Although no one expected her to replace Mimi, she was well-liked and we were glad to see Harold happy again.

None of us thought of Harold's hurried romance as a lack of devotion to Mimi. If there was any doubt about his lingering feelings for her, one had to look no further than that year's city directory, where he listed himself as Harold *Tate* Friedman. Or to the interior of his home, which was exactly as Mimi had left it—a shrine to the Tates and Gudgeons.

Sue moved into Harold's place, where the portraits of Mimi's ancestors still graced the walls, just as their sterling silver tea sets lined the shelves of her china hutch. Henrietta's marble sculpture of Queeny kept the hall door propped open. The gold-framed

Renaissance reproductions hung in the master bedroom. And Harold meant for it all to stay that way.

He loved the things Mimi had loved and, with no disrespect to his bride, wanted to preserve the life he'd had with her. The influence of his new wife, a cheery but passive woman who liked to paint, was limited to one room—the den-turned-art studio.

Although Mother and Jay thought this unfair to Sue, their more immediate concern centered on their inheritance. Neither woman had wanted to bother Harold about the family heirlooms while he was grieving, but now they felt it was time for him to honor his departed wife's wishes. Mother had a copy of Mimi's handwritten will, dated almost a decade before her death. It made her intentions clear.

> I, Mona Tate Friedman, being of sound mind, make this my last will and testament. I leave my share of our estate to my husband, Harold Friedman, knowing he will share equally with my daughters, Gwen Dole and Jane Anderson. All family pictures, paintings, antiques, china, silver, and jewelry are to remain in the keeping of my two daughters, Gwen Dole and Jane Anderson.

The following year, Mimi had written an addendum, typed this time, detailing the dispersal of the heirlooms in a document addressed to Dear Ones.

> This is a letter apart from my will. I want to be sure that certain things go to the following ones of you, as my will requests all family things to be divided between you, Gwen, and you, Jane, after you have received the following items...

Mother was to have Queeny's silver hot water jug and teapot, the portrait of Jane Bennett painted by the court artist, and the carved chest of silverware bearing the Tate crest. By tradition, the orange and blue ceramic jug that Mimi's great-great-grandfather Gliddon had used to make his hot toddy was also to go to her, the eldest child. Jay, the more artistic and fashionable of the two, was to receive the greater share of artwork and family jewelry.

Mimi knew these things would eventually pass to her grandchildren, but she bequeathed us a few special mementos.

Her antique books were to go to Mike, a cameo brooch and earrings to me, and to Tim, her grandfather's barometer and a Victorian key box, which she referred to as a hunting lodge for its carving of a dog with the spoils of the hunt.

Jay's daughter, Susan, would receive Jane Bennett's teapot, and Wendy the large silver pin of the Neville coat of arms. Mona, who had been closest to Mimi—and had changed her middle name to Tate—would be given all the china and silver marked with the initial M or T. She was also to have the Tate signet ring, another gold ring with a jade stone, and Mimi's copy of *Debrett's Peerage* as well as a book of her poems. Judy was to inherit the jewelry Harold had given Mimi over the years.

Mimi closed the addendum with her final thoughts.

> "As stated in my will, all family things will be divided between Gwen and Jane. All else I leave to Harold, who has been more loving and helpful than anyone else. His devotion has been shared by Mona, who never failed to show her love and attention to us both. I've tried to leave each of you those things for which you have shown a preference. My mother's sculptured head, work of my grandmother Tate, I leave to the one who will cherish, as I have, and care for it as a treasure of her youth."

In early 1994, shortly before the first anniversary of Mimi's death, Mother approached Harold about the items Mimi had left to her and Jay. The conversation didn't go well at all. According to some who weren't there for the encounter but got an earful later, what Mother characterized as a gentle broaching of the subject, Harold saw as a demanding of the goods. He refused to give her a thing.

February 14: Harold stunned us by saying he and Mimi made a later will and everything belongs to him. It's hard to believe Mother would knowingly disinherit us. Harold is a good man, but this is "family theft!!"

In the same way that Queeny had written to the newspaper to set right her son's World War I honor, and Mimi had attended to conflicts through letters, Mother took to her typewriter to seek justice. But, like Mimi in her correspondence to Jay, Mother didn't always know when to restrain her fingers. She sent Harold a letter that read in part:

"Please Harold, and please Sue, please read these pages with care and love, and discuss the contents between you....

"I understand the value of the common 'I leave everything to my wife/husband' will. It's protection for the remaining spouse.... But, Harold, do you really believe that Mother would have cut us out of our inheritance? Don't you realize that in her concept of your fairness and goodness, which you've always shown, that she simply expected you to follow her private and family will?

"What are you going to do with the few things that Mother left us? Sell them, give them away, will them to your grandchildren?

"The double-coloured pitcher up on the top, left-hand side of the desk/breakfront may be very valuable. Grandpa gave it to me when I was eleven, but handed it to Mother for safekeeping. The 'letter-holder' on the desk is actually a toast holder. Grandma had it on the sideboard, and it always held cold toast. She sewed for me from the snake-legged sewing table."

While emphasizing her inherent right to her family's things, Mother didn't argue the legality of the will. She appealed instead to Harold's integrity.

"The new will you and Mother drew up is valid, and I'm not contesting it. It's legal. When the Communists took over Russia, many people lost their citizenship, and it was legal to plunder their homes and churches. When Hitler took away the citizenship of certain races and religions, it was legal to take their heirlooms.

"Someplace in these many years (remember, I knew you when Helen was still alive), I displeased you, and I don't know why. I've been fair and gentle with you. After Mother's death, we knew you were relieved of being the caregiver and terribly sad at her leaving. None of us wanted to disturb you and your home. We naturally thought, bit by bit, you would rearrange your living, and give us our inheritance. We were simply waiting for you to be healed of your loss. Your putting the letter of the law above the spirit of the law has really stunned us.

"I know lots of families have to work through misunderstandings and problems like this, but I want this one over with ... We will abide with whatever your decision is, no problems and no reviews. If you decide to give us our inheritance, be sure it is with a clear heart.... If you decide to keep the heirlooms, be sure you are strong enough for the burden.

"That's the best I can do, Harold, except to always be so very grateful for the wonderful years of love and joy and care you gave to Mother."

Her last sentence of appreciation did little to offset the overall tone. If Harold couldn't be talked into giving Mother the items, he certainly wasn't going to be shamed into it. Her alluding to his keeping company with Mimi before his first wife died did nothing to endear Mother to him. And aligning him, a Polish Jew, with Hitler, was even worse than her likening him to a Communist.

Harold had usually been pleasant to his stepdaughters, unless Mimi was upset at one of them. He was, after all, her greatest supporter. Still, his relationship with the two women, despite not meeting them until they were middle-aged, had been mostly parental. As Mimi slowly faded, Harold increasingly took it upon himself to dispense advice, bestow approval, or scold when he thought it necessary. For years Mother bristled at having to treat him as a father figure who knew more about life—right down to what make and model of car she should buy—but she put up with it for Mimi's sake.

Now, with Mimi no longer here, Mother had spoken her mind. Harold, however, had a strong mind of his own and if ever he'd planned to give Mother her birthright, he no longer did. He would not relent. The paintings had adorned his walls and the china had beautified his table for twenty years. In those decades the silver and *objets d'art* had gone from being Mimi's to theirs... and now they were his.

With no response from Harold, Mother wrote again.

February 27: Sent Harold a letter and told him he could have everything. I feel betrayed, but prize my honor more than heirlooms.

Although Mother had said she'd abide by Harold's decision, it rankled her. Losing the family treasures that George James had entrusted to ships' captains or that Queeny had packed into Mimi's steamer trunks was crushing.

Mother and Jay knew that Mimi would die one day, but they believed she would, in some way, live on in the luster of the silver teapot or the worn-down gold of her signet ring. They believed it because Mimi had believed it of her ancestors. Whether she was caressing Jane Bennett's soup bowl, polishing the Tate silverware, or dusting the marble profile of Queeny, Mimi was communing with her family. Each precious object told a story and provided a link to the ancestors who had also caressed it and polished it and loved it. When Mimi gazed on the old portraits that lined her walls, she saw her own grandchildren's eyes and mouths and chins.

Mimi, who had been the connection between Europe and America, and between past and present, was gone. And now those things that were supposed to forever tie her to the following generations were gone as well.

Eventually Mother adopted the view that, more than wanting Mimi's possessions, Harold needed them. In much the same way that these treasures kept Queeny alive to her, they kept Mimi alive to him. Mother would simply have to wait for him to be healed of his loss. In the meantime, she kept positive thoughts and called upon the workings of the Universal Mind to see to it that Mimi's effects be disbursed in accordance with her wishes.

Whether it had anything to do with the Universal Mind or not, it wasn't long before Harold began to distribute a few of Mimi's things. When I told him I was writing about Mimi's life, he gave me her diaries and audiocassettes, as well as the cameo brooch and one lone earring, the other one apparently lost.

Nonetheless, it soon became clear that if Harold took to heart anything Mother had written, it was her last letter, the one that told him he could have everything. He no longer seemed to regard the heirlooms as Mimi's carefully considered bequests, but as his things to keep or bestow as he saw fit.

Like the rolls of quarters he had presented to Mimi's great-grandchildren when he saw them off in the driveway, now he gave us grandkids end-of-visit gifts. He presented Mike with the antique books slated to go to him, and then, surprisingly, the large oil painting of George Tate in his college robes. And to me he passed down the treasured court portrait of Jane Bennett. The latter was specifically to have gone to my mother so I asked her if she wanted it. She said to hold on to it, that she was just happy to have it back in the family.

Even though Mother's and Harold's dispute created tension between them—and Jay, too, who took Mother's side—it didn't cause a rift with the younger generations. Harold had always been kind to us and our children, who knew him as their good-natured Honeydo, and his affection was reciprocated. Mike never failed to invite him and Sue to his annual Christmas Eve party. And my brothers and I invited them to each great-grandchild's birthday celebration. As before, Harold and Sue remained valued members of the family.

57

Legacy

A few years after Mimi died, Mother retired from church work. She hadn't become a minister until late in life, yet she'd served more than twenty years. Now she stayed active as a circuit rider—filling in for pastors on vacation—and taped occasional radio programs. Her "Sundays with Dr. Scotti," a series on San Bernardino's KFRG, challenged her listeners with a metaphysical perspective of Bible stories and comforted them with positive messages of God's love for all.

Although she'd often dismissed the importance of family—or at least Mimi's concept of it—she was proud to show us off during our visits, and she delighted in her grandchildren. She said that when it came to kids, she was like Queeny, an observer rather than a sit-down-and-play-with-them participant. But even if watching rather than interacting, she was a beaming grandma.

She spent her summers in the pine-scented mountains at Big Bear. She loved the small-town atmosphere and became a regular at The Grizzly Manor Café, which named a breakfast plate after her: *The Scottie Bear,* with one egg and two pieces of toast.

Every year I took Jay to Mother's rental cabin for an overnight stay. On one of those getaways, I videotaped them chatting in their Adirondack chairs on the deck. Mother was eighty-five and Jay was eighty. They were talking about their childhoods when Mother, who had always kept vulnerable emotions to herself, was suddenly fighting back tears.

"I realize why I don't seem to be close to people," she said, her voice breaking. "I felt abandoned because Mother frequently left me. I was just not going to depend on other people to take care of me... or for my self-worth... or for my good feelings. I could never reach out, but I thought if I took care of my own area, I'd be perfectly safe." She turned to me. "That's why I never picked up you kids. It just wasn't safe."

We pass on more than physical legacies to our children. The actions of our forebears shape our lives as easily as their DNA sculpts our eyes and mouths and chins. Generations of at-arms-length parenting affected the well-being of those who followed, in the same way that exalted love stories molded their expectations. Mimi and my mother were merely links in a long chain.

In a lineage of strong women accustomed to focusing on their own needs, it was probably inevitable that some children would be shuttled off, some husbands dismissed. Although Mimi had left both girls with others at times, she saw it as a sacrifice, hers as much as theirs, for a better future. And she lived in an era when a better future came from finding and keeping a good provider. If she had to leave one daughter to return to America to confront her first husband, or if she had to leave the other to lend support to her second husband, then that was simply what she had to do.

Jay and Mother had each suffered a lack of consistent nurturing from Mimi but they reacted to it in different ways—Jay trying harder and Mother withdrawing. Now, during summer visits, they reflected on their early years and tried to make sense of them.

In 2002, Mother was interviewed for a newspaper article marking the fiftieth anniversary of the establishment of Religious Science in Barstow. They printed a photo of her in church robes, head tilted back with a laugh that lit up her face. She talked about her first trip through the desert town when she was thirteen and moving with her family from Upstate New York. She recalled her years as a minister. When the reporter asked her to share a bit of her spiritual wisdom, she gave him some of her best advice.

"You don't have to forgive, you don't have to forget. You just have to understand."

Mother loved inspirational sayings, but that one in particular rang true to me. Understanding one's family of origin is essential in healing from the wounds they inflict upon us.

Rereading the article, though, I wondered if Mother's words were prompted by recollections of her childhood, or if she was thinking about a more recent hurt. It had been years since Mimi died, and Harold still had many of the heirlooms. When he'd first started parceling them out, Mother and Jay were relieved, even if the items didn't always go to the person designated by Mimi as the recipient. At least they were going to Mimi's heirs. But it soon became clear that none were going to Mother or Jay.

Mother, who had characterized Harold's keeping the heirlooms as him merely unready to let go of Mimi, was forced to rethink her view when Harold gave me the tea caddies. They were the silver canisters Mimi had given Mother ages ago, the ones Mike and I had turned into outsized rattles, upsetting Mimi so much she'd taken them back. They were rightfully Mother's, but she assured me I was meant to have them. I asked Mike if he'd like the square-cornered one that I'd always considered his "rattle," but he laughed at the memory and said to keep them both.

For the most part, we grandkids—living in the busy years of our thirties and forties—didn't worry about Mimi's antiques. We weren't anxious to get our hands on her ornate silver and china. And the Tate artwork—old Italian reproductions of Renaissance religious scenes—didn't match anyone's décor.

I perhaps thought more often about Mimi's things than my brothers did because I was close to Jay, and their loss weighed on her. To my aunt and my mother, the paintings of the Madonna and Child, halo-crowned angels, and the red-robed cardinal were the reassuring guardians of home.

I often drove out to Sun City to spend the day with Jay. Over a hearty stew in her shaded lanai, we'd talk about our writing projects and our lives. And about the heirlooms. Living near Harold and Sue, she was in frequent contact with them, although neither side talked about Mimi's will.

One day, almost seven years after Mimi died, Jay told me she was concerned that Harold's cognitive abilities were declining. I had noticed it too. After lunch with Jay, I would always drop in for dessert with Sue and Harold, who had taken to repeating his stories while we enjoyed his lemon cake and a cup of tea.

He was soon diagnosed with the beginnings of Alzheimer's. With his high energy and sunny disposition, he didn't dwell on his bleak prognosis, acting as if nothing had changed. His memory, however, inevitably worsened.

Jay, who had once lost precious correspondence when her Alzheimer's-stricken husband set his mind to cleaning out boxes, worried that Harold might put Mimi's remaining items out in a garage sale. On my visits, I'd quietly scan the dining room to see if the pieces were still there.

But Harold kept a steady grip on Mimi's finery, including the Tate silverware, which Mother particularly wanted. During the wait for her inheritance—perhaps to make herself feel better—she'd bought herself an over-priced set of gold-plated flatware to bring out at family dinners. She said how much she liked it, but she didn't look all that happy. I think it mostly served to remind her of what she didn't have.

Mother liked things. Perhaps it was because she had had such a hard time connecting with people, but she took unabashed pleasure in beautiful objects.

Her desert home, now grown into a lush oasis with good-sized mulberry trees lining the driveway, was a repository of personal treasures. When she passed through her open, sun-filled rooms, she often stopped to touch one of her antique clocks, or a religious statue—she favored her Madonnas—or a Brittany ceramic vase. She acknowledged them and blessed them.

As she stroked the tops of Queeny's green dresser set—now missing the ring holder that Mother's cleaning lady had dropped and broken—she said a wordless prayer to her grandmother. As she caressed the beads on the Countess de Bélizal's old wooden rosary—hanging on the wall above her bed the way it had once hung above her grandparents'—she gave a quiet benediction for all who had touched it.

She had quite a few remembrances of her family, things given to her well before Mimi had died. But like the shepherd of the Bible whose attention was on the one lost sheep rather than the ninety-nine that were safe, Mother focused on the missing heirlooms. She wanted them back in the fold.

Another year passed, and then Sue, always a bit skittish and now stressed from the challenges of taking care of Harold, also showed signs of dementia.

The possibility of them both incapacitated raised new concerns. Sue had been healthy and an ally of sorts. She liked Jay and had said if anything happened to Harold, she'd give her Mimi's things. But in short order, Sue's children began talking about packing up their mother's belongings and moving her into assisted living. A few hasty decisions on the part of Sue's relatives, most of them unknown to us, and items could be misplaced. In the chaos of relocating, the silver could end up in an estate sale. The sepia-toned portraits of ancestors might be relegated to some antique dealer's box of orphaned prints for strangers to peruse.

Not long after that, however, Mother's call to the all-powerful Universal Consciousness to return the heirlooms was answered.

By Jay.

Although both she and Mother shared similar spiritual principles, Jay was not as inclined as Mother to leave it up to the Universal Mind to nudge an increasingly befuddled Harold and Sue in the right direction. At eighty-two, she had had enough of waiting and worrying. There was too much at stake, and ex-Army Jay was a woman of action.

In the same way that Mimi had left a final letter to Harold, she had left one to her daughters. It was dated 1974, even before her marriage to Harold, but it contained her timeless and deepest beliefs about family.

> My beloved children,
>
> If you are reading this, it is because I am beyond your vision and no longer here to say what I am now saying.
>
> Gwen dear—you the first born—it has been a great joy growing up with you. Thank you for every thoughtful thing and kind gesture you have given me.
>
> Jane darling, thank you for the tender years we shared, and for your music, which comforted me. If I ever failed you or Gwen as a mother, it was unknowingly because my love for you both taught me the beauty of unselfishness.
>
> I leave you the only gift which is eternal, the heritage of love and courage and loyal hearts. Be true in all things, thus you can do no wrong.
>
> Remember those who have gone before and who laid within your grasp the spirit of nobility and honor, respect the memory of your ancestors and honor your lineage and inculcate it within the hearts of your children.
>
> I close my darlings reminding you I shall always be with you, loving you and being grateful for you both.
>
> Affectionately, your mother, Mimi

"Remember those who have gone before…"

Jay, who had always taken Mimi's words to heart, knew her mother would never have allowed her family's things to be left in the care of those who couldn't protect them and pass them down to their rightful heirs. For even if Mimi's stories formed the heart of the family, the silver and china made up the backbone.

One morning, Jay got up early, charged the battery of her rusting golf cart, and put a stack of clean towels in the back. Then, waiting until Harold and Sue were out for their weekly bowling, she drove up to their house.

She still had a key from the years when she had helped care for Mimi, so she let herself in. Working quickly, she took the ornately framed artwork off the walls, grabbed the chest of silver as well as Queeny's tea set, and removed the venerable old toddy jug from the top of the breakfront desk. She wrapped those and the antique barometer in the towels, stuffed the heirloom jewelry in a small bag, and loaded them all into the back of her cart, with room to spare for the snake-legged sewing table. She was back out the door and safely down the road before Harold and Sue came home.

Jay knew Harold would be furious. After she brought everything inside and into her bedroom—as far from the front door as possible—she held her breath and waited to see if he would try to wrest them back or press charges.

She didn't have to wait long. He called Jay on the phone and made a terrible fuss, but she was willing to take a tongue-lashing as the price of a successful coup. In the end, Harold—perhaps recognizing she had inherited her mother's unshakable resolve, or perhaps lacking the cerebral skills to launch a counter-attack—let the matter go.

He didn't mention it again, and just as Jay and Mother had maintained a cordial relationship with Harold at the beginning of the conflict, he did likewise at the end.

Jay and Mother distributed the remaining items as designated in Mimi's will, hung the artwork on their walls, and shared the rest of the pieces between them.

Mother cleaned and polished Mimi's treasures and set them out on her dining table to admire. She loved them, and as she went through her days, each time one caught her eye, she smiled and said a simple, *Thank you, God.*

Having the heirlooms back in the family, she was at peace. But that peace didn't hinge on her personal possession of them. When winter approached, she carefully wrapped the sterling silver tea service, hot toddy jug, and the barometer in white tissue paper, placed them in holiday boxes and, at the Christmas party, passed them on to the next generation.

The End

Epilogue

The next five years brought big changes. After Sue moved into an assisted living facility, Harold's daughter took over his care. Then in 2004, Mother died of a heart attack, and in 2007, Aunt Jay succumbed to lung cancer. That was all quite some time ago. Now my brothers and I, and Jay's daughters, are the older generation, the keepers of the possessions and stories of our ancestors.

I've heard it said that those who have parted from us stay alive as long as they live in someone's memory. Perhaps that's the purpose of heirlooms—to serve as memory devices to keep our loved ones and ancestors with us.

It doesn't always work. After Mother died, I was cleaning out her kitchen when I came upon an antique spoon, engraved with "Remember Me." I often wonder who it was that hoped to be remembered. I've come to think of it as *The Spoon of the Unknown Ancestor*, representing all who have gone before, living life, collecting things along the way, and passing them on.

Mimi's heirlooms are here throughout my home, a few pieces of china and silver in the dining room hutch, the tea caddies and reframed ancestor portraits in the family room. I particularly like the painting of Jane Bennett because when I was a teenager, Mimi said I looked like Jane. I struggle to see the resemblance, but my grandmother's words make it special.

Henrietta's marble sculpture leans against the wall in an out-of-the-way spot. It ended up with me not because I was the one "who would cherish" it as Mimi did, but because Jay, who once broke her toe on it, knew I'd look after it until it could be passed on to the next custodian.

Only my favorites have made it into my bedroom. Queeny's large rosary adorns the wall above my bed, and her vanity set is arranged on my dresser. One of Mother's wooden Madonnas sits on the bookcase.

On the wall facing my bed is the painting of Mimi's home in Brittany where she charmed doves and played childish pranks. It's where she first fell in love and once saved a horse from drowning, the place that molded her until she sailed across the ocean to start a new life in America.

At a respectful distance hangs a framed photo of the Hayford Camp on the shore of Sebec Lake, where Mimi spent her honeymoon, marking the beginning of seven years that, although often trying, brought her two dutiful daughters.

Another wall holds a next-generation heirloom, a watercolor of Mimi's home in Cheviot Hills, painted by her neighbor. It was a bequest from Jay, who had been offered a large sum for it from Mimi's one-time foster daughter, Joné, now a middle-aged woman looking back on her own childhood. Jay, who was making do in her time-worn mobile home, could have used the money, but she held on to the artwork to give to me.

The piece captures Mimi's clean white house with its picket fence, blue shutters, colorful flowers, and the rooster weathervane on the roof. In the bottom corner I see the low, brick-topped retaining wall in front of the neighbor's yard. I remember walking on it, Mimi holding my hand and guiding my steps.

My elders are gone now, but along with their heirlooms, I carry their traits. I have my mother's fine hair, her love of books, and a checking account that's balanced to the penny. I share Jay's love of writing and adventure. I have Mimi's fair complexion—with the smattering of childhood freckles—as well as her determination. I have my father's hands, his frown lines, and sense of humor. From the Hayford side, I inherited the hefty bosoms, as well as a legacy of New England roots that reach back to the Pilgrims.

Like my mother, I'll stay quiet rather than risk conflict. Like Henrietta, I'm prone to let my emotions drive me, and like George James—who knew the difference between a jug and a pitcher—I can be exacting to a fault. Nonetheless, I also came by two of the best qualities of my forebears: their resilience and perseverance.

Of the traits I inherited, though, the most rewarding may be Mimi's passion for family history. I love the excitement of finding new information, the joy of sharing it, and the comfort of feeling connected to those who have gone before me.

Mimi and her daughters, Jay and Scotti, in 1980.

Notes and Sources

Easily accessible church and government documents have not been included here since this book isn't intended as a complete family record. Instead, I've focused on lesser-known sources and additional facts that, although fascinating, didn't fit into the narrative. Hopefully these details will help others in their research.

Chapter 1—A Chance Meeting

... the contractor, with whom [George] had dined just the week before. *The Diary of William Mackenzie, The First International Railway Contractor 1844-1850* (Thomas Telford, 2000) p. 455.

After finishing his university education ... I have a large portrait of George Tate in his college robe, and on the back of the painting, Mimi had written, "He is in his Oxford gown." However, I wasn't able to find a record of him in Oxford University's online database.

Further complicating things, Alain Tate in *A Saga of the Tate-Bresciani Family* (Paris, 2012), p. 15, stated George received his degree in civil engineering from Cambridge University. But their alumni office didn't find a record of him in their database either, and the department of engineering wasn't established until 1875 (almost a decade after George's death). A school representative's 2015 email says the railway may have "organised courses for promising trainees which involved attending mathematical lectures given at the University."

This headlong rush to marriage ... Since George was thirty-nine when he married Henrietta, he may have been wed before, but he was listed as a "Bachelor" on his wedding certificate and my research hasn't turned up earlier unions. The constraints of supporting his mother and sisters may have caused the delay.

Chapter 2—The First George & First Henrietta

... they found Bawtry Hall ... The first George Tate was referred to by Mimi as George Bawtry Tate to distinguish him from his son and grandson, both also named George.

The groom was the tenth ... child of a medical practitioner who died when George was twenty-one. George's mother, Leticia Wilkinson, lived to eighty-four and died at Gravesend on the Thames when George was forty-two. His sister, Betsy, sent him a letter describing the arrangements she had made to transport their mother's body the twenty-five miles west to London. She enclosed a portrait made of their mother in her coffin, which was a common practice at the time. That letter, in my possession, begins: "My dear brother, I enclose you this likeness of our beloved parent taken in her coffin. She was indeed most beautiful, like a perfect piece of alabaster."

On September 7, 1850, Letitia was buried at New Bunhill Fields Burial Ground, where her husband had been laid to rest two decades earlier. Only four years after her interment, the cemetery was filled to capacity and closed.

Henrietta was also one of ten children. She lived out her childhood at 16 Red Lion Passage, a short street of shops with residences above. The street no longer exists, but its nearby counterpart, Lamb's Conduit Passage, still leads off from Red Lion Square in Holborn, London.

... his family instead apprenticed [James John Gliddon] to a watchmaker. Wendy Norman, *The Gliddons in London 1760-1850, A Family Record by Anne Gliddon* (Steele Roberts Ltd, 2000), p. 13.

However, Henrietta's father ... still lived in London, along with many artistic, avant-garde cousins. Mimi said we were related through the Gliddons to the poet, Leigh Hunt. I have established that this twig-thin connection was by marriage rather than birth. Catherine Gliddon, daughter of James Gliddon's cousin John Gliddon, married Thornton Hunt, who was the son of the renowned poet. Norman, *The Gliddons in London*, p. 44 and 58.

Baby Henrietta arrived ... She was named Henrietta Alexandriana Ross Tate. Surely this was in honor of George's mentor in the engineering world, Alexander M. Ross, who went on to serve as chief engineer on Canada's Grand Trunk Railway.

Prince Albert presented George with a bronze medal ... Alain Tate provided the information about George's and Henrietta's medals in *A Saga of the Tate-Bresciani Family*, p. 15.

Chapter 3—The Canadian Railroad

George [was actively involved in] talks with Portuguese officials for a Lisbon line. "... the Government has acceded to part of the proposition of Mr. George Tate for the construction of a railroad from Lisbon to Santarem." *The Morning Chronicle,* London, 15 Jan 1851, p. 3.

... George surveyed the terrain [for the Canadian line]... "The line was surveyed in 1852 by Messrs. Keefer and Tate." Online article, *The Advent of the Railroads* (originally published 1901), oldandsold.com.

While he was wrapping up projects in London... George seems to have been engaged in a number of ventures at this time. A news article names him as the Acting Engineer of an Australian mining company "formed for the purpose of working large and extensive coal fields...." The Port Hunter and Moreton Bay Coal Mining Company lists him as "George Tate, Esq., C.E., 11, John-street, Adelphi, and Bawtry, Yorkshire" [C.E. stands for civil engineer, and Esq. did not refer to a lawyer but rather to someone of high social standing.] *Daily News,* London, 12 Mar 1853, p. 7.

... [the Tates] were boarding a ship to Canada. The first known appearance of Henrietta in Canada is found in a newspaper article noting the arrival from England to The British American Hotel of "Mr. & Mrs. G. Tate, child and servant." *The Kingston-Whig Standard,* Kingston, Ontario, 17 May 1853, p. 2.

In the beginning, the family lived in Port Hope. "George Tate Esq., the Resident Engineer of the company, has arrived here with his family and has taken quarters among us.—Port Hope Guide." *Owen Sound Comet,* Owen Sound, Ontario, 2 Sep 1853, p. 2.

They appear to have lived in an apartment above George's office... Mimi said George James was born in the railway building, which I found curious until I received information from a Canadian historian who wrote "... it was quite common in those days for senior officials and their families to live upstairs from their offices..." Derek Boles, Chief Historian of the Toronto Railway Museum, email of Feb 7, 2021.

[Henrietta's grandmother] ... died of a cold caused by her baptismal immersion. Norman, *The Gliddons in London,* p. 13.

... the grown-over grave was reopened ... George Tate was buried in East Finchley Cemetery's grave number E9, 37, above James John Gliddon. Information from London genealogist, Megan Owens, 2014.

Chapter 4—A Poor Choice

[James John Gliddon was] the son of tripe sellers ... Norman, *The Gliddons in London*, p. 12.

They may have had money since one of Henrietta's aunts owned prime rental property ... Owens, 2014.

[Henrietta's brother, Joshua Gliddon, was financially] responsible for two family plots ... East Finchley Cemetery Records.

Chapter 5—An Unexpected Inheritance

... **Agnes Mary, known to all by her nickname, Queeny.** She was probably named after two of her father's sisters. Agnes Maria was born when Edward Gudgeon was three, but she died as a toddler. A month after her death, another sister arrived and was named Anna Agnes. She lived into adulthood but passed away eight months before Agnes Mary (Queeny) was born.

... **[Edward Gudgeon] had been elected to the school board.** He supported free education and from 1882 to 1885 served on the school board for Lambeth, where the Tates were living. The Gudgeons lived in nearby Camberwell. Alain Tate said they were neighbors, but I haven't been able to confirm that. Still, the families must have been acquainted by 1872 when Henrietta and William Whitehead attended Edward's Liberian Ball. *Daily News* (London), January 23, 1872.

The same news article also reports a Dr. George Tate and his wife in attendance at the ball. Dr. George Tate, a London surgeon, was not our George Tate, who had passed away six years earlier, nor his son George James Tate, who was only fifteen at the time.

When [Mary Ann Fleschelle] died, she left [George James] her home and all her money. The Fleschelles and Gliddons had a long-term relationship. Twenty-seven years earlier, Mr. Fleschelle served as executor of the will of Henrietta's father, James John Gliddon. *England & Wales National Probate Calendar 1862.*

Chapter 6—A Bleak Beginning

The Countess de Bélizal . . . suggested a place ten miles north of her castle. I believe the countess lived at the Chateau de Bellevue or at the Chateau des Granges, both in Moncontour and owned by members of the de Bélizal family. *Castles and Mansions,* Commune de Hénon, www.henon.fr/Les-chateaux-manoirs.

Surrounded by farmland, the old fieldstone house . . . Mimi said her father had built Villa St. George, but an official I spoke to at Hillion City Hall in 2011 declared the building too old for George James to have built. Perhaps George James added the wing that's built out from the front of the house. It doesn't look like it's part of the original structure.

. . . the Tates' home was in Hillion's jurisdiction . . . The address of their house is now 12 Route des Greves, 22120 Hillion. Per the clerk at Hillion's City Hall, 2011.

Edward Gudgeon was laid to rest in Camberwell Old Cemetery . . . He's buried in Square 43, grave 11439, according to Megan Owens, who did not find a headstone.

Chapter 7—A Brittany Childhood

George James's sister, Maud, who had recently married, visited with her husband William Rogers. William was the brother of Edward Rogers, who had married Maud's sister, Ethel—a case of brothers marrying sisters. Maud and William wed two and a half months after Ethel passed away.

Both artists, they enjoyed capturing the Brittany countryside . . . I have a watercolor painted by Aunt Maud, and several unsigned pieces I believe were created by her or William. It's possible one of them produced the painting of Villa St. George found on the map in this book. It's doubtful it was painted by Henrietta because if it had been, Mimi surely would have made as much fuss over it as she had Henrietta's marble sculpture.

"Whoever does you good will flourish . . ." Henrietta's blessing (and curse) was related in a 1923 letter from George James to Mimi.

[Queeny] hurried the youngsters up the tree... The story of Queeny being treed, as well as the earlier one of her misplacing a stocking on her wedding day, were passed down by Mimi's daughter, Jane, known in adulthood as Jay.

Chapter 8—Unhallowed Ground

"Finally, my father, my cousin, and two friends bought a coffin." The cousin was presumably one of the Westley boys, since Mimi had no other cousins of an age that would have made their presence likely.

Chapter 10—A Different Sensibility

"My mother... was the first one to start the Society for the Prevention of Cruelty to Animals there..." I believe "there" is in reference to Hillion, because by that time the society was already established in France.

"... a hurdy gurdy, a sort of mechanical violin." Played by a crank and keyboard rather than a bow, its music resembles that of a lively bagpipe.

Chapter 11—Queeny

.... John Bennett, had been the Duke of Norfolk's house steward. John and his wife, Margaret, both worked for the Duke of Norfolk, as verified by the Arundel Castle archivist, Rebecca Hughes in an email of December 2, 2014.

John died 18 January 1847 and was buried at All Souls, Kensal Green (in 6586, reg. no. 11041). Owens, 2014.

His obituary reads: "Died on the 18th inst in London, very respected amongst his friends both in London and the neighbourhood of this town, aged 66, Mr. John Bennett, for many years house-steward to the late Duke of Norfolk." *Bury and Norwich Post,* January 27, 1847.

Queeny's maternal grandmother, Margaret... was also employed by the duke. Mimi believed Margaret Bennett (née Rockliff Croft] was a descendant of the Fitzalan Howard family, whose head is the Duke of Norfolk. Genealogist Megan Owens was not able to verify a familial relationship between Margaret and the duke.

... **[the duke's] seasonal moves from manor to manor.** Suffolk, where the duke and his staff spent autumn and early winter, was the birthplace of Margaret, and likely her husband, John. They married in Suffolk and Jane Bennett was born there, according to birth records for Margaret and Jane, and marriage records for Margaret and John.

... **[Jane's] uncle, an emissary to King George III.** I have not been able to find an uncle who was an emissary to the King. But Jane's sister, Margaret, was married to James Hankinson, who in 1843 became a confectioner in the Royal Household. And Jane's brother, Samuel, was a Tailor by Appointment to the Royal Family on Old Bond Road.

... **a second painting ... of Jane's ... mother, appears to have been done by the same hand.** I received a digital copy of the painting of Jane's mother, Margaret, from Steve Nethercote, a distant cousin I met at Ancestry.com. I showed it to Maureen Taylor, an expert in dating images. In her opinion, it was painted at about the same time as Jane's portrait, and likely by the same artist. This information is from a private consultation with Taylor at the 2018 Southern California Genealogical Society conference in Burbank.

The gravediggers ... dug open the plot ... Robert Ritchie Gudgeon, his mother, Jane Bennett, and eventually her mother, Margaret Rockliff Croft, were all buried in square 130, grave 1694 at Nunhead Cemetery. A World War II bomb destroyed the nearby Dissenter's Chapel, along with many headstones. Megan Owens took me to the grave, which now lies within the confines of a nature preserve and bears no grave marker.

... **by fifteen [Queeny] was living at a seaside convent school** ... England's 1871 Census shows her residing at St. Mary Magdalene in Hastings, Sussex. Information about the school was gleaned from *The Old Convent,* by Bernard McGinley, on page 6 in an April 2010 post at www.bohemiavillage.com.

Chapter 12—Being Helpful

"... **it was made from oil from hartshorn ...**" Hartshorn originally referred to ground deer antler and later to ammonium carbonate.

"... the women did their laundry only about three times a year." When I heard this, I thought Mimi was exaggerating. Then I read *The Horse of Pride, Life in a Breton Village* by Pierre-Jakez Hélias (Yale University Press, 1978). On page 2 the author writes "the laundry was done only twice a year, in the spring and in the fall." Helias went on to say that it was a three-day job "which corresponded to Purgatory, Hell, and Paradise, in that order." Translated from the French edition, *Le Cheval d'Orgueil*, it's a wonderful chronicle of rural life in Brittany.

"... cows were susceptible to tuberculosis..." Queeny's concern was well-founded. Before widespread pasteurization of cow's milk, bovine tuberculosis was transmitted from infected cows. Even in England, which Mimi credited as being more vigilant with its herds, the illness killed thousands a year.

Chapter 14—Bravo, Mona!

After a successful tour of Paris... The information about Buffalo Bill's visit to Brittany is from Herve Ciret's undated blog posting at unindienauphareouest.blogspot.com/buffalo-bill-en-france.

Chapter 15—Crossings

[George James's sister, Maud] was widowed at forty. None of George James's sisters fared well. It's not known how long Maud worked as a servant in Cliftonville, but in 1911, at the age of fifty-one, she was an infirm resident of St. John's Hostel for the Aged in London. Three years later, she was admitted to the Renfrew Road Workhouse from Epsom Union Workhouse. Her housing stabilized by 1921, when she is recorded with her sister, Harrie, at the Nazareth House for the Aged Poor, Incurables and Orphan Children in Hammersmith, London. Harrie lived there at least fifteen years and Maud at least eighteen years. *London, England, Workhouse Admission and Discharge Records, 1764-1930, 1939 England and Wales Register, and census records.*

[Edward] died... "of remittent fever." Death certificate and *The Hiogo & Osaka Herald,* Hiogo, 26 Feb 1870.

Edward was buried in the foreigners' cemetery . . . Information about the Onohama Foreign Cemetery is from Darren Swanson, *A Place for the Dead—the Foreign Cemeteries of Kobe and Osaka, 1867 to the present day* (The University of Sydney), 2010.

Despite the fear of coffins floating away, Edward's remained secure. But by August 1952, all of the graves had been dug up and the occupants reinterred in Kobe Foreign Cemetery (also known as Shuhogahara Cemetery). Edward's headstone reads, *E.M. Gudgeon—Died—23rd Feb 1870*. Kobe City Archives, 2014.

. . . [Oswald] was convicted of "obtaining goods by deception." From a story related in 2011 by Alain Tate and from *The Proceedings of the Old Bailey,* www.oldbaileyonline.org/browse.jsp?div=t18810131-210.

Chapter 17—The Mexican Railroad

"My father invested . . . in a railroad with two of my uncles." At that time, four of Mimi's uncles were still alive: Ethel's widowed husband, Edward Rogers, whom George James disliked; Oswald Gudgeon, the black sheep who lived in New Jersey; Emily Gudgeon's husband, John Westley, a London banker; and Charles Gudgeon, a successful merchant. Based on their resources and location, I'd guess it was the latter two uncles.

"Aunty Clara . . . asked me to go with them . . . but my father said no." It's curious in Mimi's narration that her father initially refused because he was worried about his daughter's education when in fact his son, who was younger, had already quit school to learn a trade.

Chapter 19—A Redcoat in New England

I was registered at a high school outside Dorchester . . . On another occasion, Mimi referred to attending Northfield Seminary for Young Ladies in Massachusetts, but I haven't been able to verify that.

Chapter 20—Herbert Hayford

[Herbert] had a run-in with the men of the tribe . . . This story was related to me by Herbert's daughter, Joann Campbell.

[The Hayfords] traced their roots to the Mayflower... Otis believed his Mayflower ancestors included Samuel Fuller, Francis Eaton, and William Brewster. He was wrong about Brewster but right about Fuller and Eaton. According to my research, Otis was also descended from Francis Cooke, Edward Doty, Stephen Hopkins, and John Billington. Otis's wife, Amanda Phinney, was descended from Thomas Rogers.

Chapter 21—A Hard, Hard Life

[Rose] expected to be looked up to. Jeanette Lunt, granddaughter-in-law of Rose, recalled a day they were leaving the house to attend a family wedding. Rose "was getting ready to walk out, reached for the doorknob, realized she was opening the door for herself, and stepped back. Then she waited for someone else to open it for her." Related to me in July 1999.

"A visit to her parents is advisable..." Quote from a Yale University doctor's letter attached to Mimi's passport application.

Chapter 22—Farewell to Villa St. George

[Gwen] thrived on goats' milk—sometimes suckled directly from the teat... This was told to me by Mimi.

Chapter 23—Dresses in the Closet

[Fred] drove an ambulance for the American Red Cross... It was called the American Volunteer Motor-Ambulance Corps. See Arlen J. Hansen's *Gentlemen Volunteers: The Story of the American Ambulance Drivers in the First World War* (Arcade Publishing, 2011) for more info about this elite group, which included writers e.e. cummings, John Dos Passos, and Ernest Hemingway.

Chapter 26—Starting Over

...Fred's father signed an affidavit swearing his son was nineteen... The February 19, 1917 letter is attached to Fred's passport application. It says Fred's "mother was attended, at his birth, by Doctor McCahey, of Philadelphia, Pa. who I think is now dead."

Chapter 29—Left on the Farm

[Fred] brought... a movie camera to record the family reunion. In 2012, I made a DVD of Fred's old movies and it includes footage from this trip as well as the next one in 1929.

... she signed off as Gwendolyn Tate Clara Kramer. Her adoption papers list her as Gwendolyn Clara Tate Kramer, but given how fluid names were in the family (by 1940 Jane often used Neville as her middle name), it's not surprising that the order was occasionally switched.

Chapter 33—End of an Era

Mimi regularly consulted [her father] on family history... His information was fairly good, but some claims are unproven, particularly one concerning the Marquess of Abergavenny. In 1923, George James wrote to Mimi, "The title became dormant in 1845 and is still, but had my father lived, he intended to lay claim to it."

I have not been able to establish a link to the Marquess, which George James said came through Henrietta's grandmother, Mary Neville. Even if the title could have passed to George Tate—and it's unclear to me how—Mary doesn't seem to have come from a titled family. She married the tripe dealer, James Gliddon, and ran their shop after he died. Author Anne Gliddon described Mary Neville as "a jolly, fat, vulgar, good-natured woman." At that time, vulgar referred to lowborn. The material about Mary is from Norman, *The Gliddons in London*, p. 12, and confirmation of their tripe business is from *UK City and County Directories, 1805*.

[George James] was eighty-one when he departed this life... The circumstances of his death, sitting with a book in his hands, were related by his granddaughter, Gwen.

Chapter 35—Reconciliation

... Carol had a severe skin condition ... She may have suffered from Epidermolysis Bullosa, a hereditary condition that can cause skin to tear or blister at the slightest touch. Present-day genetic testing suggests the disorder may have run in the Hayford line.

Chapter 37—A Close Call in the Pacific

... **[Jay] composed Softly, Softly Fell the Snow** ... In 1991, it was recorded on *What Child is This? The St. Olaf Christmas Festival* CD by the renowned St. Olaf Choir.

... **[Jay] suddenly saw a platoon of Japanese soldiers** ... Her firsthand account can be found in *At Ease*, an anthology of military stories published in 1996 by Reminisce Books.

Chapter 38—The War in France

Anthony Tate's recollections of the war were contained in a 1983 letter to Jay. They are used with the permission of his son, Andrew Tate. I'm indebted to him, and to Alain and Patrick Tate for sharing their memories of that harrowing time.

Chapter 39—We Are Free!

The letters to Mimi from her brother, George Edward Cecil Tate, are reproduced with the permission of his son, Alain Tate.

Chapter 42—Mrs. Dole

Then Ray proposed a deal. When I was eight or nine, Father told my brother and me how he'd got Mother to marry him. We found it hilarious, but it was the first time Mother learned Father had tricked her and she was not amused. She barely spoke to him for days.

Chapter 45—Sebec Lake, Maine

... **Wendy, a shortened form of Gwendolyn.** Reading the Hayford camp journal, I learned Herbert had often referred to Gwen as Wendy.

Chapter 47—Fate, Who Picked Me

"He told me it was at Bawtry that the Pilgrim Fathers ..." Mimi's letter actually said, "He told me it was from Bawtry Hall that the Pilgrim Fathers assembled ... and it was from Bawtry Hall that they received aid." Since Bawtry Hall wasn't built until 1785, I took the liberty of calling it a slip of the pen and edited Mimi's words accordingly.

Chapter 49—That Name Means You to Me

At the time, Jay wasn't thinking about the Japanese flag... In 2006, I took the flag to Fukuoka and delivered it to a representative of Senbo-Peace, a non-profit organization that "promotes peace and reverence for World War II casualties." They can be contacted at senbo-peace@senbotsusya.com.

Epilogue

Queeny's large rosary adorns the wall above my bed... Mother believed the rosary was Russian Orthodox because it has six decades instead of the usual Roman Catholic five. But researching the rosary on the internet, it appears to be the Brigittine Rosary, established by St. Bridget of Sweden, and used by the Carmelite nuns, a Roman Catholic order. I haven't found a comprehensive website, but there is some information at www.sistersofcarmel.com/brigittine-crown-chaplet.

Acknowledgments

Mimi and Her Daughters has been many years in the making, and over that time I have received advice and support from numerous people. But there are some to whom I am particularly grateful.

I am especially indebted to my cousin, Alain Tate, whose first edition of *A Saga of the Tate-Bresciani Family* not only provided information for my early chapters, but also led me to believe that I, too, could write a family history. Alain and his wife, Anne-Marie, invited me to a lovely tea at their Paris apartment where I met cousin Yves Tate and his wife Marie-Thérèse. They were instrumental in helping me find my way to Villa St. George, as was a determined Saint-Brieuc taxi driver and my friend, Mercedes Pujol-Garcia. A fellow first-grade teacher, Mercedes came with me and interpreted at the old house where Mimi grew up, as well as at Hillion's church, cemetery, and city hall. Our time in Brittany was an unforgettable step into Mimi's childhood.

For allowing me to use family correspondence, I am grateful to Alain, as well as to Anthony Tate's son, Andrew Tate, who gave me permission to use letters his father wrote to Aunt Jay. I thank my cousins, Monique Tate Lavergne and Patrick Tate, who also shared memories that have enriched this book.

I am especially grateful to George James Frederick Tate, who tirelessly compiled and preserved our family history, as well as to Mimi, who carried the torch. I relied heavily on her audiotapes and diaries, given to me by her husband, Harold Friedman. I am thankful to him, along with my mother, Scotti Dole, and my aunt, Jay Anderson, for sharing their stories and letters.

I owe much to my aunt, Joann Campbell, who extended a standing invitation to my daughter and me at Sebec Lake. She met our arrival each year with fresh flowers in the guestrooms. Over the course of six summers, she answered my probing questions, and if she tired of them, she was too kind to show it. She was good-humored and one year when I couldn't visit, she shipped me the troublesome canoe paddle that Herbert had once told me he was keeping for Mimi.

My cousin, Joe Lunt—who once lived with his grandparents, Rose and Wilder Hayford—was good at conveying what Mimi faced as a bride in their home. He drove me by the house where Mimi, suffering from whooping cough and morning sickness, had to "shake up the furnace" each morning. Joe and his wife, Jeanette, took me to interview his sister, Betty Smith, and a few years later, when Betty passed away, they mailed me her copy of the *History of the Hayford Family*. I'm grateful to them for such a meaningful gift and to the author, Otis Hayford, my great-great-grandfather, for keeping our ancestors as near as the bookshelf.

A cousin I met through Ancestry.com, Stephen Nethercote, provided background on the Gudgeon line, and London genealogist Megan Cherie Owens solved several ancestral mysteries. She led me to the graves of George Tate in East Finchley Cemetery and Jane Bennett, an hour away in Nunhead. I couldn't have asked for a better person to guide me through the streets of London, as well as through the English branches of my family tree.

As for the actual writing, I'm beholden to many, especially my teacher, Maralys Wills, who instructed me and inspired me over the last decade. My fellow writers have also made wonderful contributions to the telling of my family story. I'd like to express my appreciation to Dorsey Adams, Eleanor Beatty, Earl and Mary Carbone, Jane Chen, Bob Connell, Bob Ernst, Marcia Hedberg, Shannon Nelson, Pat Rinker, and Kristin Stonham. They and other classmates who have come and gone over the years offered valuable suggestions and made me a better writer, as has my editor, Susan Hassebrock.

I am indebted to my coach, Laura Perkins, who helped me over the finish line as well as to Robert Yehling, who years ago read my preface and showed me how to improve it. I'm thankful also to Jean Jenkins, who believed in me. It was her recommendation at the 2015 Southern California Writers' Conference that earned me their Outstanding Nonfiction Award for a still-in-the-works memoir of my 1971 summer in Micronesia.

I particularly appreciate those who devoted their time to reading my drafts: my younger brother, Tim Dole; my older brother, Mike Dole, who also provided me with Mimi's correspondence; my cousin, Wendy DiPeso, and her husband, Jim DiPeso, who gave an early manuscript a professional read-through; my cousin, Mona Hynch, who read the last draft and proofed the final (and gave me the sweet letter Jay wrote to Lindbergh); and my friend, Karen Hilborn, who, along with my daughter, read several drafts. Their comments and suggestions improved the text.

Despite the help of family, friends, and professionals, if there are errors, they are mine alone.

Special thanks to those who helped in the publishing process. I'm grateful as well to Eowyn Cwper, who created the map of Brittany, and to those at Damonza who designed the cover using a letter handwritten by Queeny. I'd also like to acknowledge Lauren Kahler, the granddaughter of glamour photographer Peter Gowland, for giving me permission to use his portrait of Mimi.

Thank you to all those unnamed friends and relatives who shared encouraging words, because those are every bit as important as the writerly words.

Lastly, thank you to my family—those from the past who lived lives that cried out to be captured on the page, and the here-and-now people who make me proud: Kent and Takako, Caitlin and Erik, and my grandchildren, Jasmine, Maddie, and Luke.

www.ingramcontent.com/pod-product-compliance
Lightning Source LLC
Chambersburg PA
CBHW022026050526
44107CB00118B/1292/J

www.ingramcontent.com/pod-product-compliance
Lightning Source LLC
Chambersburg PA
CBHW022026050526
44107CB00118B/1292/J